In Those Days

In Those Days

A Story of Strong Women

Valerie Strong

To order additional copies of this book, contact:
Xlibris Corporation
1-888-795-4274
www.Xlibris.com
Orders@Xlibris.com
85119

Acknowledgments

THE MANUSCRIPT WOULD never have proceeded without the help of Leonard Trawick, professor emeritus of Cleveland State University, who so carefully edited the first chapters, David Anderson, professor emeritus of Hiram College who read the entire manuscript and offered new insights, and Dick Batstone, Oxford scholar who did a laborious editing. At every stage all three helped more than I can ever thank them. In the last efforts I could never have managed without the computer patience of George and his every day encouragement, diligent reading of the text and editing of photos. To my daughter Helen I owe the restoring of old photos. Of course there never would have been a story without my family and most especially those powerful women, my mother and my mother-in-law.

My grandmother and Mother.

In The Beginning

S HE IS WITH me everywhere in this house where I live now but I have never met her. She died before I was born. I know so little about her; I don't even know the date of her birth, but it doesn't matter, I do know that as a young unmarried woman she was studying art in Paris in 1884, and it is her art that I now have in every room—her presence. On the one large wall of the house are the friends she has given me, with whom I sit to have tea or a drink. The full ruddy faced lad painted in oil, the charcoal of the handsome Byronesque lady killer, the oil of the old blind man, a pencil drawing of a middle aged woman with soft skin and eyes, a portrait of another coquettish woman looking over her shoulder, done in oil and the same model in pencil, full face, and a very narrow faced, dapper Frenchman whom I have frequently invited for an aperitif. These models brought into the studio for the students to draw, are now all these years later, my friends.

It was my grandmother who gave them to me. My mother's mother, née Minnie Jarvis of Brantford, Canada. My mother spoke endearingly of her; she was the family mediator, settling feuds between her husband's four brothers, and repairing broken friendships. It seems she was loved for her quiet, gentle ways not her formidable talent. She came to terms with the conventions of the day by never selling her art but giving oil paintings, water colors or pastels for wedding gifts, anniversaries, birthdays, thus not compromising her husband's ability to keep her. She was always engaged in an art project and became an expert wood carver; several of her carved tables are now in the same living room with her studio models.

In the large Tudor style house, named Gaywood, my grandfather had built on the Grand River in Brantford and where my mother grew up, she kept the large house and many visitors and friends well fed and comfortable, as was expected of the wife of a prosperous barrister and Queen's council, in the days when visiting was more than a quick drink, more usually an overnight or weekend stay.

I never had the wit to ask my mother more details of this grandmother, whose paintings are in every room of my small house, and who is ever present in my life so many years later. How could this young woman from a provincial Canadian town possibly have been allowed to go alone to Paris to study art, in the days when young ladies did not do such things? The only way that I can meet her now is through a miniature hanging in my bedroom of a full bosomed woman with a strong jaw and large intelligent eyes. Her role of Victorian housewife was relieved through her art, even enjoying the approval of her husband who appreciated her talent domestically. She managed her husband and lived within the conventions of the day, ('always make sure he has had a good dinner before putting forward any request' or 'never disturb a man at his place of work.') by allowing her art an outlet. My mother's stories of growing up at Gaywood, were of an idyllic childhood. My grandmother provided a stable, open house. As an only child in an era of large families, my mother's parents made sure that her friends were always welcome so there were endless house parties, skating on the river in winter and swimming in summer. Of pony and trap for trips into Brantford and visits to other large houses. The trap replaced by the cutter in winter with buffalo robe wrap, newspaper insulation under the seats and hot bricks for the feet. Collie dogs, guinea fowl, peacocks strutting their finery and screaming help, assorted fancy chickens, even for a time, a monkey. Wheels of cheddar cheese were imported from England as well as spiced beef. Root vegetables were stored for the winter in a root cellar and apples were the staple winter fruit.

My grandfather was a stickler for learning and reading and made sure that his daughter be introduced to the basic Scottish literature by memorizing Robert Burns poetry, Sir Walter Scott, Lady of the Lake, Joseph Campbell's Lord Ullen's daughter. I can see my mother peeling an apple, the way her mother did—turning the peel into a ribbon as it comes off unbroken, at last to be twisted into a rose. There would be pauses for dramatic effect as she recited 'The stag at eve had drunk his fill.' or

'Wee, slecket, cowran, tim'rous beastie,
O, what panic's in thy breastie!
Thou need na start awa sae hasty,
Wi' bickering brattle!
I wad be laith to rin an' chase thee,
Wi'murd'ring pattle.'

There would be laughter over my imitation of Scottish dialect, then a change of tone. The knife would be put down, the chair pulled closer and my mother would lean her elbows on the table.

"Only now do I realize how lonely that poor woman must have been (referring to her father's mother from whom he had learned these recitations) brought here from Scotland, to a wilderness, with no female companionship and a husband who disappeared on adventures, sailing around the world in the days of sailing ships, only to return to give her another child, five in the end. Her one wish was to return to Scotland but she died before her successful sons could do that for her." Then twirling the apple skin rose she might continue, "at least you have a choice. Women can do anything now."

Childhood

M Y OWN CHILDHOOD was perhaps not much different from my mother's except for travel. Of course there was the automobile by my time, although I remember the delivery horses in the city of Toronto. The baker, the dairy, and the various shops all made deliveries by horse drawn van: Simpson's department store was known for its smart-stepping grays. My coat pockets were gummed with melted sugar from the cubes I carried for any horse I passed. My own childhood was as unstructured as my mother's with the same Victorian codes of behavior and respect for elders.

In those days the sun rose wax-crayon yellow.

Under the sun butterflies were everywhere; sprinkling the tops of fields with live color. The names—tiger swallowtail, monarch, fritillary—a child didn't need to know, they were all iridescent magical creatures, tropical and exotic, fluttering in our northern meadows. The trick was to follow them, to get close enough to watch them feed, to watch the opening and closing of the glowing, patterned wings, or even to catch them, which we did, and had to be told of wings too delicate to touch, wings dusted with a magic powder which gave them the power of languid flight, to undulate over fields or suddenly in a fit of urgency to fly away altogether quite out of sight—to where?

Below the butterflies and their nectar plants was another world teeming with life; grasshoppers, some with wings, crickets, snakes, moles, voles and mice, and ants. Of endless fascination to a child were the ants, which could be fed or diverted, but no matter how they were distracted they never forgot their mission. There were bugs too that lived under rocks, turning up a rock or walking through the meadow we never knew what would be found. It made the stories of giants come true, for who was the child but a giant trespassing in a secret world of creatures? Sometimes we caught them, sometimes watched them, hanging on bending stems, running through grass tunnels or silently giving up sun bathing to hide in deep grass. I can remember spending hours watching, waiting, listening.

On summer nights the northern lights washed the sky with brush strokes of color, tantalizing for the fitfulness of the display, demanding concentrated watchfulness, very difficult for a child. In one moment of distraction the other watchers would claim the most brilliant sky yet; the penalty for inattention was to miss the magic others had seen.

There was no air conditioning, so hot was hot. Children waited for the ice man like gulls round a fishing boat. With huge tongs he slung ice blocks over a padded shoulder, then with a long sharp pick pulled from a sheath, he trimmed the ice to fit the box. It was these melting cold slivers we waited for. In those days there were no ice cubes.

We all swam, and I never remember swimming lessons. Somehow children learned, maybe from a parent, maybe from each other; but when it was hot we swam anywhere, everywhere, in a pool of the river, in a pond, clear or weedy, in northern frigid lakes. We jumped off logs, swung out on vines to drop into the cool depths, or just splashed in shallows. On summer nights we all played street games outside—hide and seek, giant steps, kick the can, never feeling hot, running for goal, then flopping like dogs on the grass, panting and laughing, pushing, kicking, finally drinking great gulps of cold water, or fresh lemonade as a special treat. In those days bottled sodas were a rare luxury.

And we all walked to school, to the store for errands guided by a list to be given to the grocer, to the pond, or river, to friends, the ice rink, the sledding hill, wherever fun or necessity dictated. Children had the odd jobs adults hated—raking, hoeing, weeding, fetching; and there was always someone to care for—the old aunt, who needed help with the garden, the neighbor who could no longer see to read, the mother with a new baby. Children were needed, otherwise how could all the work be done?

Children jumped, hopped, skipped, rolled, climbed trees, fell out of them. It wasn't called hyperactivity, it was called being a child. We knew to sit still too—in church, at the table, in the classroom, accompanying adults on visits. Our opinion was never sought or proffered. We listened. We were never asked what we wanted to eat; we ate what was served and said thank-you. We stole apples, or plums, not so much for the fruit but for the excitement of trying not to get caught. There wasn't much that offered such a challenge. We rode bikes without helmets, visited friends unescorted and were turned loose to wander fields and streams, turn over rocks for crayfish, spend endless hours building dams, catching frogs, salamanders and toads, fill tin cans with polliwogs and minnows, find bird nests and nests of mice sometimes with naked babies pressed into the delicate linings. There were always orphan creatures to be brought home to be raised or more usually die, with the accompanying ceremonial funeral complete with marker. The cemetery, which could be at the edge of the lawn under a tree, enlarged with the inevitable deaths of wildlife and pets. There were cocoons to hunt for, brought into the house and pinned on the back side of the curtains where they would hatch at unexpected times during the winter. Around the porch light huge moths like winged mammals could be found on summer mornings, the plump furry abdomen between large-eyed flat wings. These were always kept as special trophies. They fit perfectly into a cigar box lined with cotton wool. Some were intricate shades of brown, others green, the patterns and circles of muted color, the deep texture like the finest velvet fabric, to be stroked gently with one finger.

Touch was important to a child: the soft but very live nose of the horse, the soft but very limp ear of the dog, the soft deep fur of the cat, the fragrant softness of the peach, the waxy softness of a rose petal. There were prickers too: berries gathered through skin-shredding thorns, nettles' instant stings raising welts for days, thistles in the grass to make barefoot children dance.

And there was taste in those days. Cold milk poured from glass bottles taken from the ice box, the floating lumps of cream slicked from inside the tumbler with a finger, too good to miss. There were no frozen foods, so fruit and vegetables were eaten in season. In Canada, the first spring tonic was maple syrup, served in a saucer with a spoon, as desert. The first rhubarb was also considered a spring tonic, whether stewed or made into pies. Each year we waited for new potatoes, asparagus, new peas, crisp carrots, pulled from the ground and merely brushed off before eating. In August it was tomatoes, hot with sun, that were best eaten right off the vine in the garden, the juice trickling down the chin and corn, picked minutes before cooking, sweet, dripping with butter. Strawberries, sold in split-wood quarts, could be found at the green grocer by smell, but even better were the tasty wild berries of the fields. There were wild blackberries too, blueberries, and nuts. Children seemed to know instinctively, how to find all these as well as which gardens to raid for pumpkins, apples, plums, or peaches dripping with juice.

Cold was cold, to be mitigated indoors by a coal-fired furnace, outdoors by layers of woolen clothes; sweaters, lined wool coat, a long wool muffler to wrap around the neck and pull up over the nose and mouth when the wind was biting, a stocking cap to pull over the ears, double wool mittens and the hated galoshes or overshoes, hated because it meant jamming this year's shoe into last year's overshoe. Thrift was built into society. If cleanliness was next to godliness, then waste was wickedness. Lights were turned off after leaving a room, slivers of soap were pressed onto the new bar, hems were taken up and let down, clothes were passed down and on and on. Food was never wasted, and children cleaned their plates. Kitchen scraps and bones went to dogs and cats; special foods for them were unknown. In those days there were no paper towels but every household had a rag bag with polishing rags, wiping-up rags for kitchen, bathroom, floors, wiping-off rags for boots, and messes. There were no paper napkins, only linen ones kept from week to week in one's own napkin ring.

The medicine chest held Vaseline, witch hazel, iodine which was applied to scratches and skinned knees with a glass rod and hurt, gauze and adhesive tape. There were no Band-Aids. If we were too sick to go to school, we stayed in bed with books and games and a mother to read to us, bring soft custards and weak tea. When diseases such as measles, chicken pox or whooping cough hit, then not only did children stay in bed, but a quarantine sign was posted on the door.

Bundling up for school in winter took energy, and once there it took time and energy to unbundle, standing in pools of melted snow in the halls, bringing the cold, snow covered woolens in to melt, or be turned back at the door to shake off the coat or stamp feet harder. As with swimming, we could all skate. Boys played hockey, girls tried to imitate Sonja Henie and any slope or incline turned into a sled or toboggan run. After a new snow we made angels on the way to school and snow men after school, and played games of fox and hare whenever we found a sparkling fresh field, running in circles making the first tracks, trying not to be caught.

In those days autumn leaves were raked into piles, it seemed to children, just for jumping in, covering each other in, rolling and burrowing in. In the end the leaves were burned in smoldering leaf bonfires, and that pungent odor, by association, carried others with it—the smell of crisp days, winter vegetables, the school room, apples, roasted chestnuts. Every season seemed to have its own odor, but the smell of coffee and bacon meant morning not a season.

The damp soil and soggy woods of spring were of a nose tingling aroma as rich as dark chocolate, quite unlike the sickly sweet hyacinths old ladies loved to plant at doorways. Summer flowers were never sickly, just fragrant; the old honeysuckle, lavender, alyssum, roses. There was the scent of mown grass, or hay fields. The meadows were rich with an undefinable stiff fragrance of maturing flowers and grasses which invited stretching out in, secret nesting in, and lying back in to put names to clouds as their shapes changed overhead.

Winter was the smell of wet wool, coal smoke, wood smoke, children's breath and bodies held in too close confinement. It was the season of cooking odors—cakes, pies, pickles, roasts, and the smell of fresh snow; like fresh rain cleansing streets, yards, gardens.

Sounds were seasonal too. To me lying in bed on a winter morning, the sound of a snow shovel rhythmically scraping the walk meant that it had snowed in the night, and was more effective than any alarm or parent's call to make me jump out of bed. Ice snapped on the deep frozen pond or river where we skated and the grate rattled in the furnace, when once a week clinkers had to be removed. In summer it was birds and crickets, deep gulping frogs, bees in the clover. There was the bang of the wooden screen door on the porch, the steady whir of the reel mower, restful in its rhythm, the slow scratch scratch of the handy man cleaning out the beds, or his snips clipping hedges, gentle summer sounds without motors. But the most comforting, tantalizing, cozy, relaxing, sleep inducing, all's-right-with-the-world sound for a child in any season was the cat purring on the shared pillow.

All this we never thought about, never asked why, only absorbed.

A child wasn't encouraged to ask much, only to follow orders, finish tasks or keep out of the way, and above all be polite, especially to those who were, if not disliked, then certainly not favorites, like the smelly elderly aunt who had to be kissed. By keeping out of the way, we children could avoid errands or work and had time to read, laze about, write, daydream, draw, build, take things apart and put them together again, put on plays with cast, costumes, curtains, music. There was time to watch the creatures brought in from outside to be housed in boxes, jars, the bath tub, bookcase. They were studied, not for any reason, only to see what they did. Like the polliwogs that could grow legs: everything else seemed to be born with its legs, but a child could watch a fish turn into another creature altogether, just the way the cocoon turned into a butterfly. Why couldn't we turn into another creature? It seemed only a question of deciding what to be. Inevitably these captured animals escaped to find new homes somewhere in the house and reappear, slithering, scurrying, hopping or crawling, as the case might be, when, to the delight of my fun-loving mother, the adult most fearful of that particular creature, was being entertained. At the time she proffered regrets, wiping up the tea spilled in fright, but later at the dinner table she would give us a vivid reenactment of the episode mimicking gestures and voice, making the family complicit in what to my mother was a huge joke, until even my father was brought laughing to his favorite aphorism "Ho, ho, the breakers roar,"

In those days we created our own world, our own fun, our own adventures. We were never bored.

Travel

IN THOSE DAYS transatlantic travel was by steamship. My mother was restless and of independent means, so travel was the norm for her even though at the time it was quite scandalous for a married woman to leave her husband and travel on her own for no reason. The only child of a small-town Canadian barrister, she brought to her marriage the security of a private income provided by her doting father. "So necessary for a woman," my mother had told me. Remember, in those days there were few occupations allowed a woman: nursing, school teaching perhaps, and not even these if she were married. Her income depended on her husband. My mother had married a man who avoided confrontation, and did not want to travel, so she took my brother, Leonard, four years my senior, on a round-the-world tour and traveled with me on various shorter trips. It wasn't until years later when my father was living with me that I realized how difficult life with him must have been for my mother. He was always agreeable, pleasant, well mannered avoiding confrontation by agreeing to everything. She loved discussion, argument and change. His defense was to agree to all her plans and then wiggle out, which of course infuriated her. "Why didn't you tell me right away that you didn't want to go around the world?"

"But I would like to, just not right now." And so she learned to go her own way when she could no longer endure being stuck in one place.

One of these trips was my introduction to England. It was probably mid thirties, pre World War II, and for me there was no hint of the horrors to come. The crossing took fourteen days, sailing from Montreal to Plymouth. It was late winter: the seas were as rough as the North Atlantic can be and I was violently ill the entire time, able to keep down no more than teaspoon doses of Lyle's Golden syrup and dry ship's biscuits. In those days there were no seasick remedies other than the frequently proffered advice of mind over matter. It has never worked for me, then or since.

Sick as I was, I can remember lying in the bunk watching my mother dress for dinner. She selected jewelry from a Chinese lacquer box decorated with gold and red dragons, fitted with trays to hold rings, necklaces or brooches. The wardrobe trunk stood open in the cabin, a portable dresser—holding gowns folded on hangers, gloves, underwear, stockings, scarves, all in their own flower-papered drawers. Hats were kept in a separate hat box and overcoats in a steamer trunk in the trunk room. These were the days when travel took time and dress was not to be compromised. For a young child the evening ritual of a beautiful mother preparing for dinner was like Cinderella invited to the ball. There were decisions in which I was included: "What about this with that? This color with this? No? Quite right, won't do." Laughter, always laughter. "What about this?" Brightening from the doldrums of seasickness, I would go into fits of giggles when she hoisted a skirt, wagged a sleek leg naughtily, and knotted a scarf round her waist. Her eyes sparkled as she swayed with the list of the ship, laughing at the storm. "All the more fun for those left standing," she would say, describing to me, who couldn't bear the thought of food, the excitement of the semi-deserted dining room, table rails up, only the ship's officers and a few stalwarts able even to make it to the dining room—and then there was the challenge of dancing across a rolling dance floor. There I was with the most exotic, beautiful, fun-loving person I had ever met in my short life—and she was my mother.

The evening adventure was recounted in detail next morning when I was tucked under a steamer rug on deck, refusing the cup of hot Bovril. I listened to the hilarious mishaps of the evening—of running down the dance floor, kicking off high heeled shoes for better footing, being steadied by the handsome second officer, pointed out to me when he passed, drinks spilling despite the railings, soup spilled down the penguin suit of the most pompous man aboard, the sly smiles of the officers, and the immediate ministrations of my mother as she rubbed the liquid well in. Names were whispered into my ear to match the fool, the bore, the honeymoon couple, the recent widow.

I listened to this mother whom everyone on the ship seemed to know and for each of whom she had a joke or story. They were drawn to her, and she to them, and their stories were recounted to me in my seasick misery as another mother might read fairy tales. I heard the pathetic account of the old maid school teachers returning to England after a life in Canada, stories of endurance and loneliness they had never told anyone before. The young man sent by a domineering father to join an uncle's law firm in London, had poured out all his fears of being treated as a colonial, much the case in those days, and how he didn't want to study law anyway. There—that elegant middle-aged couple strolling the deck pointed out to me—they seem so carefree, my mother said, but they had lost an only son when he was eight. Sunk under the blanket in the deck chair I watched and listened, accomplice in the events, as I learned that meeting the unexpected, making mistakes, pricking the prigs, upsetting the formal, were the fabric of life, and that everyone not only had a story to tell, but a secret sorrow.

The boat docked. I only remember being carried in strong arms into a warm, dark interior, a glowing fire and the final bliss of a deep feather bed and the first restful sleep in fourteen days. There were hushed conversations: a doctor was brought, I had suffered too much from seasickness. White-capped maids offered little sandwiches with weak hot tea, plumped pillows and chatted in a language which sounded very much like English but was not understandable. The retching ended and little by little appetite and spirits returned. It was an old fashioned inn in Plymouth that provided this refuge, with inglenook and dark panelled walls brightened by horse brasses, for me a place of mystery and adventure. My mother hired a car to take us into the English countryside, onto the moors, which was the beginning of my love affair with England. Maybe it was the first firm ground after days of misery, the solicitous attitude of everyone toward the too scrawny child, or the clear beauty of English spring and the moors, but the memory has remained vivid through my life. There must have been a picnic on that first outing because I remember exploring the hedgerows, finding bouquets of perfume-bottle-fragrant flowers, listening to birds—maybe sky larks—never heard before and running in circles imitating the new lambs. What else happened in England? How long did we stay? The details are obscured by the poetry of the English landscape which I absorbed, even at that young age.

There was another sea voyage, this time through flat Caribbean waters with warm breezes and flying fish and porpoise cutting playful arcs at the bow. Sea gulls snatched bread from the air, squabbling and crying. At last now I could enjoy the ship, even deck tennis and shuffle board, played with adults. Instead of Bovril, I could order my own lime squash from the bar with airy instructions to put it on the chit. There were sailors to talk to as they worked at the painting or brass polishing, those unending tasks on a ship. Never missing a brush stroke they told me about the Caribbean islands, and I questioned them about their life, where they had been, where they came from, so now I had stories of my own to tell a mother who listened with delight.

The ship stopped at several islands, sometimes dropping anchor in the harbor where noisy, laughing boys rowed out to dive for coins in the clear water, coming up like seals, water running off their lean bodies, then with enormous grins holding the trophy high. How I envied them their skill, boys my own age, as quick and sleek as fish in the water, never missing the flashing coin. The islands were wondrous, all different, some volcanic, some coral, but all with unfamiliar vegetation and people. There was time to go ashore, by launch when anchored out, otherwise down the gangplank onto the teeming, noisy quay, noisy with people not motors. The streets were crowded and everyone seemed to have something to sell, all excitingly unfamiliar. There were colorful fish, displayed as artistically as ribbons in a window, and fruits, strange and fragrant. There were straw baskets and hats, bright cloth, shouting, calling, waving, singing and laughter, women carrying loads on their heads, which I unsuccessfully imitated back on board, with books. To me all this unrestrained confusion—noise, color and odor—was a tingling paradise.

The island of destination was Barbados, where my mother had friends, and where we quickly settled into a hotel with a large choice room on the ocean side. The waves crashed all night just below the balcony. Next day a move was made to a room on the street.

"The waves never stop," complained my mother, "at least the street is quiet at night."

That's how it was in those days. The night streets were quiet. Even during the day, there were no more than a few buses, no motor bikes, few cars but crowds of bicycles, donkeys, carts and a lot of walking and carrying of bundles and wares. There was the early morning serenade of street sellers—*dolphy-doll-phin, flyyy-ing fish, fre-ssh fruit.* Wonderful strong deep songs for selling.

There was school too, a convent with wimpled nuns who seemed to me to be unapproachable, in their white robes held at the waist by rosary beads, crucifixes and keys. The school uniform was prosaic enough with blue cotton frock, but the straw hat I loved with the ribbon of school colors, green and red circling the crown, the same colors as the school tie. But best of all was the open-sided classroom where birds flew in and out and chameleons darted across rafters. Out of school there were endless unsupervised hours spent swimming in lagoons, wading in shallows, searching for all the new water life, a new watery meadow to explore. There were, as on land, gentle shy creatures and those that would raise a fierce welt if any part of it were touched.

It was on this island that I learned to walk, really walk, for hours. Frequently after school, my mother would start off with sketch book and pencil and the two of us would wander through cane groves, through villages, past shanties usually surrounded by small fenced vegetable plots, always stopping to talk, quickly surrounded by children and women of all ages. My mother would tease the women about their husbands, "Where are the men?" she would ask, which always brought laughter. "They off enjoy thesself we lucky they bring home a fish. They say they work hard, mmm,mmm, mens all the same." After a few more comments on the failures of men, my mother would end with words of advice, "Just remember that no man is worth a woman's tear." Which brought laughter and approval. As she sketched I had goats and donkeys to pat, which I ached to take home. Sketches were handed out like candy and accepted with the same delight. Chickens ran everywhere like the children. No one was hungry, the children were beautiful, barefoot and strong and shy. Imagine having donkeys, goats and chickens right outside the door! I thought that this life with children and animals mixing in an unrestricted stew must be the most perfect way to live, and why couldn't we move here to live in just such a house with the door open for any animal to stray into?

The word had gone out that the lucky could have a picture of their house or portrait of themselves, so our stops became mandatory through pleading invitations. In the midst of this teeming life we walked for miles, my mother teasing and laughing with everyone while she sketched.

In those days children were not tested in school, not in the way they are today. There were no bluebirds and robins, just pass or fail. Some were bright and everyone knew who they were, and some were not and they were known too, facts of life. My mother took school rather casually. My brother and I were supposed to do our best which resulted in good marks or poor. If they were poor it was not because we didn't work, it was because this was not a subject for us. There was no thought of tutors or fitting into the future, be it the next grade or college. It was taken for granted that there were certain subjects that were loathsome to learn so it was much better to do something else. With language however, there was no compromise. Mother accepted no excuses for sloppy speech. To speak correctly, not just grammatically, but expressively, to say what was meant, to articulate, not mumble, select the appropriate word, was as essential as good manners. Reading too was important and cause for discussion. The scenes described in Dickens or Scott were reformed in my imagination until they became as vivid as illustrations. The characters were compared to some people we had met together—"just like that old buster with the twitch, on the ship," or—"remember that Mrs. Snit with the frightful hats, she could have posed for a portrait of . . ." Literature became a way of meeting more people, even villains, liars, cheats I had never met but read about now with avidity and the excitement of confronting evil. Literature sent me on new voyages.

I had read *Captain's Courageous* just before another North Atlantic crossing, this time to France, from Montreal to Cherbourg. After the first days out, the initial swells flattened to dead calm in a pea soup fog. If the ship had been a sailing vessel it wouldn't have moved. As it was, the steamship continued to cut through the water to the drone of the fog horn, while I, with each moan repeated at unvarying intervals night and day, became obsessed with the danger of running down a fishing vessel. The ship, always a self contained island, was now wrapped in an isolating shroud of fog, thick, dank and bone chilling. The incessant horn played on the nerves, warning, always warning of death. The steady deck instead of offering the joy of breezes and open views, was no more than a suffocating crypt to escape from—but there was no escape in that gagging white air. The prow rent sea and fog, from the stern the wake foamed white far below, to be covered instantly by the fog blanket. Who is out there? Who is the fog horn warning with endless rhythm, night and day, never stopping, repeating again and again until anyone would want to scream? Where are the lonely dories being worked by the fearless fishermen of my readings? Was it possible that this big ship had already run over a dory and no one knew, only the fog horn droned on and on and the fishermen were left to die? Compulsively I stayed on deck listening for the sound of bells from the mother boat of the fishing fleet, or the cries of men who hear danger.

Finally, driven to summon untapped reserves of courage, I addressed an officer who had spoken to me on his rounds on deck. He had laughing eyes and a kind word for me who could never begin to answer anyone at that age, or for years. I was what was called a shy child, in those days considered correct. In my case it was because my mother was such a good raconteur, I listened in awe. What would I ever have had to add? Perhaps the officer really liked children, perhaps missed his own but more likely he paused on his pacing of the deck to talk to my mother, with whom he no doubt had been dancing the previous evening. In any case I felt that I could approach him. I poured out all my pent-up fears for the fishing vessels and the dories. To his credit the officer took a child's fears seriously. Together we went to the bridge and the chart room; together we studied the map, the course of the ship, the fishing grounds, the steamship routes. His finger trailed across the paper laced with lines meaningful only to the initiated. The assurance that no fishing boat or dory had ever been hit on this route removed the threat, the morbidity, what seemed to me the death knell of the incessant fog horn. Next day as promised, the befriending officer took me on a privileged tour of the entire ship, engine room and kitchens included. And of course the fog did eventually lift.

These ocean voyages always ended, this one in a country where there was more than dialect to overcome.

That is when I learned French. Plunge in was my mother's advice—into life, into cold water or hot, into fun, into a new language.

Another convent school with a beautiful garden where the Mother Superior took the foreign child alone for French lessons. She was old and gentle and small and it seemed that what she loved most were flowers, so that is where the lessons started, learning the names of flowers, no grammar, no verbs. As we strolled through the garden she would point to a flower or bend to smell a blossom, say the name in French, and wait for me to repeat. *Marguerite,* pointing to a daisy, *une rose, quelle parfum.* She would push the flower into my face to drink in the deep fragrance. It did not take many of these walks for a rapport to take place between us. Soon I was finding beetles, bees and toads to give names to—butterflies, crickets and ants. The frail nun delighted in the response she had awakened and the progress that I was making in French, never mind that I couldn't ask a question or say hello, she had taught me the names of all the flowers and creatures of the garden.

The daily classroom was another matter. Unfriendly children, a tormenting lay teacher, strict discipline of a kind I had never had, and memorization of everything from the first morning prayers, to irregular verbs in every tense and mood, "*eh bien, au subjonctif maintenant,*"—to geography, which meant the rivers of France and all their tributaries, the mountains of France, capitals of the departments of France and the produce from each. The children unable to recite correctly sat near me in the last seat of the last row where I remained for months, in misery and humiliation, exactly as the teacher intended.

The Fables of La Fontaine were a literature study, if memorization can be called study. I took my required homework of *La Cigale et La Fourmi* to the Mother Superior, and on the garden walks the fable was committed to memory. The Mother Superior must have had some idea of my misery in the classroom because she coached, not only pronunciation but when it came to the voices, she herself imitated the voice of the cricket, sweet and gentle when she said to the ant:

> "*Je vous paierai,*
> *Avant l'oût, foi d'animal, intèrêt et principal.*"
> The scolding voice of the ant took over for:
> "*Vous chantiez! j'en suis fort aise.*
> *Eh bien! dansez maintenant.*

We both laughed. My mother however told me that the moral was all wrong. The ant was very mean spirited to refuse help to the cricket who had given such joy to everyone all summer, while the ant was intent on no more than the selfish amassing of goods.

Mother Superior had told me to think of the garden when I was called on to recite, that way, "*tu n'auras pas peur.*" When I was finally called before the class, the sadistic teacher, thinking the assignment impossible for me, hoped to make an example of *la petite etrangère,* ready to gloat over my embarrassment and incompetence to send me back to the last seat yet again. I stood boldly staring straight ahead, to the opposite wall, to a point just above the graphic painting of Christ dying on the cross, blood dripping from his wounds, took a deep breath, smoothed my *tablier* with moist palms, thought of the garden and my only friend in this school, Mother Superior, then boldly recited the fable of the cricket and the ant including the sweet voice of the cricket and the mean voice of the ant, without flaw. The children clapped, the grim teacher's mouth twitched, as much of a smile as could be expected, and never recognized her own voice in that of the ant. From that day the children were friends and the teacher tolerable. Mother Superior became an accomplice in the preparation of future memorizations.

France, except for the torment of school, became another nature preserve. This shore of Brittany was rocky, with high tides and exciting winter storms that whipped the waves into mountains to crash against the promenade, salt spray rising in a tangy mist. When my English friend, Monica, was home on holiday from her English school, which was the only time we saw each other, we would leave the beaches and rocks when the weather was rough enough to make the crossing by *vedette* across the estuary to St. Malo, a daring adventure, always hoping the return trip would be canceled. Then we would have had to take the bus upriver to cross on a bridge; but to our disappointment the ferry was never canceled. Monica was up for anything and seemed to know the whereabouts of the best pastry shops, even kiosks that would sell cigarettes to us. Sharing cigarettes with Monica seemed very worldly and daring. I probably wouldn't have thought of smoking if it hadn't been for her, my mother smoked constantly and had never mentioned to me that it was forbidden. With Monica there was the thrill that she thought what we were doing was quite wicked. In turn I could show Monica caves, the best tidal pools, home to mussels and snails and crabs and surprises of strange fish trapped between tides. There were unusual sea birds, ducks, terns, gulls. With her, and the new freedom of a bike, a French bike, we explored the surrounding countryside to look for wildflowers and feed grass to horses that hung their great heads over walls.

My mother acquired a fox terrier pup from the coffee vendor in St. Malo. Scamp became my alter ego bubbling over with the mischief I felt, but dared not exhibit. He was never on a lead, but growing up I can never remember any dog being on a lead. My mother always had a dog trailing at her heels, present at tea parties, the library, grocery store, never given commands, invisible with good behavior. Scamp was another type, with endless energy perfectly matched to that of a young child. He created chaos everywhere, giving me side splitting stories to tell to my mother at home. He hit the beach running as only a terrier can, destroying the carefully modeled sand castles with the ruthlessness of Tamerlane destroying a city. Without missing a beat he grabbed and tossed over his shoulder, hats, towels, shirts with the skill of killing rats in a stable. He was at the end of the beach before the devastation had been realized with shouts and shaking fists from parents, sobbing and screaming from children. Like veteran thugs we never recognized each other, I sauntered casually through the curses and screams, never acknowledging that I could even know such a dreadful dog and Scamp, for his part never came near me but kept to the fringes, until up on the Promenade we joined up like jewel thieves discussing the loot. After one of these beach raids we would stay away from the beach for a few days to allow children and adults to let down their guard. Scamp provided much amusement and conversation for my mother who delighted as much as I in his escapades.

"What happened today," she would ask, cocktail in one hand, cigarette in the other.

"I thought we should let them recover at the beach today so we went for a bike ride in the country."

"What happened?" She knew there was a story.

"It was so funny Mum, I don't think he'll chase another chicken."

"Did he kill a chicken because if he did we must pay?"

"No but it was so funny."

"What happened to slow him down?"

"A huge rooster flew out, jumped on his back, hung on pecking all the time. Scamp couldn't shake him so he just ran in circles and the farm family were laughing so much they were crying and so was I. When the rooster finally flapped away, Scamp practically crawled over to me on the road, he was so ashamed and never left the bike all the way home."

"Now you know the meaning of the expression 'hangdog'", my mother said.

It was a wrench for me to leave my best friend when it came time to leave, but we were lucky enough to be able to return Scamp to his former home where the terrier character was understood. Even all these years later I cannot see a terrier without a catch in my throat, and the vision returns of that black and white streak destroying the peace of the beach.

In those days the fishing fleet of wooden sailing ships where work never ceased, set out from St. Malo to the Grand Banks of Newfoundland, those dangerous waters I knew so well could swallow a dory. They sailed under the statue of Jacques Cartier, who stared out toward Canada and the St. Lawrence river he had claimed for France. He was a heroic figure for a child who had herself come down the St. Lawrence on an ocean liner.

Each year before leaving for the Grand Banks a festival was held for the blessing of the fleet. The ships were fresh—new sails, new paint, even the sailors in new clothes. There were cages on deck with chickens, even a pig to provide some fresh meat: in those days there was no refrigeration. Although the voyage was dangerous, and there were always one or two vessels that never returned, the blessing of the fleet was festive, with the optimism of a safe voyage and rich catch, salted away in barrels.

The women, who in those days in Brittany wore the traditional lace coif of their village and full black skirts with embroidered hems and aprons, were like crested birds, no two species quite alike. The quay was crowded with families and friends of the sailors who followed the priest from ship to ship as each was blessed. Then when the tide was running, sail was set, women wept, sailors waved and shouted and very sedately the fleet sailed west toward the Grand Banks. They would be gone at least six months.

Scamp and I in France.

Word of the first returning ships spread through the towns and brought everyone out to the promontory. Shops closed, and businesses shut down to attend to the more important business of welcoming the ships back from the other side of the world. I couldn't wait to take the vedette to St. Malo to watch with the rest of the town and cheer along with everyone else when the first sail was seen. Then for days as the ships straggled in there was joy and fear—there were no radios or global positioning units in those days—until at last all were accounted for. That year all returned safely with full holds of salt cod, the mainstay diet for much of Europe in those days. But I could never forget that the sea was more foe than friend.

France was the country of tantalizing odors. Just walking down the street was fairy tale temptation. The bakery where the loaves were bought hot and crisp every day, the patisserie with odors of marzipan, fruits, and chocolate, the roasting coffee, the fragrance of oranges, or any fruit that was in season, vendors of cherries and strawberries found by following the nose and cheeses, musty, runny, creamy, tangy. There were the odors of urine too, never masked by the salty air; the men, like dogs, used any nearby wall. There was the wonderful smell of horse, in those days the round-rumped gigantic Percherons or smaller Belgians were seen everywhere working fields and pulling wagons with slow, deliberate power.

My special delight was the large dog which pulled the little milk cart that stopped at our door every morning before my mother was up. Jeanette, the maid would hold out her pan to be filled with rich milk from the milk can, then there was the platter for the *petit suisse,* little logs of fresh cheese covered with a ladle of cream. While this was being done I would be talking to the dog, a mellow eyed, chunky, black and brown animal. The milk of the morning was immediately put on to boil, for the essential start to the day, even for children, of cafe au lait.

War

INTO THIS WORLD came war. The adults discussed it endlessly. It was called the war of nerves. The Maginot Line, which the French had absolute faith in, that cement and steel fortification running from the Swiss border to Belgium, all agreed could never be penetrated. Even with the demands of Hitler for a corridor through Poland to Danzig, and threat of invasion of Poland, France was considered safe. The news was serious enough though for it to be broadcast in the town square by loud speaker. In those days few had their own radios. This war of nerves continued until Hitler overran Poland, and Britain and France declared war.

That summer I had been meandering into the countryside exploring back lanes on my bike, watching the harvests. There was activity everywhere as the crops ripened. In the orchards, pickers were gathering apples, loading them in baskets to carry to the cider press; wagons pulled by tandems of great horses filled barns with hay raked by hand; stubble fields were yellow with stooked grain and fat cows still browsed the thick pastures. The rich plenty of France was undiminished and it seemed, could never change.

It was an early autumn day, bursting with ripe beauty. In the town square the crackling loudspeakers shattered the air with the declaration of war that would shatter lives.

Attention, Attention, froze everyone in place, a message of national importance to be announced. In solemn tones the declaration of war was announced to a silent crowd—men, women and children. The French knew about war, the wasted lives, wanton destruction, suffering. It seemed only yesterday that they had fought the war to end all wars. The crowd shuffled feet, some muttered "Boche" and spat, but it was a sober crowd that broke up, each with their own thoughts.

At home my mother and I discussed the future. Now my mother regretted that she had not sent me back to my Canadian school with one of the mistresses who had offered to escort me, at the end of the summer holidays. After all, many English families were thinking of Canada as a safe haven for their children, entire schools were being evacuated to Canada. Still, even with the declaration of war, France was safe—there was the invincible Maginot Line—or so reasoned my mother and many others. Of course I had no conception of war, even of death, and was keen to stay in France where I had settled in.

Then came news that shocked the world. The Athenia, a civilian ship bound for Montreal had been torpedoed in the Irish Sea. For my mother and me it was chilling. This ship was to have been my escape, chaperoned by the three mistresses from the Canadian school who had booked passage on the Athenia, to return from their summer holiday in time for the start of the new school year. All three were on the Athenia. Those were the personal implications, but for the rest of the world it proved the German ruthlessness—to attack an unarmed civilian ship defied the rules of war. Did war have rules? To the British it was open defiance of the invincibility of the British navy. The Germans had struck a cruel and sobering blow that war would be waged on any terms.

Galway in Ireland took in the rescued, four hundred and fifty of the original one thousand four hundred passengers. Of the three mistresses, one was never heard from again, one made it to the life boat and returned to Canada, the other, a Scottish mistress I had liked for her readings of ballads and poetry of Robert Burns, returned to Scotland where she died shortly after. It was said she had suffered too much from exposure before being rescued; the torpedo had struck in the evening when passengers were dressed for dinner.

With declaration of war, the rhythm of life changed; men were called up, blackouts enforced, and rationing started. Winter was spent listening for news of the next German advance and deadly bombings. By spring it was evident that the Germans were not to be held in check, and when the invincible Maginot Line was broached, my mother had had enough. We took the ferry from St. Malo to Southampton, which was under barrage balloons and strict blackout. Then by train to Liverpool where we waited aboard ship until a convoy was assembled. The U-boat war was in full swing and solitary crossings were out of the question after the sinking of the Athenia. Now civilian ships were as much a target as war ships. It was only later that I learned that my beloved St. Malo, medieval buildings, tangled streets and ramparts built for defense in another age—would be bombed flat, but not before the town had been the evacuation point for over 21,000 allied troops unable to withstand the German invasion. France was occupied.

The crossing with convoy took longer than the usual fourteen days. Guns had been mounted on the decks, and for days the ship ran in zigzags, to make a torpedo hit more difficult. There were other ships within sight and at the edge of the flotilla, like sheep dogs the navy destroyers, ready to foil any submarine attack. There were friendly over flights of British planes too, scouting for U-boats. All these precautions were supposed to make the dangerous voyage safe. This convoy docked without incident in Montreal, but many did not.

Len, four years older was always my hero.

Canada

CANADA WAS A shock after blackouts and rationing and the endless discussions of German tactics and bombing of civilians. This country seemed carefree; the lights in Montreal taunting more than cheerful, the food too plentiful.

My mother settled me into my old school, and we both listened firsthand to Miss Wright, the one mistress who had survived the rescue after the sinking of the Athenia—of how the three were together, dressed for dinner as was the custom in those days, seated at table, then separated in the confusion that followed the torpedo strike and the rush for life boats. "I was the lucky one—I don't know why." A refrain often repeated by soldiers surviving in the midst of slaughter.

In those days school was not meant to be fun and teachers were not friends, in fact children were united against the adult world. The multitude of petty regulations—gloves and hat on and coat buttoned before leaving the school, sleeves on the playing field not rolled higher than the elbow, shoes polished, lights out, beds made, everything eaten that was served, no running in the corridors, and on and on. There were so many of these rules that it was very easy to do something daring and naughty, against the system, without doing anything really bad.

Like sneaking around the corridors after lights out, reading under the blankets with a torch, purposely losing gloves or hat just when it was time to leave for Sunday church, to say nothing of climbing out on the roof to talk to boys from the nearby boys' school who had defied their own rules to stand at the bottom of the drainpipe and even on occasion climb up, to our subdued squeals.

Despite the restrictions, or perhaps because of them, the girls' imaginations soared and self-expression came through study, discipline and training. Some of the best teachers I had were at boarding school in Canada. There I was taught by brilliant women, usually English, who had advanced degrees from the best universities and had come to Canada to earn a living. They did not teach down to a prescribed age level, it was taken for granted that children would understand what was taught. These teachers were an interesting collection with such an assortment of idiosyncrasies that by comparison, in later life, no one seemed strange. There was Miss Lamont, the history teacher who talked to herself. When she took evening study, sitting at the desk facing the class correcting papers, there was little study done by the girls who held in giggles, as she swiped across one paper with a scowl, and at another was all smiles, muttering as she did so. We always wondered whose papers she was correcting and the bolder girls even walked behind her to try to read the name, pretending to need a book from the shelves. She was a brilliant teacher, using the Socratic method to pull out answers. With her, ancient history was as vivid and important as that of the present, to which she referred. We did not memorize events, but considered cause and effect, as well as personalities and institutions, and in these classes we started to think, debate, reason. In a real-life struggle against fascism, we learned about the first democracy and the duties of the citizen and the state.

Then there was Miss Macy, our English teacher, one of the few Canadians. The question everyone had about her was—did she get her one dark brown dress cleaned over the holidays, did she ever wear anything else, maybe when she wasn't at school? But we forgot about the smelly dress to hang on every word she had to say about Keats, Shelley, or her favorite, George Bernard Shaw. She was sharp, incisive, quick, and expected the same. In her class there was memorization, but it was more than memorization. We had to know what the lines meant and recite them accordingly. The essays were marked severely for grammar, spelling, punctuation, logic. It was this teacher of English who sparked my interest in art history by bringing into class cardboard mounted reproductions of various paintings representing the mythological or biblical subjects alluded to in our readings. In those days there was no audiovisual, overhead projectors, or slides. There was instead a teacher who could bring those faded pictures to life with questions and explanations and even suggestions to see the real paintings some day—when all this was over. For those girls, like me, lagging from haphazard previous schooling, there was much catching up to do, but always someone to help.

In those days there was still a subject called geography, separate from history. This was for me a daydreaming class, memories of mountains, fields, rivers. I could not study shore lines or agricultural produce without returning in memory to the lanes of France, the rich farms, the tide pools, the coral reefs, those places where I had meandered. There were sports too, each in season. Everyone participated unless excused by a doctor. The goal was to teach sportsmanship, not necessarily to win.

And so I developed, mentally and physically, and, strangely, enjoyed school, the camaraderie of the girls, and the lessons taught by respected teachers.

All this was to change drastically.

La Titulaire :

UNIVERSITÉ DE PARIS

FOYER INTERNATIONAL DES ETUDIANT

FONDATION GRACE WHITNEY-HOFF

93, BOULEVARD SAINT-MICHEL - PARIS (V

CARTE DE MEMBRE ACTIF

1947 - 1948

Miss Valérie Stong

La Secrétaire :

A French student.

Growing Up

IT WAS NOT a surprise to anyone that I wanted to become a veterinarian—what more natural for someone who loved animals? It certainly was not for love of science, which was one of those yawning gaps in my education. Now with my parents' drastic move there was a chance to fulfill this dream.

My father had decided to buy a farm and become a farmer. He would never have called himself a "gentleman" farmer, but that is what he was. To begin with he was a romantic, pressing his case for buying a farm to my mother, with descriptions of jugs of creamy milk to serve visitors, milk fresh from the cow, vegetables grown on the place and eggs gathered moments before baking the cake. Mother, ever ready for a new adventure, agreed, fully aware that work is involved on a farm, especially when all able-bodied men are away at war. The farm was bought in Michigan while I was at school in Canada—bought for the pretty rolling hills, not for the fertility of the soil. On my first summer holiday I fell in love with the fields, never mind that the whole place was run down; there was a wood lot, stream, barn with hay loft and stalls for horses. Best of all, I explained to my parents, there was a vet school so close I could practically walk.

That was how I started Michigan State University—by passing entrance exams which seemed trivial to me, with the goal of becoming a veterinarian—far too young, knowing nothing more than how to write a good essay and speak fluent French, and nothing of the opposite sex.

While I was contemplating vet school, my brother Leonard had joined the Royal Canadian Air Force, and was able to visit my father's impractical farming venture only on unannounced and infrequent leaves. He would blow in, handsome in his uniform, tall and straight, now with a dashing mustache on his upper lip. He had always brought a fizz into a room generated by his easy manner, extreme good looks, wit, energy and laughter. Now he was glamorous, a service man. He was in looks and temperament what my mother would have been had she been a man. Len, four years older, had always been my hero, able to do anything; fix anything, make anything, draw anything, fearless and daring. Now instead of his usual tirades against the establishment or compassionate stories of the underdog, he brought with him stories of airplanes: explanations in technical detail of what makes them differ and how to recognize one from another, illustrated on the back of a napkin; the wild Aussies in the mess hall who wouldn't eat beef and the sergeant major who called them all goons. None of his stories were boring, even the technical, and all were laced with humor.

He had decided to join up along with friends, and was sent off with advice from my father, who knew only too well the rebellious nature of his son, "kiss the hand you cannot bite." On his first visit Len poured out plans to put the farm on a paying basis, outlining schemes for a flock of sheep, beef cattle and of course honey bees, as now with sugar rationed honey would soar in price and honey alone would make the farm pay. My mother mentioned to him that she would be the one person to manage all these animals she knew nothing about, especially bees. What she did not tell him was that he knew no more than she about farming. "All you need is one of those bulletins put out by the agriculture department," was his advice and he was off to Prince Edward Island, not to be seen for months.

The Dean of the veterinary school discouraged women, especially in the critical war years, they only take up a man's place then end up getting married, he reasoned. In those days there were certain professions it was difficult for a woman to enter, so I spent most of my time not in veterinary school but exercising the beautiful Arabian horses stabled in the barns at the edge of campus. The Liberal Arts curriculum which I finally enrolled in offered little challenge—literature, history, French, Latin, German etc. At the end of four years I had become a young woman, graduated with honors, made many friends, earned a full scholarship to Paris for a year, and fallen in love.

It was the adolescent *coup de foudre* for both of us. Kimon and I had met at the international club which was no more than a room where foreign students could gather to talk or hold dances. As I was still mostly tongue-tied at social events I found it easier to mingle with foreigners who, even if with thick accents, were fluent talkers. The glib joking banter of the average college student I never got used to, and it only made me retreat into awkward monosyllables. When I had complained to my mother that I never had anything to say, she had quoted Eleanor Roosevelt to me (it seems that she had had the same difficulty) "Just listen. Everyone likes to talk about themselves. All you have to do is draw them out." What I learned is that a Greek never has to be drawn out. They just talk.

At the international club I was more at ease than at any of the dorm parties or dances. There was never a problem talking to Helge from Norway, Izmit from Turkey, Antonio from Italy, to laugh about the new ways here in America. For me, with a boarding school background, it was not just American ways but attitudes beyond my limited experience. I must have looked a blue stocking with waist length braids wound round my head, no make up, no concern with style, faintly English accent and reserved manner; all of which must have been as off-putting to the opposite sex as the glib inanities were to me. No wonder I found social events paralyzing.

We soon formed a group with Kimon, Helge, another Greek, Andreas, and me, frequently joined by others to swell the numbers to ten or more. We sat at the local cafe, eating ice cream, went to movies, plays, concerts and lectures sponsored by the university. There were always heated discussions, everyone talking with their hands, about what we had seen or not seen, about politics, the war and communism. With all the excitement of the studies which would launch these young people into the thick of postwar life when they returned, there was a longing and nostalgia for what had been left behind; parents, younger siblings, friends, customs, landscape. With the expansiveness of students, invitations to visit each other on home turf were passed out along with stories of how we would be entertained, the sights that could not be missed, from the fiords of Norway to the fountains of Rome and the temples of Greece. We became involved with each others studies; Andreas was promoted to lab assistant resulting in a larger stipend, Helge was put in charge of a new psychology study, with the assurance that her name would be attached to the final report. (Not always the case). Kimon, who was in anguish over changing his major had advice from us all and I who had already changed mine felt the most liberated. I was not basing my studies on making money to support families or siblings, nor did I have to show parents that their sacrifices for my education had been worth it. In this respect I was very North American.

With Kimon I was never tongue-tied. I listened to his plans for the future and the reasons for wanting to change his major from chemistry to history; he had at last found a field into which he felt he could pour his soul, a field where he could examine the causes and results of human behavior—he had just finished reading Toynbee—and he knew that he would rather spend his life in a library than a lab. The sure knowledge that there would be no place for a history professor in Greece, whereas a chemist would always be welcome kept him awake many nights. How to earn a living doing what you knew you would love? This is when the first inklings of making a career in the States crept in. Here it would be possible to have a job as a history professor; then he listed the friends from Greece who had decided not to return.

Kimon and I shared many common interests, most especially nature. Kimon spoke longingly of hiking through the mountains and described to me the smell of thyme and pine, the delights of the Greek sea, the rocks, the flocks of goats with their bells moving through the aromatic scrub, and the tough men who herd them, standing out in all weathers on the mountain. Of course there were stories about the occupation, and of his family and friends at Athens College. I heard how his friends had all longed to get away from Greece after the war to study abroad, to return with new ideas to rebuild the country. We took long walks through the extensive campus and to the barns where I introduced him to my beloved Arab horses. Eventually he came to the farm where my parents took him in with open arms. My mother found him charming—so good looking—Kimon was tall, lean, with reddish hair and of course spoke beautiful English. My father was more suspicious as he knew there was a serious attachment starting which in his eyes had no future. "Dating" for my father was an unknown word. A young man courted with the object of marrying, but what was happening here did not fit anything he had been brought up with. A man does not lead a woman on, nor does he take on a wife until he can provide for her. He himself had not thought it possible to marry until past thirty and established. I was his only daughter and certainly not ready for marriage, most certainly not to a penniless student and what did we know of this young man's background? We had not even met his parents.

But we were both too young, with all the passion, inexperience, stubbornness and confidence of youth, and not to be dissuaded. For my father, the scholarship to study abroad came at just the right time—time for his daughter to recover from this infatuation.

When I arrived at Le Havre with the same steamer trunk my mother had traveled with years before, and after a similar grim crossing, there was a dock workers' strike—so all passengers were held on board for two days. The war had ended and the country was rebuilding and trying to pick up normal life. France was coming out of the occupation with bitter memories. Although repairs were being made to all services, there was not enough of anything—buses, manpower, or even food, which was still rationed.

I was lucky enough to be lodged at the Foyer International with a roommate, Janine, from Algeria who had gone through the war in that country. Her parents, who lived on a fruit plantation, sent food packages, usually dates, which were considered the staff of life. It was a time of strict rationing, even the sterno, which was necessary for us to make the weekly two-egg omelet from pooled ration cards. (It was from Janine that I learned the strict ritual of omelet making). The depressing food at the Foyer made the limited menu at the Canadian boarding school seem lavish by comparison. Students foraged, finding edibles that were not rationed, or ate the slops at the Foyer. Just the sight of the lentils and lungs, looking like something the dog would throw up, was enough to put me off any food for the day. Students were unsupervised, unlike American women college students of those days who had to follow rules that were much more like my boarding school. It is hard to believe now, that the American college student of those days, late forties, had to sign out on leaving the dorm after dinner, sign out for week ends and have parents' permission to visit friends. Here at last, there were no regulations, only a tip to the night watchman to open the door after midnight.

In those days although students were poor, they didn't take on jobs like American students. The university was free for those who had qualified through rigorous exams, and a student's job was to get an education. In the best of times, students were expected to eat what no one else would eat and live in squalid quarters with minimal plumbing, but now it was even worse. Luxuries taken for granted were sporadic or nonexistent—heat, hot water, good lights. At the Foyer, even though we had the luxury of hot water once a week, at least the rooms were airy. What was lacking in private space was made up for in public space, which continues today when comparing American and European society.

There was the whole of Paris, cold, damp, but ever fascinating. The city became a classroom of vistas, visions, and misty streets, never to be forgotten. Art and architecture were part of everyday scenery—churches, streets, bridges, museums and galleries without end, and the river with boats, fishermen and lovers. There were lectures at the Sorbonne in overcrowded halls, heated by the press of bodies, and museums which could be taken in slowly, savored, and returned to. There were book stores, cafes, parks, promenades, boulevards, all-night parties and my first champagne, music and theater, all but free for students who didn't care where they sat.

The city, usually swirling in mist, was transformed by the sun into a *fête*. Couples indulging in that French word *flaner*—stroll, which doesn't quite express it—embracing on benches, riding bikes hand in hand, crowded in outdoor cafes; fishermen on the quays: children in the parks riding in bright goat carts or donkey back, sailing boats on the ponds, or watching puppet shows. Oh the French! Downing oysters at stalls set up to sell these seasonal treats, carrying home the groceries in string bags, fresh baguettes under an arm, haggling at market stalls, taking children to school, eating, drinking, talking. There were too those familiar odors which always mean France: bread baking, coffee roasting, fresh fruit, fish, and the odor of the pissoir. The city was a rich mix of people, energy and bustle. In those days pollution was an unknown word; there were few cars or motorbikes. It was possible to enjoy walking the streets, the quays, the boulevards, even to talk and be heard. Despite the food and fuel restrictions it was a magical time to be in Paris; there was the relief of having survived the occupation and the optimism of a new life ahead.

In those days when an adult child traveled abroad it was understood that there would be no home weekends or Christmas or anything else. It was for the year, or two, or whatever the allotted time was. Nor were there long-distance phone calls every day or ever at all. Transportation was long and arduous and French phones barely worked domestically, much less for overseas chit chat, so communication was by letter which took anywhere from ten days to a month, more usually a month. Letters were looked forward to, longed for, and the writing of them was important.

But I had fallen in love before this trip, and unfortunately, no number of letters could suppress the longing for reunion. Kimon and I had sealed our love during these months and despite my father's reservations, but with my mother's connivance, when the year was up I returned with steamer trunk and memories of Paris and spring holiday in Italy, to Canada to be married.

Marriage

I N THOSE DAYS marriage was expected to last—until death do us part. There was no trying out of partners, like courses at school, to be dropped if they were boring or too difficult. Couples went into marriage with the idea that it was for life, and because they were so much in love at the time it was easy to accept: they couldn't imagine that they would ever want to leave each other, that this love could become tiresome or diminish. What I got from the marriage was the only man in the world—brilliant, good looking, witty, hard working. Could anyone ask for more? During the year I had been in France Kimon had made his decision. He was a history major. He was taking a double load to fulfill requirements, and now was considering medieval history as a possible Ph.D. major. Western Byzantine was how he put it to me. But there was much more to this bargain. Kimon was the only child of Greek parents, real Greeks, living in Greece. I inherited new parents and came into the arms and hearts of two extraordinary people and was accepted without reservation as the daughter they never had. This only son had taken the path of so many young people in Greece who couldn't wait to leave the country after the hardship of war. He was given a full scholarship to study in the United States, and a chance to establish a good career.

49

The difficulties originally presented by the families on both sides of this transnational marriage were not even considered by us. We were too full of ourselves: our unreserved optimism, our broad mindedness, our disdain of impediments. Lack of money, different cultures, unfinished education, primitive housing, were a joke, not even a challenge.

What I took to the marriage was the innocence, naiveté, faith and trust, of my own and of those days. To be so deeply in love and trusting of this one man, to bind one's life to him, to take literally the words—for better or for worse—would be considered by most young women today total stupidity. For me, as for many young women in those days who stood by student husbands, taking in stride the worse, hoping for the better, fulfillment came through the husband, never for self. Difficulties were dismissed, even flaunted.

My brother was finishing his degree in philosophy from the University of Toronto, after his discharge from the air force. He and Kimon had seen each other over holidays in Toronto during my year in France and had become fast friends. Len was living in the house, a pied-à-terre, which my mother had bought after selling the large Victorian she had inherited. It was in this house that the intimate wedding reception was held after the Church of England ceremony in the chapel of my old school.

There was much going back and forth to Toronto in those days and for Kimon and me, many visits to the farm in Michigan, from our base at the university. During that first year of marriage, 1949, where the big switch from chemistry to history (practical to impractical) was made, we were given married student housing—a trailer at the edge of campus. For us, basking in the glow of first love, a palace could not have provided more happiness. I arranged the wedding gifts, English china tea cups and silver tray on a shelf, and tried new recipes on a hot plate. The few friends who were still on campus came over for coffee and desert. As well as continuing my paying job of exercising the Arabian horses, I had odd jobs at the university book store.

In those days marriage was meant to last.

The visits to the farm were like coming in late on a comedy of errors, where the performance is in full swing; the actors are known but the outcome doubtful. As one actor leaves stage right, another enters stage left, unknown to the first. My mother was planning social events, or driving off to Toronto, my father was often travelling on business, which left Len, having finished his philosophy degree at the university of Toronto, to do something practical by helping my father make the farm pay.

He started by buying twenty bee hives without knowing a thing about bees, other than what he picked up from reading *"ABC and XYZ of Bee Culture."* For months our dinner conversation was diverted from heated discussions of social injustices, Plato, Toynbee, the Lecomte du Nouy, and "the guy who just got out of jail for not being able to pay his electric bill," with detailed monologues on the life cycle of the bee with accompanying drawings of the differences between the members of the hive, elaborately produced on any scrap of paper. When my mother complained about stings, Len announced casually that it took a certain number of stings for an immunity to build up; she simply hadn't had enough yet.

At the time the boisterous, rowdy, argumentative dinners seemed normal. It wasn't until later that I realized few families engage in such a rush of talk. Perhaps that is why the Greeks endless passion for talk did not seem strange.

My brother was forever championing the underdog with vivid personal encounters to illustrate his point. "The guy couldn't have been nicer. He has this old car and just drives all over the country finding jobs anywhere he can. I thought he could help out here on the farm."

"I do want to be a good Samaritan, but Jove, I don't know." My father.

"Nonsense. What would he do? The bees are in their hives. Where would he stay, who do you think would do the cooking, and what would happen when you all take off, as happens?" My mother.

"Len you would have loved the lecture last week comparing our democracy to the democracy of ancient Greece." Kimon.

"Yeah slaves in both. Don't think we don't have slaves today we just don't call it slavery." Len about to launch on the injustices of our society.

"The Bishop will be visiting this Sunday, so we must all make sure to be ready on time." My father heading off the tirade.

"Why should we be on time just for the Bishop?" Mother asking a question she knew would upset my father.

"It's to keep up another defunct social institution." Len

"It's more of an ecclesiastical method of governance."

Kimon.

"Ho, ho, the breaker's roar." My father's favorite expression to avoid confrontation.

On one occasion Len rushed to greet us when we arrived, with smoke pot and bee hat in place.

"Jeeze, am I ever glad to see you. I'm ready to go round the bend. I've got to get that swarm out of the tree before they take off and do I ever need help."

"Tell us what to do," Kimon naively said.

"First off I need to cut that branch so I can put the swarm in a hive I have ready."

"That branch?" Kimon pointed to a buzzing knot of bees on a high limb of the sugar maple. "How will you ever get up there?"

"Well I thought Val could go up." This was said as easily as if I were still the ten year old younger sister, when I tested the soap box racer, the kyak in the pond in February, the ladder to the tree house. "I'll hand her the saw then I'll be underneath on another ladder to hold the hive the swarm will drop into."

Resuming my childhood role, I said, "Just keep the ladder from wiggling." Refusing didn't occur to me.

"No Val can't do that she might fall." Kimon felt honor bound to step in and save my life. The childhood dynamics of big brother little sister relationships were lost on him. He had one foot on the ladder leaning against the tree, when my mother appeared to say that a cake had just come out of the oven and no one was going up the tree, bees be damned.

"It's one thing if you want to kill yourself," she told Len, "but quite another if you want to kill all those around you."

Enthusiasm for honey marketing diminished after the bottom fell out of the vat when the honey was being liquidized on the kitchen stove. (It had formed a solid lump when left too long in the cold). The chore of scraping, wiping, scooping, lifting honey from all over the kitchen floor and stove took days, and months more to wear and wash off an indefinite pull on the shoes when walking through the kitchen.

Then there were the sheep. The flock Len bought at auction to turn a profit, were too elderly to survive, much less lamb, which meant bottle fed orphans in the kitchen or in the barn needing constant care, or the "dead" man coming to pick up the carcasses. The chicks bought to lay those fresh eggs, if they survived, turned out to be mostly roosters and no one in our family would kill them for dinner. No sooner had the various projects failed than Len married a Toronto beauty in a huge wedding and, with new bride, was off to New Brunswick as a social worker.

By the time he graduated Kimon had applied for and was granted another full scholarship to the graduate school of the University of Wisconsin. We two had became we three with the birth of our daughter Io, born that year 1949, on Easter Sunday. I had been born on Christmas day so my father, whose life revolved around the church calendar, declared our daughter's entrance into the world a "divine birth."

"Nonsense," my mother joked. It sounded too much like 'immaculate conception' to her. "It all came about in the usual way."

We drove in our Crosley car with all our worldly possessions, through Chicago, along winding hilly roads, always a test of the unpredictable brakes, (no throughways in those days) to Madison Wisconsin, to the Cabin Camp—graduate student housing. It was indeed a former tourist cabin complex taken over by the university in their desperate need for student housing after the war. Plumbing was no more than a communal wash house we trudged to through snow drifts, with wringer washing machines on the lower level. In those days there were no disposable diapers and in Madison, frequent winter days of twenty below. We were a pioneer group of wives, all waiting for husbands to finish degrees—not to buy the new car but to live in a house with running water. To this day water gushing at the turn of a tap seems a wonder not to be taken for granted. Letters to both families, (I did the writing in those days, Kimon's time being too valuable) described none of this. There was no mention of hauling water in a bucket from the wash house, frequently in 20 below weather, of the thrill of the young wives when the automatic Bendix machine was installed—on trial—of hanging diapers on the line to dry (no dryers in those days) and bringing them in frozen, stacked like boards to dry overnight in the one room. No one was told that the baby slept in a drawer because there was no room for a crib, of cooking on a hot plate, or the extravagance of indulging in a twenty-five cent milk shake at the university dairy. The families were told of bright winter days, the wonder of being able to walk out onto the lakes—walk on water—with baby and pram, the pale northern winter sky topping snow drifts, the speed of the ice boats on the lake, the ski jump on campus, the streets blocked off for children's sledding, and the skating rinks everywhere, where entire families spent the evening or the days on weekends, recreating with color and movement a Breugel painting. They were told of baby's first smile, of baby's beauty, of baby's rosy cheeks, of baby's good health, of baby crawling, standing, walking, of the miracle of this baby, the perfection of this baby compared to all other babies ever born.

Kimon loved his studies, everything from paleography to medieval philosophy and he even enjoyed his role as graduate assistant. He came home excited, pouring out his day to me—lectures, reading and discussions with undergraduates, and I a voracious reader, told him of my latest book or of the book being read on the university radio station which I arranged my day to hear. One of these, *The Sand County Almanac, by* Aldo Leopold, was so evocative we took a rare weekend off to visit the sand counties. We were always short of money but in those heady days it didn't seem to matter; everyone we knew was in the same boat. We exchanged baby sitting to see free films at the university, *Bicycle Thieves, Open City, Rules of the Game.* In a simple way we had fun; endless walks pushing the pram, Willow Drive, Picnic Point, the barns, the dairy. Looking back it was a carefree life. Through stringent economies, we had enough to live on, no debts, shelter of a sort, a stimulating intellectual atmosphere, and no demands other than our own. We were very much in love, waiting for the end of each day which separated us, to be reunited.

We did it. From one degree to the next, living in sub-standard housing, a cabin with no running water, in a climate that was barely fit for polar bears. We did it with help from parents, on both sides, grit on our part and the knowledge that our discomforts were only temporary.

We three became we four by the time the Ph.D. was in hand. Alice was born at the university hospital in Madison on a bitter January night too cold for the car to start. "Just push," Kimon said jumping into the driver's seat. "Then when it catches run up and get in quickly, before it stalls."

"I'll spend the night pushing. Let's trade places. I know how to jump a car." And so it was that I drove us to the hospital with barely minutes to spare, and no pushing.

For the Good of All

"ACCEPTED" DOES NOT convey the obsession the Greek mother of an only son had for his wife and children. Coola was ever present in our lives, even from thousands of miles distance and even, as things were in those days, with rare telephone communication and slow letters. We were never without her. The letters did come through with regularity, filled with impossible but very Greek mother's advice. "For the good of all, you must talk to the president of the university. He will get you nice house to live. You must ask."

"For the good of all do not take studies where you will not make money (Kimon had just told his mother of the switch from chemistry to history) how will you get good job?"

"For the good of all, do not stay in such cold. Go to Florida (a big Greek community in Florida), very like Greece there." The closing words were the same in every letter, the imperative—"Be Happy!"

We hadn't been married more than a few months before Coola arrived to see her son's bride for herself. She was an extraordinary woman in every way: in looks, intellect, ambition, energy, creativity. She stood out in a group, handsome rather than beautiful, with strong, chiseled features softened by lovely coloring, trim figure and chic dress. Her quiet manner hid a restless mind, brimming with ideas for everything—books, plays, poems and moneymaking schemes. She believed that anything was possible, and for her it was—she had proven it. She was a success as novelist and poet, she was a leading dress designer (money making) and was unexcelled at interior decoration. Kimon had often said that if his mother had been his father they would have been rich. Her life had been a constant pitting against the odds; most recently, she had survived the occupation. Providing for the whole family, including grandparents, during the German occupation of Greece when people were starving to death, had meant an exhausting daily hunt for food where there was little to be had, and quietly, unknown to anyone, she had worked with the resistance in the mountains.

I thought that her obsession with the health of her son was a result of the occupation until I met other Greek mothers later—they were all the same, critical, nagging and at the same time protective. She stayed for a short visit, but long enough for everyone, including my parents, to learn that her son was special amongst all sons. She forked the white meat of the chicken from her plate to his, leaning across others to do so, she switched dessert plates to give him her slice of pie or cake, which might be bigger, or better, or have more cream or more icing, or she let everyone know his favorite flavors to make sure that we always catered to his taste. She would suddenly jump up, interrupting after-dinner coffee and conversation, to change chairs with her son so that he would not be sitting in an imagined draught. None of this went down with the stiff-upper-lip, children-fit-in, never-complain, attitude of my parents. And it was all to the complete embarrassment of her son who would spend hours pleading in Greek not to be treated like a child. The constant arguing was a lesson in endurance which none of us had ever met.

Greeks are brought up on argument, or to be more generous, discussion. In the round of everyday life it degrades to bickering. If one says it is black, the other automatically with great vehemence, says it is white. If one says it is a good day, the other will have to say, no it is not, and for fifteen minutes explain why, all the time being interrupted.

Greeks speak all at once, so full of their own ideas that there is no need to listen, only interrupt. But even with these idiosyncrasies we all loved Coola. She was the most kind, loving woman, and for her daughter-in-law there was no limit to her generosity. For her, the in-law did not exist, I was her daughter, with all that implied for a Greek mother.

Coola's first visit was short, just a peek at the new wife, but as the babies came she could not contain her desire to hold her grandchildren.

"For the good of all," she insisted I should come to Greece with the grandchildren. Theodore, Kimon's father, had never seen his grandchildren, his new daughter, nor had her own parents seen their great grandchildren.

I agreed to make the trip to Greece—with two infants. It wasn't a trip that I had to make—it was proof of the power Coola had over both of us, even from such a distance and with communication as it was; to her nothing was difficult, she could not be refused. It was a journey a mother might make as a refugee to flee flood or earthquake, but when I think how innocently I set out I am amazed at my own underestimation—or stupidity. Remember in those days the visit still meant an ocean voyage, this time not only across the Atlantic but through the Mediterranean. There were no disposable diapers, no baby foods, and no nursemaid. Not that I hadn't been warned.

Friends and relatives agreed that it was insane. My own father reminded me that Coola was always jabbering in Greek with her son and once in Greece, everyone would be jabbering in a language I didn't understand. An aunt took me to one side and confided in a lowered voice that Europeans had an entirely different attitude toward women, which I wouldn't know about as my husband was "like us." Friends, confusing Greece with the equator, encouraged having shots for every tropical disease, the only encouragement came from those who had no children. They were envious of this opportunity to visit Greece, the temples and ancient sites. The ocean voyage alone would be worth it they told me. Imagine two weeks of leisure and luxury. It sounded delightful and with the optimism of youth, that is what I picked up on. My own mother thought of the adventure, dancing every night, and all the fascinating people I would meet. But she was savvy enough to give me a private stash to tip stewards when I needed help.

Kimon saw us off in New York with the same old steamer trunk, this time filled with presents for everyone in Greece, no evening gowns, velvet wraps or jewelry. My clothes were minimal drip dry supplemented by suitcases of diapers. It was only waving good-bye to Kimon from the deck that I faltered, with serious second thoughts of the months that we would be separated.

That two-week ocean voyage was a contradiction of all the travel slogans. The sunny Mediterranean, once we got there, was so sunny we nearly stifled. I remembered too late an Englishman explaining to me the meaning of Posh. "Port out starboard home. Very important sailing out to India, my dear." It meant that each way the cabin would be on the shaded side of the ship. After airing, feeding, washing not only the children but the diapers, and running after the two-year-old all day, by the time the dance band started up and the Mediterranean moon shed a romantic light over the water, I was in bed gathering strength for the next day's ordeal which started at five thirty or six. How I ached for the familiar routine of home, the routine which makes life with small children possible.

The two-year-old was at the undressing stage. She undressed casually, like any good stripper, not all at once but leaving an enticing trail, a shoe here, a sock there, as she roamed the ship finally rescued by passengers or crew, in the lounge, hall, or deck smiling proudly, stark naked. Another favorite pastime was to drop my clothes, usually underwear, out the porthole which opened onto the deck. I would much have preferred they drop into the ocean as my undies were my last priority, and certainly not to be retrieved by strangers. A crib had been brought for the infant so she was safe at least from falling out while she slept, but as she was one of those wiry, active babies, twisting and turning and trying to stand, it was another constant worry that she might climb the sides and fall. My mother's pourboire money was a life saver.

There hadn't been time to think about our arrival and how I would fit into my husband's home until the boat finally docked in Piraeus.

Then it hit as hard as the blistering sun. I looked out at the chaos of third world dockside, which Greece certainly was in those days—heat, dust, donkeys, scrawny cart horses, men yelling and loading huge bundles onto hand carts. I felt like a character in an E. M. Forster novel in the days of the Raj, stepping off the P & O in Bombay. How was I to manage? What was I doing here? I didn't even speak the language other than the few phrases Kimon had taught me. I had heard about his father, Theodore, a gentle quiet man, and the grandparents, especially the grandmother who had raised Kimon and to whom he was devoted. There were few relatives thank God, but of course friends to meet, friends of the family and friends of Kimon. I had to face them all and pass muster alone. Why wasn't Kimon here with me to pave the way? I stared in panic at the winches, shouting porters, jostling carts. The mountains Kimon had described so often as being pine and thyme scented refuges lay like bleached bones under a fierce sun—Hymettus, Parnes, Pentelicon, the guardian mountains of Athens.

The confusion of the dock carried over into the ship's lounge, where passports were being checked. It should have been no more than a formality, but it took hours, all the time the heat in the stifling room mounting, officials perspiring, passengers shouting, slapping their papers in front of the presiding officer after pushing to the head of the line. Why was there so much argument and shouting about showing a passport? It was my introduction to the Greek survival mechanism. Where there is any hint of bureaucracy, regulations of any kind, whenever they are faced with getting on or off, into or out of anything—bus, boat, theater, no matter how much time is allowed for the process, no matter that tickets have been purchased in advance, they feel compelled to be first. A primeval survival instinct takes over. Men and women, normally gracious and hospitable, will elbow aside or trample anyone who is in their way. Caught in a human crush, pushed toward the gangplank, one babe in my arms, the other so close to the ground she was in danger of being squashed, I wished I were in France where a woman with a child is treated like a queen, deferred to, where the only thing better than having a toddler is to be about to produce one, where bus seats are reserved for *femmes enceintes*, where cars stop for them and packages are carried for them. But I was not in France. In the panic of getting off the boat I came against the survival frenzy in full force, and found that I had one of my own. I was not, after this long voyage, going to be tipped with my babies into the murky port waters. I stood at the head of the gangplank and turned to face the press of bodies behind me. In clearly enunciated English I ordered that no one step forward until I reached the dock with my babies. It worked.

At last there was Coola. Her delight at seeing us could not have been more than mine at seeing her. With efficiency she passed us through the formalities of customs, all except the trunk which for some mysterious reason would have to be released later. Never mind. She got a taxi, all the while hugging the children and when not looking at us and saying how beautiful, she was outlining the plans. "Theodore still in Volos, cannot come to Athens—next day we go to Volos by train—very nice hotel here in Athens—how beautiful—*chrysomou,"* hugging the infant. "Why she want to talk to donkeys—very funny." She laughed at the two year old reaching out the window for the donkeys she saw on the streets.

There was the cool balm of the hotel where the family were known and where Kimon had stayed before sailing for America, and now here were his wife and children. The whole establishment turned out to see us. I had a small insight into what royalty must suffer from constant admiration. Because I had married a Greek, the boy they had seen to manhood, I was accepted immediately. I was no stranger in a strange land. It didn't matter that I didn't speak their language, their country was my country, even more, I was their guest. This tradition of hospitality, *philo xenia,* I found everywhere in Greece, in those days before the masses of tourists, when homes and hearts were opened to the stranger. Coola apologized for not taking time to go sight-seeing in Athens (thank God) by explaining that the family were all too excited at our arrival to wait another day. So, "For the good of all" we left by train the following morning for Larissa where Theodore would be waiting for us with a car to take us the thirty miles to Volos. That night Coola arranged for the chambermaid to watch the children while we went to a neighborhood restaurant, for an early dinner at ten thirty. There, over my first taste of retsina, we talked of Kimon, his plans, always with amendments by Coola, the more amusing aspects of the sea voyage, and my relief at having arrived.

Yaya, had the reputation of being very stern.

Papou, in his day both a wit and a rogue.

In the garden in Volos.

At Home in Volos

AT SEVEN NEXT morning we were on the train platform surrounded by a mountain of luggage, very little of which was mine, even with bottles and diaper bags. Travel for the Greeks is another survival episode: not only would it be impossible for a Greek to make any trip without dozens of possessions, contained in everything from carton boxes secured with twine to baskets covered with cotton stitched to the rim, they must have as well as their own water, food and clothing, boxes with specialties of the region for themselves or for gifts—it could be anything from a large fish, sweets made by a grandmother, peaches from a relative's tree, cheese, hand woven cloth, even water from a home well. Coola who had proven that any obstacle can be overcome, thought nothing of traveling with two infants in blistering heat for four hours on a crowded train; that in itself was not enough for her. She was loaded with supplies she assured me were unobtainable in Volos, which explained the boxes and crates, but indicated to me that we were headed to some primitive outpost, and what would I do with the babies? I felt slightly more at ease when she told me that the big round box was a lamp shade made to her specifications here in Athens, because

Volos workmen were not good enough. At least I thought, there would be lights and electricity.

The train was a surprise; modern, clean and fast, by the standards of those days, given by the Italians as part of their war reparations. Even so the heat was exhausting. We left the clutter of the city behind and slipped between the mountains Pentelicon and Parnes, in ancient times covered with pine forests, now barren, exposed to every fantasy of the sun. Now I understood Kimon's criticism of what I considered fertile midwest farm land and woods. "Too green," he had said, "there is no place for the sun to play, no bare rock." I had wondered then why anyone would trade bare rock for lush vegetation. As I watched those bare mountains change from rose to white, purple shadows slashing valleys, I understood the aesthetics of these stripped classic mountains. Is this what inspired the Greek ideal of moderation, I wondered? Not too rugged, not too sharp, not too high, the ideal of balance and symmetry. Coola reminded me that this was Attica, what she called the real Greece, the wild Greece I would see soon, farther north.

Even the plains were parched and dry. I was not prepared in summer for the dormant season. I had left hay-making and corn growing, trees casting deep shade over soft lawns, only what was expected in summer. How, I wondered, could anyone scratch a living from these parched stony fields? Coola explained smugly that Greece has the most perfect climate in the world.

"No rain for three months. Perfect for everything," she went on. "We live outdoors, with no bugs, eat, swim, even sleep outside when is hot—beautiful—never worry about rain like Europe—Switzerland always wet and cold—all summer—but green—yes."

It would be as difficult to explain to a visitor from the tropics that our barren winter trees are not dead, and that in summer they are as lush as any tropical plant.

As we approached Larissa about noon, even I started to consider my appearance, especially compared to Coola, who had somehow remained unrumpled through the ordeal of wiggling and climbing infants—Italian silk knit dress somehow intact, hair perfect, shoes of the latest style and always the showy sapphire ring and pearl necklace. I, on the other hand, in my best drip dry shirtwaist, which was supposed to be wrinkle free, and sensible shoes, looked the way I felt, trampled and mauled. It was only because I was meeting Kimon's father for the first time that I considered dress handicaps—what would he think of me looking like a frump? At last we pulled into the station where Theodore was waiting for us, looking more like Kimon's elder brother than his father. His boyish grin took over his square face, then as close to a giggle as I ever heard him, he hugged me then picking up little Io, repeated, "My darlings, my darlings." The break in his voice, for a man not given to emotion, not only wrapped me in his love but put any trials of the journey into perspective. This burst of emotion was counter to his usual composed, reserved manner as there was nothing of the hail-fellow-well-met about him. His eyes sparkled with humor and his direct gaze and square jaw indicated a determined man of principle, and yet there was a certain shy charm. Meticulous and orderly habits were apparent in the perfect white linen jacket and shoes without a speck of dust.(No mean feat in Greece of those days). His movements were so unhurried each gesture and step seemed to be studied. Except for the same long thin fingers, I did not recognize much of the son in the father. There were similar mannerisms however, the same grin, the same walk, the same hand gestures. He was a man of integrity, a man who could be relied on, and indeed he was too honest to make a good business man and this was his failing. Perhaps he should have been a scholar.

With the boxes strapped to the top of the taxi and Theodore pressed into the front seat with the lamp shade, we set off across the plain of Thessaly on a road the Americans had built after the war. There were flocks of sheep and turkeys, guarded by shepherds, gleaning from the long-since harvested grain fields. This plain is one of the most fertile regions of Greece.

At last we saw Mount Pelion towering over the town of Volos. Kimon had told me so many stories of roaming the mountain as a child, of the villages, of the chestnut groves and apple orchards, of the runnels of pure water which gurgle beside those stone paths, the *kalderimia* . . .

I wanted to explore all of it right away. But we were going to Volos, situated at the foot of the mountain facing the bay of Pagase, which enjoyed all the benefits of nature. The villages appliquéd to the mountainside are no more than an hour's climb; half an hour along the coast one can swim in the ink blue waters of the bay or stretch on the sands of the beach at Alykes. The site of present-day Volos dates from the middle ages; the ancient cities of Demetrias and Pagase are now archaeological sites outside the present port city. It was from here that Jason and the Argonauts set out in the Argo made of oak from Mount Pelion. The mountain was home too to the Centaurs. Coola told me that in a fog, seeing a peasant riding toward her on a sturdy mountain pony, she herself had seen the half man, half horse.

Quickly I settled into a new life. Everything new—parents, grandparents, friends, climate, food, habits, language. Kimon's grandparents, greeted me with such pleasure, laughing, hugging, holding the children, Yaya the infant Alice and Papou little Io. Yaya I had thought, might be especially critical of Kimon's wife as she had taken care of him until he left for school and they were devoted to each other, but there was no hesitancy on her part—I was another daughter. Despite her strong features time had taken its toll and she was now a rather pathetic figure: bent and wrinkled, dressed in black as was the custom for the elderly, she seemed to be in mourning for life itself. She had the reputation of being very stern and deeply religious, and because he had none of these qualities, of making her husband's life a misery. Papou was straight and dignified with a shock of white hair and full mustache, but his mischievous eyes gave him away. In his day he had been both a wit and a rogue and had lived up to his reputation of being the handsomest soldier in Thessaly. Undoubtedly he brought on his wife's abuses, but it was known that he never crossed her unless under the influence of drink, to which he was driven, on frequent occasions, by her tongue. Then he said things he would never dare to say at any other time, and she became the submissive wife.

Theodore, ever dapper looking more like Kimon's elder brother.

The strength and vitality of this old couple amazed me. They were true children of their land, as tough as the olive tree, as hard and strong as the mountains. Often when I was up at dawn with a child, I saw them already breakfasting on a bit of bread, cheese and the thimble of Greek coffee. Every morning about eight, Papou would walk to the cafe where he would meet his cronies to carry on the endless discussions, so essential to the Greeks. Here in the coffee house Papou was respected, his opinions were valid, he was admired and deferred to. It was so unlike North American society where old people are put out of sight, where their ideas are old-fashioned and where they become helpless because they cannot drive a car. Papou, although suffering from bad eyesight, was independent and walked anywhere in town as he had done all his life. His world remained intact.

The very day after my arrival the procession of relatives started which continued for about a week. I had not expected such a small family to muster so many aunts and cousins. A gift of flowers or a sweet of some kind was sent beforehand. Then the visitors would arrive, two or three at a time, usually at about seven in the evening. They were all aged, all dressed in black and all filled with curiosity about Kimon's wife and children. We would sit on the terrace and talk, at least everyone else would talk, as these ladies knew no English. Soon the little maid would bring the preserved fruit, the *glyka tou koutaliou*, the specialties of Volos, preserved walnuts, cherries or kumquats. They were brought in a dish on a tray accompanied by a glass of water and a spoon. The guests took one spoonful of the thick very sweet fruit, put the spoon in their glass and drank the water. The same *glyka* were served to us when later we returned the call with the same formality. Nearly everything is served with water for good reason, it is either so sweet or so strong that water is needed to wash it down. Ouzo, the national drink, a white, very strong anise-flavored brandy, the coffee, and these thick preserves were all hard for me to take without the cold water wash. A bit like the gulps of orange juice I remember taking as a child, after a dose of cod liver oil.

The aunts and cousins would sit uncomfortably on their chairs for about an hour, for all the world like sweet faced nuns. Then with much handshaking, nodding and smiling they would depart. This ritual kept up for several days, much to the enjoyment of Yaya who seized this chance for a little gossip.

Having met with the last of the relatives I felt that my initiation into Greek life was complete. Coola, however, tried to make my breaking-in gradual. My mother-in-law had memories of her visit to us in the States some months after our marriage, which were now served up to me, literally. I wasn't a really bad cook as a bride, but I must have been a plain one. Now, she wanted me to feel at home even in the matter of food. I was to have what I was used to. This, in her opinion, was Campbell's soup. She had bought it by the case in Athens at exorbitant prices. These, were the "provisions" we had traveled with. Regularly each day they were served up to me. The grandparents, not considering anything from a tin fit to eat, prepared their own meals, delicious aromatic Greek dishes, and every day these tempting concoctions wafted past my nose while I sat down to my bowl of Campbell's soup. At last, when I could stand it no longer, I told Coola that I would really love to have the same food the grandparents ate.

"I didn't think you would like," she replied, "and I know you eat much Campbell's soup in America."

"Yes, but just think of all the soup I can eat when I go home." I persuaded her not to open any more tins, much to the pleasure of Yaya who must have thought me a barbarian to spurn her good Greek cooking. From then on I was allowed to live on a Greek diet.

Theodore, who was most particular that everything, including food, be of the best, trusted no one with the shopping. He would go down to the quay at dawn, when the boats were returning with their catch. The fishermen respected his fastidiousness and saved any special fish or lobster for him. Yaya might buy vegetables from the street vendor who displayed produce picked that day from baskets tied to the back of the donkey, but Theodore did the daily grocery shopping, never trusting anyone else. As a result, a steady procession of small boys made deliveries to the house all morning: peaches, figs, apricots, grapes, melons, perfuming the house. With each new delivery the aroma would draw me to the kitchen, all the time playing an identification game. Fig? No. Grape? No. Ah yes, peaches, and there they would be, often on a bed of their own leaves. Making these identifications was like opening a bottle of perfume concocted just for me. Bread was delivered fresh from the bakery around the corner, milk, cheeses wrapped in paper, jugs of fresh drinking water from the mountains and thick yogurt in terra cotta pots. I had learned to like yogurt as a child in France, but the yogurt in Greece was special. I remarked to Theodore that I could live on it.

"I'm glad you like it," he said. "I always get the best and the best is made with sheep's milk. It is more expensive but, as you say, more tasty."

Although I had been brought up on "good plain food," I took to the cuisine of Greece. In those days in North America cuisine was an unknown word; the promotion then was called "home cooking." Meat, potatoes, gravy, overcooked vegetables, cole slaw, jello salads, cream pies, ice cream and of course Campbell's soup. Herbs, unless served in an ethnic family were unknown except for the sprig of parsley to make a BLT look fancy. Olive oil was used to soothe earache, olives themselves tasteless things from a can, only good for a martini.

Here I was eating eggplant, zucchini, peppers, tomatoes, green beans of a type I had never seen, and of all things grape leaves! Salads were tomatoes, cucumber, feta cheese, round olives from Pelion, all wetted down with olive oil. The *moussaka,* stuffed tomatoes and peppers, *imam baildi*, beans in tomato sauce, all soaked in oil, were a taste discovery. As good as they were, returning home, I never mastered the art of reproducing the flavor of the dishes prepared by Yaya. I watched her every move, took notes, questioned quantities, but never could I make anything to compare. Now I realize that it was the ingredients, vegetables picked that day, not just her skill as a cook which made the difference. The fish was especially delicious and prepared as fish should be, either broiled on a little charcoal grill or fried in olive oil. In restaurants the available fish were brought on a platter and the fish of one's choice was then taken to the kitchen to be cooked. Coola enjoyed beer with her meals, Theodore water, but I liked the excellent native wines; although I became accustomed to *retsina*, the typical Greek resin-flavored wine, I preferred the natural chilled whites.

I was beginning to feel very much at home in Greece. The food, the people, the routine which I had thought would be so strange, I took so much in my stride I could hardly imagine that I had ever led a different life.

It was not enough for Coola to express her affection in words, typically she took up the ultimate challenge. She mastered English. From the day of our marriage her letters came written in English, imperfect and amusing, but English nonetheless. It was a task few women of her age would have undertaken, and even fewer women would have done for the sake of a daughter-in-law. It is to her great credit that she learned to speak and write English with ease. For my part, I knew the alphabet and a rudimentary vocabulary, having studied New Testament Greek, so that by the end of my visit I was able to understand most of what was said, but was unable to express myself adequately. I must confess relief that I didn't have to address my letters to Coola in Greek, and my shame that I made so little effort.

Theodore, although he had heard much about me and had often seen my picture, had never met me before this first visit. So clearly did he imagine me, however, that he knew the cornflower-blue linen in his shop was just my color. He put aside a dress length, but when every bolt had been sold and an opportunity came to sell this remaining piece he could not refuse. Once it had been sold, he regretted the mistake he had made. This was to have been for his daughter and it should never have been sold. When, some time later, he saw the exact color and material again he immediately bought a length, paying a premium price, of course. Coola made it into a slim shift with hand tucked bodice, stunning in its simplicity. For years I wore this blue linen with great pride and love. Today, a half century later, when I turn back the tissue paper wrapping from the linen, now faded to winter sky blue, my hands tremble with emotion in memory of Coola and Theodore.

Coola was an outstanding designer, setting the style for the ladies of Volos and later from her shop Style, for the ladies of Athens. One look at my drip dries and she put aside all other commissions and set the four girls, who worked in a downstairs room, stitching to transform me quickly into the bride she could be seen with on the street. Italian silks were brought in from Theodore's shop, Egyptian cotton in every color, linen for a suit—"you need sleeves for the mountain evenings"—this for the morning, that for the afternoon. She did all the cutting and fitting, leaving the actual sewing to the seamstresses. Not only did she outfit me personally with dresses, lingerie, coats and jackets, but she ordered linens for our home as well. She brought fabrics for my approval, to be turned into sheets and table cloths, and then called in a special embroiderer to execute the design of my choice. Even little Io stood for fittings, much to her annoyance. But her pleasure was great, when she could wear her hand-smocked dresses and adorable little coats and jackets.

Theodore's shop resembled him, orderly and conservative. Only the best was displayed on his shelves lining the walls: English woolens, Italian knits, Swiss tulles and Damasks, Irish linens, Greek silks and Egyptian cottons. He enjoyed opening his doors each day and he enjoyed conducting his business. As a man of routine and habit, he was not troubled by the monotony of the job. People were in and out all day, both patrons and the usual hangers on that every store has in Greece, even the butcher. These shop-sitters, as I called them, could be seen sitting on cane chairs at the entrance or just inside the door, wherever it was best to catch the passers by, or meet cronies. Often when I stopped, Papou would be sitting inside Theodore's door, on his way to or from the coffee house.

It was not long after I arrived that I heard the discussion between Coola and Theodore of Papou's pilgrimage. Each August it was his custom to visit, on foot, the feast of the Church of the New Apostle in the village of St. Lavrendi some eight miles away. This year the family thought that Papou was not strong enough to make such a long trip.

The church was named for a young man from the village who had been taken prisoner by the Turks, during their occupation of Greece, and carried off to Constantinople where he was tortured and put to death, his body tossed into the sea. According to legend the waves carried the body back to Volos where the young man was made a saint and a church named after him. To this day the villagers believe that prayer in this church effects cures.

It is typical of many solitary Greek churches built on a mountain side, fertile ravine, or rock outcrop. These little churches are built as thank offerings by a family, husband or wife for deliverance from illness, birth of a longed-for child, or safe return from abroad, and offer solace to the shepherds, or peasants working their fields, but formal festivals with a priest are held only once a year on the feast day of the saint; then everyone for miles around walks to the church, bringing offerings, flowers, oil, whatever the family can afford.

This year despite the warnings of the family, Papou set out at five, to walk the path as he had done all his life, to attend the celebration and feast of the church of the New Apostle. It was all up hill, in the heat and dust of summer. He was not alone of course, but it was a grueling walk for an old man. I could only think of the congregations at home which spend thousands on parking lots so the faithful will not have to walk, and worship may be made easy.

By nine that night he still had not returned and Yaya had lit a candle before her icon and was quietly weeping. It wasn't until ten thirty that we heard the gate close and the sound of Papou's cane on the path. He stumbled in utterly exhausted but smiling and proud. Again he had made the pilgrimage. Happily sipping tea, he described his thrilling ride in the back of a jeep, as if through the hardship of a bone-jarring ride over those mountain tracks he had relived his life as a young soldier. Slowly, savoring the pleasures of the day, he recounted the details; the stop for ouzo, "How many?" Yaya couldn't help shouting. He ignored her and talked of the services, the priest, of old friends met, others who had died since last year, the gossip of the government directives, (the issue at the time was the banning of goats from certain mountains to regenerate the forests). He had done what he had set out to do and enjoyed it all.

Yaya's piety took the form of rigorous fasting which she forced on her husband, although he did not consider self-denial necessary for a good place in the life hereafter. For weeks it seemed, fasting for some saint or other, the old couple would eat no more than a little paste-like substance ground with Yaya's pestle and mortar.

"It is ridiculous," Coola would say, "for this old couple to eat nothing for so many weeks, and Yaya makes poor Papou do what she thinks necessary for salvation. The difference, that she needs this, but Papou, so gentle, will be accepted like he is."

Remembering the problem of overweight at home, I said, "It is probably why the old people are so healthy."

If Papou had the coffee house, Yaya had the supervision of the house. The twelve chickens confined to a corner of the walled garden were her charges, as were the flower beds filled with color, the roses climbing the walls, the jasmine which scented the entire yard at night. She was in charge of the servants, whom she never trusted, although I couldn't imagine sweeter, more accommodating help. The attitude between the Greek mistress and her servants is like that of fencing opponents: the one is always trying to outwit the other. But there were obligations on both sides. When we sat down to the main meal midday I would see two small children in the garden, squatting without moving, never making eye contact. When I asked about them, Coola said casually, "They are the children of Helen the maid. She bring them here to eat our food. I tell her we pay her less for that but she know that will not happen. Who will she bring next?" There are always hangers-on in Greece, the more prosperous expected to assist the less fortunate. This assistance can take many forms, like feeding the small children, filling out forms, assisting in the bureaucratic labyrinth, arbitrating in family feuds, or giving paid days of absence when employees need to aid their own sick or dying.

Every day flowers were arranged in vases throughout the house, everything was aired, polished, dusted and scrubbed: it was spring cleaning on a daily basis. The rugs would have been taken outside and beaten except that it was summer, when they are stored, leaving bare, cool floors. Bare floors were more of a challenge, just what Greek housekeepers want to keep gleaming and dustless in a world of dust. This miracle of dust-free floors was accomplished by skating around on woolen cloths. The extra laundry which I contributed with the children was all done by hand and spread in the sun to bleach. Every article of clothing was examined for repairs so that at the end of the day not only was the laundry ironed, and folded but mended as well. Just thinking about all this cleaning routine I found exhausting, even if there were servants.

It was about this time we began to wonder if we would ever see my trunk again, the trunk with the waffle iron; waffles were another culinary memory of Coola's visit to America, and she was becoming impatient to make them. Theodore had filled out dozens of forms and despite all the assurances we had had in Piraeus the trunk still had not arrived. There had been so many orders and counter-orders that even Theodore, who had lived his life with government incompetency, became enraged. We made several trips to the city hall together to fill in and sign all the sheafs of paper required to release the one trunk.

These visits were an introduction into what was in those days still a pervasive Byzantine bureaucracy, where incompetence and endless delays were the rule. Many years later, in Cairo, trying to buy a train ticket, I was reminded of what it took to retrieve the old steamer trunk in Volos; the demanding voices, the indifference of the officials, the rubber stamps, the shunting from one *quichet* to another, and endless queues for yet one more signature or stamp. Inside what would have been an imposing building, had it not needed paint and repairs, there was nothing to inspire confidence in completing the task at hand. Peasants lined the halls, squatting on their haunches, settling in for an endless wait to the resolution of some matter of boundaries, missing animals or custody. At one end of a long dun colored corridor, a violent argument was taking place, one man waving a fist in the other's face while the man being threatened stood feet apart, arms stretched wide to his side, in a hit-me-if-you-will pose, I am innocent. There must have been twenty others taking sides, shouting full volume. Suddenly, an official popped out from an office, screamed at everyone to get out, and like a Jack-in-the-box, popped in again. The antagonists stopped mid-threat, and the invectives, previously screamed at each other, were now directed at the office where the official had vanished. How they had the energy to even murmur was a wonder. I was sick with the heat, and ashamed to be constantly mopping my face with the linen handkerchief Theodore had handed me, as fresh as a new sheet of paper. Finally, after at least an hour, we reached the secretaries, sullen men, who were to give clearance of our trunk.

They sat on straight kitchen chairs at desks which looked like discarded kitchen tables, and without acknowledging us continued scratching with fine nibs into thick dog-eared ledgers, dipping their pens frequently into wells of purple ink. Theodore, having navigated bureaucracies far worse than this, tapped his dust free shoe and mentioned a name. Immediately, the exotic penmanship ceased and we had the attention a circus dog gives his trainer. Papers came out from yellow files, questions asked and answered and at last, there remained only that I swear that I was not trying to sneak contraband such as explosives, foreign currency, or precious gems into Greece. Just as I was about to sign at the bottom of a page of fine print, all Greek to me, one official with a sudden concern for duty, decided that the whole document would have to be translated. I must know what I was signing, I was told. Theodore's translation would not do, as for some reason he was considered an evil accomplice. After Theodore, without success, had explained the ridiculousness of it all, (logic only makes functionaries more stubborn) we were directed to an office in the annex across the street where there was an official who was considered competent to make the translation. Theodore went off and returned only to say that the designated linguist was out for the coffee break. At last our dutiful clerk relented so far as to say that if I understood French, a language in which he was proficient, he himself would read the document for me in that language.

"Thank God for French," Theodore sighed. "I'd hate to have to wait until the coffee break is over."

The trunk did finally arrive, just before I was ready to leave Greece, and Coola was able to make her waffles once before I left.

In the routine that was established I was treated like a queen and the children like princesses. I was allowed exercise through walking or swimming, certainly not through any kind of house work. The sounds, except for the honk from one of the rare motor cars, or the even rarer shock of the telephone, were all the rural sounds of a past century; the call of the drovers to their animals, the raindrop patter of donkey hoofs, the rumble of heavy carts, the clang of the carriage bells, roosters crowing, dogs barking, cats fighting, women screaming, men yelling, donkeys braying, all in the center of a twentieth-century city. I loved it.

Most of all there was time. Everyone seemed to have it. There was time to enjoy the latest Hollywood productions in the open air, time to drink coffee or ouzo, to talk or play *tavli* at the cafes, time to loiter, time it seemed, for the entire town to fill the waterfront promenade in the evening, time for long drawn out meals, time for siestas, time to watch the fishermen mending nets or preparing their brightly painted *caiques* for a night on the bay, time to watch sunsets and the play of colors on the mountains opposite, time to visit the churches and light a candle.

We would wait until six, when the sun was low, before going out in the evening. We usually had the two-year-old Io with us, Io and her bear, for the two were inseparable. On our walk we nearly always passed the church where we would take a few moments to enter, light our candle and say a prayer. In Greece religion is very much a part of everyday life. The church is open at all hours for prayer and meditation and not reserved for a best bonnet display on Sunday. Shrines and crosses beckon for a moment's pause at every corner and crossroad. Many times in the church, Io had watched wide-eyed the solemn women in black cross themselves, kiss the pictures of the Saints and kneel on their "marrow bones" (my father's expression) to pray.

On one occasion we had stopped on the promenade before the church to greet friends. When we turned round for Io, she was gone. The search was on. Finally, seeing the church doors open, we thought of looking there. Sure enough Io had entered, taken a fist full of candles from their pigeonholes and with the help of the dame in attendance, lit every one of them. There she was, standing in the glory of their light, one hand clutching Bear, the other busy making the sign of the cross over and over.

Sickness

COOLA HAD GREAT ambitions to show me as much of Greece as possible. She was an intrepid traveler and was pleased to have this excuse to roam Greece after the confinement of so many war years. War had not ended in Greece with the end of the war with Germany. Civil war had taken a toll, said by some, including my in-laws, to have been more vicious than the occupation. Rebels came down from the mountains to kill, burn and plunder and the kidnapping of children was a vivid outrage. Now at last it was safe to visit villages and the mountains.

Two small children only made the challenge greater for Coola. If the baby had not come down with a virulent form of dysentery she probably would have had her way and we would have been on the go constantly. Now, with the baby ill, for the first time I felt lonely and homesick. All the words of warning came back. Self-incrimination haunted me; how did you think you could trek around the world with an infant? How could you have been talked into this? You must be insane. Couldn't you have waited at least until she was two? What will you do now? How are you going to explain your concerns to these doctors? Desperately I longed to be home where I could speak the same language and finally,

I had to admit, where everything that entered an infant's mouth was boiled. There were many times when I wondered who the "all" were that this was good for, and especially why I had ever thought it would work. For the first time I considered the fragility of life. Here I was in a foreign country, (and in the depths of my despair I was thinking foreign, not second home), facing the fact that the healthy baby I had brought into the world might not survive. My options were so limited—what was I to do, what could I do? I couldn't take the next plane home. There weren't any. Stories of foreign missionaries burying fever-struck babies in India and Africa haunted me. Was I to leave a tiny grave in Greece? It was the helplessness that consumed and frustrated me. Of course everyone was good, understanding and helpful—too helpful, and everyone had a remedy. First I was told that all babies and small children got sick in summer—summer sickness—nothing to worry about. The old ladies in black, cronies of Yaya, visited every morning, looked at the infant, pinched it's cheeks, squeaked endearments through toothless gums, while I stood by in a bewildered half reality at this gathering of witches. Would they cast a spell on the child? Were they good or evil? What charm could I produce to ward them off? Surely the child, if she survived, would be traumatized for life. Their potions were benign and ineffective; one suggested barley water, another suggested rice water, another no water at all, another goat's milk, another corn starch in the bottle. Yaya who had taken over the infant from the first day, who had fed her yogurt from her finger, (probably the cause of the infection) reassured me with stories of how her two children who had died, had not had at all the same symptoms as little Alice, and look how strong Coola was, her one surviving child. I was not to worry, she knew how to raise an infant. Look at Kimon, she had kept him alive through chicken pox, measles, flu and look how strong he is now.

Every doctor in town was called in—all three. One trained in France, one in England, one in America. This was only after all remedies had been tried, the diarrhea persisted and the child was losing weight as fast as she should have been gaining at that age. I was beside myself with worry and knew without doubt that more than barley water was needed.

It was the American trained doctor with his imported streptomycin who turned the tide—but only just. To say that we kept the child alive is saying all. Irrationally I thought that if Kimon had been with me this would never have happened, and he was so far away I couldn't even pour out my worries to him. Why distress him? There was nothing he could do from that distance. My letters were full of the daily trivia; swimming at Alykes, Io's doughnut shaped beach playmate whose mother followed him around with a spoon of food to shove into his mouth at every moment, and there at the beach, wouldn't allow him to go into the water, and that I had finally taken to fried squid as our beach meze. I did however have Theodore change our return passage to an earlier date. When the diarrhea abated somewhat I finally insisted that everything be boiled that went into the infant's mouth, including water. Yaya couldn't understand. "The water comes from the mountain, it doesn't need to be boiled." This time I had my way.

Monitored by the various doctors, especially helped by the antibiotic, the child finally took a turn for the better, which was not to say that she was totally cured. It wasn't until six months after our return, and treatment by the professionals at the University of Wisconsin medical school, who diagnosed a virulent intestinal bug, that she finally made up for her bad start. When Kimon met us at the pier in New York, the thrill of our reunion was dampened by the sight of the mite I held in my arms looking like a poster for orphan relief.

Excursions

A T LAST THE baby's health did stabilize enough to enjoy evening outings along the quay, sitting at the cafe eating one of the sweet, sweet, Greek sweets, always served with a glass of cold water; *baklava, kataifi* which looks like shredded wheat, or the specialty of Volos, *halva sapainos* which to me tasted exactly like what the name meant—soap. There was the *hypovrachia*, submarine, not to be at all confused with an American sub sandwich. This specialty, also called *vanilia,* was a gluey, white mass like mastic, served on a spoon in a glass of water. My favorite was the delicious *granita*, a mushy sherbet made with fresh, pure fruit. We would sit under stars close enough to pluck, smelling the salt of the sea, cooled by breezes off the bay, while Io fed the cats, and Coola entertained us with stories; she was after all a story teller, but it was the addition of Theodore's cryptic comments and very dry British humor inserted in perfect English, that added the zest. The stories usually started with a comment about a passerby:"you see that couple there," pointing to an old couple walking hand in hand, "like young lovers," she would say, "well when they first came to Volos . . ." The stories were pathetic, tragic, comic and never repeated.

Slowly over that languid summer, languid except for the baby's illness, I put together the family history. The life now was so peaceful and serene, that it was hard to come to grips with the tragedies which were the fabric of every family. All the cheerful faces we saw around us: the laughing youth, coy young girls, the peaceful old people, had stories of persecution and survival and valor worthy of the histories of old. The grim realities became more vivid in the casual telling, Coola carrying the narrative, Theodore with his own apt comments.

The family struggle had been long and hard, as is the story of every Greek family, rich or poor, fortunes had been made and lost many times. Theodore was born in what was then called the Greek city of Smyrna, on the coast of Asia Minor. At the Treaty of Versailles the Greek cities of Asia Minor were retained by the Greeks, but the Turks, not accepting the treaty, declared war and sacked and burned the cities, killing all Greeks, men, women and children. Theodore, a young man with a good education, fluent in five languages, now found himself protector in this chaos of war, of three women: his mother, grandmother and aunt. In the terrifying panic and flood of refugees, Theodore managed to put his three charges on board a refugee ship bound for the mainland of Greece. By this time everything that could float was packed with people fleeing for their lives and repeatedly he himself was barred from boarding. In desperation he swam from one ship to the other in the harbor, calling out, in the vain hope that he would be rescued; to remain in the city was sure death. Finally, he pinned his hopes on one ship pulling out of the harbor and swam after it. The futility of his act and his persistence must have softened the captain's heart, for he was thrown a line and hauled aboard.

Once in Greece he had to find his three women in the flood of refugees who had been dropped at ports all along the mainland coast. And so started Theodore's search from city to city until he finally found them in Volos. It was in Volos soon after the reunion that Coola and Theodore met and fell in love. It was not easy for a young man with the support of three old women to consider taking on a wife but I am sure Coola persuaded him that "all things are possible."

"He was so elegant, slight, like a faun, with gloves, wearing spats, carrying a cane," Coola's description was as she had first seen him walking the promenade. "He needed all new clothes so bought only the most elegant. What I saw him wearing was all he had."

"And Coola had just returned from Paris with a dress which set the whole town talking." Theodore picked up the story. "It was good because that is what started the business. The other ladies of Volos felt like frumps."

"Then we had to have elegant materials to work with, so that is what started the shop. We are a very modern couple, like those." Passing by were a young couple we saw every day taking their dog for a walk, not only did they have a pet dog but they walked arm in arm.

"What makes them a modern couple?" I asked.

"They are always together like Theodore and me. They walk together in the evenings. The old style couples don't do this. The men are ashamed to be seen so much with their wives and spend their time at the coffee house. The wives run their home and the husbands do nothing when they return home. Theodore is more like an American husband, very modern like you and Kimon. You have seen him clear the table from dinner. I have taught him to do this. I told him what husbands in America do in their home and I told him we can save money and have the servant leave early if we can do this work ourselves. Theodore clears the table very well, never breaking the dishes, but did you notice how he closes all the shutters first so no one will see him doing a woman's work?"

Together they had made a comfortable home, cared for Theodore's women until they died, and then took on the care of Yaya and Papou, Coola's parents; it was unheard of for old people to be shut away by themselves. Coola collected local Greek art and furnished their house with fine carpets and furniture. Then just when they could pride themselves on their hard work and accomplishments, including the rearing of an only son—Kimon—war broke out and Greece was occupied.

First came the Italians. An officer commandeered the main part of the house for himself, where he took up residence with his mistress and lived like a pasha, while the family made do in the basement. Next came the Germans. The officers billeted with the family, were polite, friendly and even relaxed in the evening in the salon where they enjoyed music, books and commented on the Greek art on the walls. When these cultured officers left, they took with them every piece of furniture, paintings and the objects they had admired during their intimate visits with the family, even the piano.

The war in Greece did not end with the fall of Germany.

There were the grim years of civil war, with resulting hatreds from murders, kidnappings, burning of houses and villages. Again the family struggled to set up, and succeeded. Kimon who had been sent for safety to the mountain during the occupation to live in a hut with a peasant woman, returned and was sent to Athens College for an education. From this prestigious American Foundation school he graduated and was awarded a full scholarship to study abroad.

"You did after so many setbacks resume a normal life." I commented in awe.

"Here we don't know what is normal," Theodore chuckled, as if all the tragedies had been mere adventures. How true. Tragedy—death, loss of home and livelihood—was so much part of life it could not be dwelt on. Survival was at stake, which meant looking forward.

It was not long after my return from this visit to Greece that we had news of the devastating earthquakes which almost destroyed Volos, a city with a population of about eighty—thousand, as well as many houses of the mountain villages. It seemed that even nature conspired to toughen an already tough people, never allowing for a moment of complacency. Theodore described the quakes to us in a letter; he was on the street one morning, the ground shook, the buildings staggered and fell like a child's tower of blocks. He wondered when the moving earth beneath his feet would open and swallow him up. Now after the destruction by the earthquakes, the rebuilding, the starting again. It would seem to me, one who has endured neither hardship nor privation, to be just too much, more than one lifetime can take. This little family story is not an isolated case, it is the pattern which runs through Greek lives. Disaster does not hurt these people less, but it is accepted as the inevitable design of life.

Although we were not able to travel far from Volos because of the baby's illness, Coola made sure that I saw as much as possible. It wasn't hard to change atmosphere, literally, by going up Mount Pelion to one of the villages above Volos which hug the mountain like barnacles on a ship's hull.

For Coola these were old haunts revisited, a part of the world she loved. It was the first year since the liberation and civil war which followed that it had been safe to visit, and we frequently went for the day to enjoy the cool air. I didn't know then, with these casual visits, how important this area of Pelion would be in my life and later, even in the lives of my grandchildren. The baby we left with doting Yaya and all the new instructions, but Io came with us on these excursions, passed between us on terrifying bus trips, held alternately by each of us when she fell asleep. For Coola, nothing could dampen her enthusiasm for these all day excursions, and I tagged along in her wake.

"We had civil war after the Germans," Coola said matter-of- factly, "many houses destroyed."

She pointed to ruins, houses blown up, roofs off, windows gaping. Violence seemed more disgraceful here, where the simple houses were built for survival and protection of man and animal.

All were lovingly crafted of local stone and wood, in symbiosis with the surrounding nature.

From the first village we visited, Portoria, half way up the mountain, the views were breathtaking: Homer's wine-dark sea, the Bay of Volos, spilled at our feet protected by a circle of lavender mountains. The square took its size from the massive, over reaching plane tree, (I came from a country of trees and I had never seen such a protecting marvel) the limbs, each as large as a venerable Canadian maple stretched over the flagged square like the strong arms of a guardian, offering the ultimate protection the inanimate can provide for the human. Almost saying, "Under here you will always be safe," The square was ringed with coffee houses and restaurants, a tobacconist and a general store. The ubiquitous old men were talking, playing *tavli*, or caressing their *koboloi,* there was the sound of water running, directly from the mountain, into a stone basin where beer, wine and watermelon were chilling. Tragedy seems worse in a beautiful setting; at times troubles seem more unfair when everything around is serene and beautiful, and now I wondered how anyone could violate the basics of nature presented here: stone, aged tree and water, masterly arranged and preserved by the hand of man. And yet tragedies had repeatedly invaded this place. It was Portoria that drew Coola and she intimated on our walks through the village that it would be good to have a house here to come to every summer.

She would say to me, "You like this one? Too old, many problems." I should have realized that what Coola contemplated she accomplished and that these were no idle questions. She wanted to buy a house in Portoria.

The very architecture of the Pelion houses, built as fortresses, against the Turks, speak of tragedy. As with the Irish under English domination, Greeks suffered under the Turkish occupation of Greece which lasted from 1460 until independence in 1833; schools were banned and worst of all, small boys were taken regularly to serve in the Turkish Janissaries. These houses of Pelion are unique and have, since my first visit, been registered as national treasures, not to be destroyed by the modernizing frenzy of wealthy outsiders who have bought them for summer homes. The architecture may be unique to Pelion, but the villages themselves typify everything Greek; the central square with plane tree and fountain, the houses allotted space unfit for cultivating cling to a steep hillside. The streets, no more than stone paths beginning or ending in stairs, meander through the village; *kalderimi,* these paths are called, designed for the convenience of mules with an upright stone placed where a mule can catch his footing. Along the edge of the lanes and narrow streets the gutters rush with water, diverted at intervals to provide irrigation for a plot of land. These paths are not only the streets of the village but the roads of the mountain and in the days before motor transport they linked all the villages of Pelion. On later visits to Greece we walked many of these ancient roadways, always in awe of the labor it had taken to make them.

After a walk about the village in the grueling sun it was a treat to sit under the centuries-old plane tree. Every so often, climbing the steep streets I had to pause to catch my breath, while old men and women walked past effortlessly.

"There are no heart problems here," I panted to Coola. "No," she replied, "everyone live too long."

Sitting in the deep shade of the square we were cooled by the sound of running water from the fountain. The lunch—it might be stuffed tomatoes, crisp fried potatoes, green salad, bread hot from the oven, beer or wine iced in the trough of the fountain, the bottle wiped dry as the waiter brought it to us, seemed fit for the Gods. What more perfect for dessert on a hot day than a melon cooled by the crystal mountain water? The air was fresh, cool and even on a hot day invigorating. Io would toddle about the square, which was somnolent after the noon meal, feeding the cats, which in those days haunted the restaurants, and were always chased off by diligent waiters. Now with patrons satisfied, waiters nodded on chairs tipped back against the building, and the cats prowled. In those days too it was not hard to find a donkey, almost anywhere.

I have often thought that originally donkeys must have been created, not as beasts of burden but to delight children; they look so much like the fanciful creation of a child's imagination. Fuzzy animals, child-sized, with soft white noses, and who but a child could conceive such ears, comical either erect or drooping? Who but a child would have given this creature such dainty feet and taught it to walk with such precision, quite out of character with the rest of the thrown-together body? And only a child would have topped off the creation with a huge voice out of proportion to the size, sounding like the breath being squeezed from a troll. Besides finding animals to befriend and feed, Io amused herself, with dabbling in the fountain. The entire square was her playground, with no restrictions.

Often, on these lazy afternoons, sipping chilled wine after an aromatic Greek dish, while Io explored, Coola would continue her story telling. The themes were universal of the beautiful talented daughter gone wrong, the unfaithful husband or wife, or the no-good son. But as ever in Greek affairs these episodes were complicated by the way in which the families reacted to these misfortunes. One husband, whose beautiful wife went off to Athens with a soldier, shut himself in his villa, (which was still pointed out by the locals) closed all the shutters and never came out again.

The daughter of one of the most respected families in Volos returned with her husband, after living several years in Switzerland. The townsfolk greeted her with strange giggles and embarrassed glances, and the point was frequently made that she must be happy with her husband. The daughter couldn't understand this behavior, until her mother explained that in trying to simplify life she had sold a great deal of furniture after her daughter's marriage. It seems that among the articles sold was the desk which contained, in one of its drawers, all the daughter's love letters. These letters of course had become the delight of the town.

There was the story of the unattractive newspaperman who very late in life married a very young and beautiful girl. When told by several of his friends of his wife's infidelity he countered with, "I would rather eat a spring lamb and share it than eat an old goat alone."

The Greek nature is very proud and family honor is sacred. My mother-in-law was horrified in reading of the crime in our daily papers when she visited us.

"Do you have no crime in Greece?" I asked her.

Her answer was, "No, we are safe on our streets and do not kill each other this way. It would be dreadful, unheard of in Greece. Only would a brother or father kill the lover who had wronged the sister or daughter, to protect the family honor. But this is something different," she told me, as if this type of murder can be excused.

Once after visiting friends whose three marriageable daughters had served us the *glyco*, Coola remarked, "It is too bad Mr. Andros' business does not do better; with three such daughters it is very sad."

"What have the daughters to do with the business?" I asked.

"But did you not notice, the girls, although very clever and polite, are not beautiful? It will take a great dowry to marry them off and Mr.

Andros cannot afford it, especially three times. He should try to marry just one and give her all, then he will be left with only two. If he divides the money between them, he will be left with his three daughters all his life."

Then she told me the story of a brother who, when his father died, was left as head of the family with the task of finding husbands for his sisters. He could not marry himself until his sisters were settled, and so because his sisters were not beautiful and he had not enough money to compensate for their homeliness, he remained a bachelor.

These endless tales revealed a new mentality. When I thought about the restrictions placed on these families, of conventions defied only at great risk and sometimes death, I was thankful not to have been part of it.

"This is the old Greece, the Greece of the villages,"

Coola explained. "Now women do everything, they study abroad, choose their own husbands, we are becoming very modern. But I have always been modern," she said with characteristic candor.

She insisted on visiting the villages of Pelion which were close and well known to her. The fact that we had an active two-and-a-half year old didn't faze her. We strolled the *kalderimia* of the Pelion villages, craning our necks to look up at the top-heavy fortress houses, where windows ring the overhanging upper floor built as a lookout. As we walked Coola would be greeted by the women we passed, everyone seemed to know her.

To my thrill, on one occasion, we were invited inside one of these strange houses of Pelion. An old woman wearing the traditional heavy wool skirts greeted Coola from her doorway. The greetings started, I was introduced, the novelty from America, and in a minute the other women of the house appeared all smiles, urging us in—of course not a man in sight. The ground floor, where we entered from the street, was windowless used for storage and the animals. The living quarters were on the second and third floors. The house was truly a fortress; the walls four or five feet thick, the doors so massive it was an effort to swing them closed. When I commented to Coola about the beauty of the massive door set in the whitewashed surround one of the women produced, with great pride, the foot-long key. The mistress of the house was proud to lead us through the doorway, across whitewashed steps and pavement past the inevitable pots of geraniums. To step from the heat and the dazzling entrance into the deep cool interior of the house was as refreshing as a drink of cold water. The stairs to the living quarters and the bare pine board flooring were bleached through countless scrubbings. I was amazed at the taste and artistry shown throughout the house and above all the cleanliness. With all my vacuum cleaners, washing machines, electric this's and that's, my home was never so spotless. The curtains at the windows looked as if they had that day been laundered and hung. Copper pots and pans gleamed. The simple chestnut-wood tables were covered by the finest needlework cloths, the fanciful, bold, traditional designs of the cushion cover embroidery brightened the entire room. We were shown the summer and winter living rooms. The winter living room was small with a fireplace in a corner; around the room ran benches, inviting and bright with embroidered cushions. The walls were bare white plaster, the floors covered with the colorful geometric rugs found everywhere in Greece. One could imagine the family round the fire in winter, snug in the glow reflected from the warm colors of the embroidered and woven covers. The handmade objects—the chairs, weavings, tables, all created by the family or past generations, created a room of a sophistication hard to match in today's quick-fix society.

On the third floor we stepped into a huge room cheered by the many windows we had seen from outside. Here again a bench ran round the walls. This was the room, we were told, where the family gathered for feasts, dances and parties, where there would be room for the dancers to swing out and for the onlookers seated on the benches to clap time. Here all the relatives could gather for any occasion.

Our hostess asked us if we would like to meet her daughter whose baby had been born ten days ago and who would be sorry to have missed the visitors. We were shown into the bedroom where the shy daughter was still confined. The baby lay asleep on the bed beside her, swaddled tightly and very much resembling a mummy.

"The poor little thing," I said to Coola, "he can't move a muscle."

"This is their custom," she said. "All babies are swaddled. They say it makes them feel secure and contented."

The baby looked contented all right but I couldn't help wondering about the practical aspect of unwinding the infant each time he needed a change. Our hostess, with many smiles and handshakes, urged us to visit them again when we were in the village. With all the hardships and poverty I knew the family had to have suffered, we left feeling nothing but admiration for these strong people. We had been received with such dignity, pride, vitality, graciousness and poise, qualities many ladies of so-called cultivated society lack.

In those days the villages functioned as units, self-sufficient in almost all things. Everything needed for survival could be found in the village or as close as the next house, survival being dependent on cooperation. Walking the paths in the forenoon we might see a procession of young girls or children, carrying to the wood fired communal ovens round trays of stuffed tomatoes, peppers, whatever was to be served for the main meal. The ovens not only baked the village bread, but served for personal baking, especially on feast days, with a procession of trays filled with special breads or sweets. Why should every household have its own oven when the baker fired his every day?

"Now we go to Hania," Coola had said on one visit, as usual deciding where we should go and what we should see. "They know Kimon there—you must visit," again the imperative.

We walked some distance outside the village of Portoria, to a hillside overlooking an apple orchard. There before a small stone shed, enlarged by a few extra rooms tacked to one side, Coola was greeted by an old couple as if she were an apparition. It took some time before all the greetings were made and questions answered and before Coola could say to me, "Hania, Kimon was here very often to eat. It is very long since we meet. These very good people. They hate Germans very much." Hania means inn, and indeed those tacked on rooms were for passing travelers, which I thought stretched the notion of an inn. We were going there because Kimon had come so often as a boy when he was on excursions. In a nostalgic mood he had told me of the delicious sausages made by an old couple on the mountain so I asked Coola if this was where the special sausages were from.

With laughter she repeated the question to the couple, saying in Greek, "You see your sausages are famous even in America."

I was seated as if I were a state dignitary, at a table in the shade of a grape vine. Of course they remembered Kimon and of course they welcomed his wife. I went through my head nodding and smiling routine and chattered away in English and even threw out my few new Greek phrases, with Coola eagerly translating the trickier spots for me. When I told them that Kimon had said that there was only one place on Pelion for sausages, the old couple laughed and the wife at once disappeared to bring out the delicacies. All eyes were on me as I took the first bite, expecting me to be as keen over them as Kimon. One nibble was enough for me mentally to curse him. My mouth and throat burned. How could anyone like it? Outwardly I tried hard to smile and not show my dislike.

"How do you like our sausage?" was the immediate question, husband and wife bending forward to assess my reaction.

"Is this the same Kimon liked?" I asked tentatively, trying to sound casual.

"Yes, yes, the same. Have another piece."

I couldn't, I just couldn't. I would rather have eaten live grasshoppers at a Chinese banquet. It was no use pretending. I couldn't eat another piece.

"We don't have such sausage in America," I said. "It is so very hot, I must get used to it, the wine is better," I panted, reaching for my glass and draining it at a gulp.

Now everyone laughed. "If it is wine you like, I'll bring you some more and some fresh cheese and bread." the innkeeper chuckled.

Walking back from Hania I understood the real reason for visiting the old couple. Coola said, "That couple very brave. They help many get to the sea during the occupation. All safe here. Greek men on German black list."

I had not heard of the black list. Coola explained. "Nazis make list of anyone they don't like," was the way she put it, which was more or less true. Many were university professors, writers, anyone who had spoken out publicly or in some cases were simply known for their "subversive" ideas—against fascism. These people were to be rounded up, interned or executed according to their crimes or influence. Anyone who knew he was "marked" tried to escape to Egypt, a safe haven for refugees during the war and close enough to Greece to become a favored escape route, many starting from the small fishing coves of Pelion. It seems that Hania was used as a refuge en route to the sea and a boat. Of course Coola herself had been involved with some of these escapes, thus the special relationship with the old couple.

One of the best excursions we took was to the village of St. John, on the other side of the mountain where Pelion looks down on the Aegean. Because I knew that Kimon's family had gone to St. John every summer for years, and had heard so much about it I felt that I already knew the site. As soon as the mountains were safe after the fighting from the communist war which shredded Greece after the defeat of the Germans, the summer tradition was picked up by the families who could, to leave Volos during the hot summer months for the mountain villages or the seaside. Hotels filled again with women sitting on the terrace talking nonstop, needles flashing through intricate embroideries while undisciplined children ran wild until all hours of the night, mothers shrieking at them constantly with no effect. On weekends husbands joined their families adding another level of noise. But this was not for us. Our excursions were day trips only and even then I was uneasy, always the health of little Alice in my mind. The bus ride to *Aiyous Yioannis* (St. John) could only be taken on faith. To say that it was uncomfortable was the least, it was death defying; never have I been so scared. Coola reassured me by saying, "Greek drivers are the best, never accident," but even she crossed herself when it seemed that two wheels hung over the edge of a precipice. During the first part of the trip, traveling along the fairly level road at the base of the mountain, I was in constant fear that we would kill children, donkeys, and drivers.

The bus slowed for no one or thing. The stones, dust, and potholes in the road meant nothing either, on we went like a runaway team scattering all living things before us. At times the peasants driving or riding their donkeys would deliberately block the road.

"Motor drivers and mule drivers hate each other," Coola explained. "They like to fight in this way, they are very funny." They played what we would call a game of chicken. Neither giving way until the second before inevitable death. Then the bus driver would lean out his window, shouting and cursing and shaking his fist at the donkey drivers. "It is too bad you cannot understand his curses," Coola said. "They are so clever at cursing. Something like, 'may all your goats be male and all your children female.'"

The road wound through endless olive groves, the trees staggering off in every direction as far as the eye could see. The olives from Pelion are the best in Greece, according to those who live on Pelion, and of course, the oil from them the very finest. As the road mounted and left the olive groves, we came onto the open rocky pastures where shepherds were tending their long-tailed sheep.

Once we caught sight of the Aegean, the excitement, if you can call it that, began. The road we took now was carved into the sheer face of the mountain; for here Pelion does not rise gradually and protectingly from the sea, allowing villages and cities to nestle in her shadow; but rather, rising from the Aegean, she defies all comers. She carries her head in the clouds and the sea plays at her feet. Man and his villages are not in the scheme of things. But man had cut a place for himself even here on this rocky shelf. The narrow road of loose stone and gravel had no guard rails. Its turns were so sharp that at times I was sure we must have one wheel over the edge. The only time I dared to look down, the sight of the waves dashing against the rocks far below left me ready to throw up. Only now, did Coola admit that she hated this drive, and never once did she look seaward, "Don't look do like me, I don't want you to be fright," she said, and when she thought the driver was being distracted by the lively conversation he carried on with those around him she called up for him to pay attention to his driving, and of course this was all he needed to enter into a lengthy and lively narration as to how many years he had been driving this road, without an accident. (It would only take one, I thought, and you wouldn't be here to tell the tale). To explain his story adequately he would turn completely round to look at Coola and illustrate every phrase with both hands off the wheel. I noticed several passengers crossing themselves.

"It is always the same," Coola moaned. "These drivers talk too much."

Kimon's story came to my mind of the indelible impression he had had when as a child, he had been walking this road after a storm and saw the tire tracks of a car, tracks which ran right to the edge of the road, and then nothing. He had told me that he could never forget how sick he felt following those tracks with his eyes and then looking down at the pounding sea below but probably no sicker than I was feeling now, years later.

Through some merciful providence we arrived safely at the village. Coola told me we would walk down to the hotel on the beach and take the mule to come up. For about half an hour we zigzagged our way over the most primitive path, the two year old finding it great fun to slide over boulders, or to be swung over shrubs and rocks. Every so often we could glimpse the beach and the little white hotel by the turquoise shore. By the time we had scrambled to the bottom I had blisters on both feet.

The couple who came to greet us, were all welcome and filled with questions which had to be answered before we could be shown to our room. "From America? Po,po,po." While Coola gave a synopsis of our life history, little Io's cheeks were pinched, my hand stroked, and glasses of cold water were set before us. Then the meal was ordered. To say ordered sounds as if there were a choice. In fact we were offered the catch of the day, fried potatoes and tomatoes. In such a place there could be no menu. But as always we were treated as honored guests. The so-called hotel was nothing more than a long whitewashed stone building with a palm thatched verandah. All four rooms led off this. We were shown to one immaculate little room, with iron cots, where we could rest and change our clothes. It was a tonic after the bus trip and the treacherous walk to plunge into the waves, taste the salt, and enjoy the giggles of Io splashing in the water. After the dip we walked along the beach and inspected a fishing boat which had been hauled up for repairs. Mellow from lunch on the terrace in the shade of the thatch, I thought that I had never visited a more idyllic place. I should have loved to stay at this inaccessible hotel for months, to swim and hike, to climb and explore the mule paths, to watch the ever-changing ocean, to see the sun rise out of the Aegean. I did not know then that as a family we would often visit *Aiyous Yioannis,* and that eventually we would make the trip on paved roads.

But we had come only for the day and when Io awoke from her nap we had to mount our mules for the long trip up to the road. Now I understood why the mule is so valuable in mountain country. I had ridden horses all my life and I shuddered to think what would happen if a horse were ever put to such a path. At times, afraid the mule would fall, I was all for dismounting to aid the poor beast to gain a foothold on sheer rock. When Coola passed on my fears and compassion for the mules to their owners, they only laughed. She translated for me: "a mule will never place his foot if he is not sure he can take the step." As for the load he was carrying they said that this was the lightest load he had carried in many days, for it was their job to haul supplies to and from the hotel below. I consoled myself, as I always did in Greece, at the sight of the half-starved, overworked animals, that their masters were no better fed, nor did they work less.

In the bus on the way home, a man introduced himself to us in English. He wanted to tell me he had been to America twenty years before.

"It was dreadful," he said. "I went there to make money and when I got to New York there was nothing for me to do. I stayed one year, saving every cent and living worse than a dog to get enough money to return home. Never will I leave Greece again," he went on. "I am not rich but I live a decent life, clean, in a good climate, with my friends and family all around me. I am known and I know everyone. Here I have time to drink my ouzo and talk."

I was apt to agree with him that perhaps in America, after spending a lifetime striving for better and more, we are too old or too tired to enjoy our acquisitions. Life has passed us by, without our living it. Coola, I remembered, had worried very much about what she thought was our hard life in America. She had been appalled on her visit at the struggle and rush of American life.

"You have no time to think," she often told me, "and this is necessary."

Speaking of the do-it-yourself vogue: "You must always do everything yourselves, this is not good. Your husband should do what he is trained to do, and then pay the carpenter, gardener and painter."

I agreed but pointed out that we, at least, could not look forward to such luxury. My husband intended, upon the completion of his doctorate, to enter the notoriously underpaid academic profession. Coola could not understand why professors were not held in higher esteem. "In Greece a professor is the most respected member of society. He is a man of learning. In Greece we respect this very much." Or so it was in those days.

During her visit to America we had made the mistake of calling on one of my husband's professors. Taking advantage of the summer holidays he was in the process of redecorating his house and when we called he was at the top of a ladder rolling paint on himself and his living room ceiling.

Coola could not believe her eyes. "It is dreadful," she remarked after we had left. "This professor is like a laborer." We explained that he could not afford to hire everything done and engaged in jobs like painting which he could do himself, to economize.

Coola's firm response was, "Kimon, you must not be professor, is not good for you. Once you studied chemistry that would be good for you, or architect, that is what I would be if I were a man. See about it, Kimon, for the good of all, but do not become professor. You must be happy."

My husband, having had advice from his mother all his life, fortunately or unfortunately, went his own way. Fortunately or unfortunately, he became a professor of history with a meager salary, and ended doing, with great enthusiasm, much of the restoration work on an old house: ripping off porches, dismantling ancient furnaces, painting being one of the easier jobs.

Every August Volos held a fair where Coola thought I might be able to find some typical Greek craft work to take home. The fair, which was set up on the edge of town, attracted villagers from the mountain and the plain. There were sideshows and shooting stalls but the atmosphere was not one of fun and festivity. This was a glorified market day and the purpose was serious (survival again), and any fun to be had was quite incidental. There were bleating sheep, braying donkeys, and Greek music whining at full volume from speakers hung to poles. Improvised coffee houses had their collection of men, and colorful gypsy bands had gathered to sell beautiful ponies. As well as livestock and produce, crafts made during the winter were displayed for sale. I was especially interested in the rugs, the woven materials and the ceramic work. The word ceramic comes from the Greek and there is still creative pottery available, although the stalls at the fair mainly displayed copies of ancient vases and the overused image of the Parthenon done in cheap bold colors. Except for the utilitarian earthenware and some decorative wall plates there was very little of interest. Then we came to a vendor who showed the lovely pots and plates done in the traditional designs and colors, nearly all with the deep blue of the sea.

"I wish that I could take one or two of those home with me." As soon as I had spoken I realized my mistake.

"Then choose," was Coola's simple answer. It would be nothing for her but I was not up to the challenge of burdening myself with breakable, heavy pottery. Only by refusing even to consider such a folly did she finally agree.

"For next time," she compromised.

At one stall embroideries, as decorative as a painting, were laid out on a table. If I had ever been able to make anything so beautiful I would have framed it for posterity, certainly I could never have sold it. With smiles the saleswoman unfolded each piece to explain the designs and stitching, Coola as impressed as I, translated for me, explaining that this was a design from Thessaly, another from Pelion, yet another the design from the edge of a traditional costume apron transposed for a table cloth. Despite the selection Coola had already made for me I could not resist a small cloth, with stylized figures in bright colors.

Among the rugs and woven blankets were the eye-catching bags. These tough woven bags were carried by every shepherd, peasant, or mule driver. They held the meager bread, cheese or olives or the occasional tool. They seemed so smart, durable and colorful that I bought several for gifts, as shopping bags. In a few years these bags could be seen in the States carried by every college student. We also bought several of the woven rugs, geometric in design, some especially lovely ones using only the natural wool colors, ranging from white to black. For the first time I saw the woven shag rugs, which at first glance look like fur, the *flokati*, which have since become an international favorite. They were so luxurious looking and in those days, unusual, that Coola bought a lovely white one for me to take home.

Here at the fair the traditional costumes were still worn.

In the heat of a Greek August the women wore several black wool skirts, the outer skirt pleated down to the ankle, and spotless white woolen stockings I would have considered appropriate for skiing. Their blouses had long black wool sleeves, and although I had heard something about wool clothes providing insulation in hot weather, just looking at them made me itch. Most wore decorated heavy leather slippers on their feet. These peasant women treat the sun like an enemy and do their utmost never to expose themselves to it, even to tying a black kerchief around their heads. It made me wonder if the Islamic tradition of covering the woman's head had not a similar origin, protection against the sun, and not for modesty at all.

The men wore loose black trousers which tapered in below the knee and the same heavy white wool socks. Their full sleeved blouses were white under their jackets and their tall hats set straight upon their heads. The men could be seen standing in groups fingering their *koboloi*, conversation beads. These amber beads, an inheritance from the Turks, were the only frivolous touch about them.

The women, not allowed such lazy fingers, were spinning as they talked. On our outings we had often seen, a weary peasant woman returning home, barefoot, her shoes carried over her shoulders to save the leather and her hands busy spinning or knitting as she walked, squeezing every ounce of labor from herself. The somber clothes and busy fingers seemed to symbolize the endless struggle for survival by people who work like their own mules all their lives.

Suddenly, it seemed, despite the trauma of little Alice's illness, it was time to leave for Athens and home. We were all in tears, Yaya and Papou no doubt wondering if they would ever see their great grandchildren again. Theodore decided to stay in Volos to keep an eye on the shop and house.

It was painful to say goodbye to a man who had become such a good friend, with whom I had had so many long discussions, exchanged views on English authors, mystery stories (which we were both addicted to), England and America, society and customs. With his shy charm, sharp mind and unprepossessing ways, he was one of the most interesting, lovable and even sophisticated people I had ever met—and he was my father-in-law!

The last ten days were spent in Athens, where I was at last able to visit the Acropolis and other sites Coola would not let me return without seeing. In those days, Athens, a capital of some one million, had a village-like atmosphere, so much so that it was a surprise to find it such a humming cosmopolitan center. Almost everyone could speak several languages, and catering to this, almost any kiosk sold French, German, Italian, English papers magazines and books. Representing the entrepreneurial talent of the Greeks, were the new boutiques sprouting from the walls, displaying European fashions in locally made shoes, hand bags, men and women's clothes.

There was nothing flamboyant or presumptuous about Athens, perhaps because it lacks a whole age which produced so much in art and architecture in the rest of Europe. Athens has the Ancient and Modern, but the Renaissance and Baroque does not exist. For four hundred years Greece was occupied by the Turks and during this time, in an age that was so productive in the rest of Europe, it was if a blanket had been held over Greece and the country all but smothered.

One very important visit had to be made to a bare rock of ground at the foot of Lycabettos, facing toward the Acropolis and the Parthenon. It seemed such a miserable plot it was hard for me to engage in Coola's enthusiasm.

"This is where I am going to build," she said with certainty. "This is the time to buy. In a few years all land taken, too expensive then."

How right she was, how shrewd and how ambitious. She did in a very few years build a beautiful apartment building on this barren rock, which over the years, through frequent visits, became a second home for our children.

In those days, my impressions of Greece were of a land of blue seas and imposing mountains, clear skies and crystal atmosphere, the land of the olive and the fig, a land with a simple beauty which is enhanced rather than disfigured by man's works, a land which makes the myths seem possible, which makes all the fantasy, humor, wit and tragedy of these tales spring to life. The spirit of Greece, as I felt it, was best presented in the tale of Baucis and Philemon, the poor old couple who offered their last crumbs to entertain wayfarers, the gods in disguise. How bountifully hospitality had been extended to me I realized with anguish, when I was about to board the ship to return to America. Although I was going home I was also leaving home. Greece had cast her spell, Greece and her people. My one thought was when and how soon I would be able to return—but not with small children.

Home? At Last

I T WAS A very spoiled family who returned home to Kimon. The baby Alice had been constantly held in Greece and had become the mascot of the ship on the return voyage. She looked so pathetic, with huge black eyes staring from the thin little face, the child-loving Italian crew had adopted her and passed her around from one to the other. Even the tough deck hands held the baby, cradling her with all the tenderness of a new mother, while cooing melodic Italian endearments. By the time we got home the baby had decided that she could not tolerate life unless she was in someone's arms. The two year old, who had had every whim catered to, threw temper fits all over the floor if her slightest desire was thwarted, and I myself hardly knew how or where to begin the overwhelming round of daily life. All at once everything devolved upon me. The baby cried, the two year old threw her fits and Kimon hung around expecting something to eat.

For several days I stood in the middle of the floor wringing my hands uselessly, paralyzed with all that needed attention, and not knowing where to begin. There was the incessant laundry, it had been so easy in Greece with the maids and the sterilizing sun, and the meals I had no hand in. Where were the aromatic fruits, thick yogurt, shiny eggplants, tomatoes hot from the sun, orange-yolked eggs, olives, green, black, purple, sour, salty, arranged like a mosaic, bread hot from the wood oven, pistachios to eat from a paper cone? On a walk with the children where could I sit for a coffee and watch a drama unfold around me? Where on the street could I buy a warm flaky *tiropita*? Cleaning had never been a concern but now our cabin seemed miserable in the extreme. But it wasn't the primitive Cabin Camp conditions which irritated: I knew that was temporary, I had been jerked from one society to another too quickly. How on my own I was! No extended family, and I realized with despair that this is the way we keep house, bring up children, live, in North America. How did mothers survive? No aunt, grandmother, or woman friend to take over when exhaustion hits as it must do when there is an infant. No wonder there was child abuse. Before the trip to Greece I had accepted the new mother role as it is ruthlessly handed to us; always feeling exhausted and frustrated, I had accepted never being able to think or read, accepted the never ending mindless tasks, but now, I had found a slower pace, a different age in Greece with many hands to help, willing and smiling, and perhaps because it suited my temperament I had expanded in it.

There was so much that I missed. I missed the knots of people on the street or wharf; it could be the loading of a wagon, the repairing of a road or even a fisherman looking down the length of his pole; in Greece they would attract hangers-on, their own faithful. It was a wonder how so many people could spend the morning watching a fisherman paint his *caique,* or circle a hole in the ground where digging was under way, or give advice as to how to patch the road. I missed the bray of donkeys, the smell of animals, the fragrance of fruit, the sea, sun, sky, mountains. I even began to miss those sticky sweets, the resinated wine, and yes, those shrill voices come to pinch the babies' cheeks. I missed the long evenings of story telling, the disputes at the coffee house with screaming, and gesturing better than any American TV drama could provide.

Now at "home" again I felt that I was caught on a senseless treadmill. Coola was right, "There must be time to think, a time when there is nothing to do. We all must think. I won't have time for another thought for years I said to myself bitterly as I tied on an apron before tackling a stack of dishes.

"Well," Kimon said, "you weren't exaggerating when you said you were treated like royalty."

"We'll all have to come down to earth, just be patient with us, it's a dreadful shock you know to come from everything to nothing."

It was a strange statement to make. After all, I had visited a war-ravaged country, with few of the conveniences we consider necessary, not even cars, and I had returned to what was, to most of the world, the epitome of luxury; yet I felt deprived. Americans, I realized, lead lonely lives. No coffee house, no personal contacts with grocer, fisherman, baker, bus or taxi driver. All the people who keep us going are kept at a distance so that our privacy is not invaded. We never have to shove or push, scream or yell, or argue over or for anything or everything; even emotions are subdued; at funerals, there is no wailing, grief poured out for everyone to hear, to know of, to participate in, stronger even than the oppressive fog of incense.

It was the rapid change in the infant that finally eased the transition. In two months she had gained so much we couldn't believe it was the same child.

"The next trip Coola and Theodore will have to make to us,"

I said firmly. "No more travel with infants for me, next time I go abroad I'd like to have children who could take care of me." Alice's illness had been too much of a scare.

Reunion in Hiram Ohio

I T WASN'T UNTIL three years after our return that the subject of a reunion was broached.

By this time Kimon, with Ph.D. in hand, had accepted an appointment as assistant professor of history at Hiram College in Ohio, a state we knew nothing about. In those days this liberal arts midwestern college was not much different from the way it is now. Buildings have been torn down and replaced, not always for the better, but the general atmosphere remains one of tranquility and stability. The village and campus still present a peaceful New England scene, which then we especially appreciated for our two small children. Large maples shade green lawns, the town circles the campus with a few houses and, in those days, all faculty were provided housing, or at any rate, as President Paul Fall told us at the time—"a roof over your head."

The first housing had a very long roof; a barracks at the bottom of the hill, overlooking the football field, that had been built as temporary housing for the returning G.I.'s, abandoned now that crisis had been met, but resuscitated for the recent faculty housing shortage, in fact for us. The living room with torn sofa and broken easy chair was the center for long corridors which ran on each side. Off the corridors were rooms with bunk beds: one, with concrete floor, rows of basins, shower stalls and toilets, was a more than adequate bathroom. There was no kitchen. No place even to boil water for the longed-for cup of tea. It was not an auspicious start. Any stoicism I might have had vanished after a grueling trip from Wisconsin with two small children (no freeways in those days) in a heat wave, (no air conditioning in those days) not only to an empty larder, but no larder at all. It was too much. I burst into tears. We were supposed to have left the Cabin Camp and graduate housing behind; we were supposed to better ourselves. Certainly this was not the reward I had waited for.

While Kimon tackled the authorities, sure that we had come to the wrong place, assuring me that there must be a house somewhere, I stepped out the front door with the children, onto the soothing green expanse of the football field, and across it into the cool depths of my first Ohio hardwoods. The psalm, so often repeated at the Canadian school, returned with vivid meaning; *he maketh me to lie down in green pastures,* except that I lay down in the deep shade, the still waters were still to be discovered. Body and temper cooled. The children played, frisking like puppies, while I stretched into musky leaves and dozed. By the time we returned to the barracks, our new home, my perspective had changed. The children were running in delighted circles to flop and roll in the clovery grass, (no weed killers in those days) and I could only think how wonderful it was for them to have this huge playing field outside their own door, so what if we didn't have a kitchen, things could only get better. And they did. Apologies and explanations were given, (mix-up in days) promises made, (kitchen tomorrow—not the way it happened, but there was hope). Other faculty took us as a refugee project, with offers of food, beds, rooms, camp stove, anything we needed or didn't need, and there was no need to cook because it seemed the entire college had set to for us.

In those days a small liberal arts college was intimate.

Not only did the faculty know each other and live on campus, but the faculty knew all the students and entertained every freshman who entered in the fall. It was a bewildering change, after a big university and comparative anonymity, to have one's life known and monitored by the whole town. The telephone operator could find or comment on anyone from her central switchboard. "He has gone to the library," or "Mrs. Hand just left in the car," or "just a minute I can ask Mr. Frost where the meeting is" or "the Tylers are having a party tonight, so Mable might be there—she should be."

It was almost like being back in Greece, the extended family being the whole town and college. The barracks were wonderful for small children who could ride tricycles up and down the long corridors on bad days, the football field was a source of fun when practice was in session and excitement during games. Just on the other side of the field was the mystery path meandering through mixed hardwoods over ancient stumps, decayed fence posts, and fairy-like clearings to a stream (the still waters) and sugar house.

Baby-sitters were always available, we were young, energetic and optimistic. The huge bathroom became home to stray or orphaned animals, and a new puppy. My brother Leonard arrived one morning, unexpectedly as usual, with an orphaned lamb.

"I've got the bottle, just feed it every so often," he advised.

"A real lamb! Will it follow us everywhere we go like Mary's lamb?"

"Right on," was the answer. "Just try to get away. They bond you see, and think whoever feeds them is the mother. I was going to bring them a couple of ducks," he turned to me, "but I thought the lamb would be better, more fun."

"Uncle Len you are the best uncle anyone could have," Io hugged the soft animal.

"How did you know that we needed a lamb?" Alice asked. No wonder Len was a hero to our children. They never knew when he would drop in or what he would bring. Best of all we had the space, children, puppy and lamb were all safe outside the door with their private lawn and secret woods.

Perhaps because we were young, energetic and optimistic, or it may have been my father's refrain—"own the roof over your head," we longed for our own house. When one day a friend told us that a house in the village was coming up for sale we decided that this was the time to buy. We knew that Coola and Theodore were becoming impatient to see us. Several times in recent letters the possibility of a trip within the year had been mentioned. If we bought a house now we would be well settled in to welcome them.

"We just cannot have them come to this," I said to Kimon sweeping my arm round the dormitory. "Your mother would know she had been right all along about you being a professor. She would really be appalled if she thought a shabby place like this was provided for faculty."

"You're right," Kimon agreed, "we should be decently settled in our own home when they come."

We would show them that life in the U.S. could be pleasant, not luxurious on our salary, but decent and dignified. We would receive them into an attractive up-to-date home of our own with all modern conveniences, we would take them to the theater and concerts and on shopping sprees and we would have a bower of flowers for them to sit amongst in the garden. They could take the long walks they enjoyed so much, and devote hours to the grandchildren they knew now only through photographs. I was sure they would delight in the round of our daily life as much as I had their life in Greece. They would have a complete rest and change.

We took the plunge and bought the run-down house in the village. Little did we know as we signed the deed how all our plans were to backfire. As events worked out we would have been much better off as renters in the minimal college housing during the next year than as harassed overworked house owners.

The house we bought, and I fell in love with, was a hundred and fifty year old derelict with possibilities. I had dragged home stray cats, dogs and birds all my life, so it was no wonder that my heart went out to the neglected house, obviously it needed a good home. When all our friends thought we had gone mad, Kimon and I saw the property as we would make it. Even before the deed had changed hands we had mentally redone the house. We saw the sagging porch torn off, the shutters replaced, the classic Western Reserve doorway exposed. We saw the neglected grounds tidied and beautified by blazing perennial beds and masses of old fragrant roses. In our minds, it all proceeded without effort. The porch was gone, there was no debris to be hauled away, the roses were climbing and blooming at the entrance, the rooms needed only a paint job, all so easy with a roller. The plan was to spend the summer on renovations so that when school opened we would move into a comfortable house, with every amenity and great character.

As it happened, the house was not turned over to us until August and the estimates from professionals were so exorbitant that we were forced to take on all but the skilled work ourselves. As if that were not bad enough we had an excited letter from Coola to say that they would be able to come sooner than expected and were making plans to be with us that very autumn. Now what?

Since my visit Papou had died and Coola had moved the family and her business to Athens. The apartment building on the land—the rock she had showed me before I sailed for home—had been built; that was a feat in itself, with difficulties unlimited that we had heard about through letters. Difficulties not only with workmen but the bureaucracy which required permits, endless waits in government offices, and constant delays. Two of the five apartments had been sold to finance the building so that quality of construction would not be compromised. The view, as seen from balconies stretching the width of the building was of the Parthenon and Acropolis on one side and the rock of Lycabettos on the other.

As if this were not enough, with the move to Athens, Coola had now established her business in a chic shop in Kolonaiki and named it Style, where fashionable ladies came for fittings, where three seamstresses worked in the inner rooms fashioning Coola's designs, where fabrics she brought from Italy and Switzerland lined shelves. In the meantime, what had I done? Walked the woods, cleaned, cooked, carried on conversations with preschoolers. I was suffering from housewife inadequacies.

I did understand Coola's obsession to be upper-middle class which meant everything new and modern. For a Greek of her background and time the rush from a medieval society into the twentieth century was headlong and ruthless where it involved old possessions or buildings. I remember her telling me that she got rid of all Yaya's copper pots, "always in the villages, those pots, now we have new aluminum, never need tinning." In a few years Germans were haunting every shop in Greece for this old copper and buying it up at exorbitant prices.

Understanding all this did not help me with the oppression of my own inadequacies and the miserable place we were bringing this couple to.

"What are we going to do with them in the middle of Ohio, not even a house, just a derelict army barracks even the Greek army would spurn. They can't come now," I moaned. "There are no flowers, no roses."

"No bathroom, no kitchen, no heat," Kimon continued.

These were some of the deficiencies in our new house that we found only after signing the papers. The wiring was a fire hazard, the furnace obsolete, the original lead plumbing already leaking, the kitchen no more than a sink hanging on a wall. The walls could not be painted, they had to be stripped of generations of wall paper which had covered not just cracks but holes in horsehair plaster. The same was true for the floors, old poplar and ash boards, covered with layers of linoleum that had melted through the years into a smear of thick black asphalt-like glue, all but impossible to remove.

"We have to put them off," I insisted. "What about the cold, winter will be coming?" I was desperate. How could I return hospitality in this derelict, how would I find the time, with all the renovation work we had allotted ourselves? I knew enough of Coola's values, her feelings that a good education and advanced degree excluded you from any kind of manual labor. I remembered the small boys making deliveries to the house in Greece where not even six peaches are carried home. They were not coming all this way to sit and watch us strip wall paper. On the other hand we couldn't disappoint them and they might not be able to come later. We would just have to conquer the most difficult jobs before they came and put the rest aside. Surely if the furnace worked, we had a bathroom and kitchen, and the place looked fairly clean we would be able to relax. But delay after delay frustrated our plans. Everything took longer than expected. The electrician always went to Canada for fishing this time of year, the furnace man hurt his leg, the plumber found more work than he expected and would have to replace all the pipes—old lead, poison, he told us.

When three weeks before the expected arrival of Coola and Theodore, we were still torn up we realized there was no hope for it. We would receive them in the barracks and take them for walks in the woods. Would that compensate? It would have to.

I made myself a pest with the workmen. I explained the situation; elderly parents from another country, visiting for the first time, not just visiting but visiting America, the land of warm houses and bathrooms. Their patriotism came through. "Don't you mind," I was finally told, "everything will be working that we can do, now for the rest . . ." our man of the hour gestured at the walls only partially stripped, shreds of paper in tangles on the floor. "You say you doing all that?"

"Don't worry about my end," I said with a confidence I didn't feel.

"Perhaps," I consoled Kimon, "they will think it fortunate they came in time to help. You know how your mother always writes that she wishes she could be near to help with the house and children."

"Help yes," Kimon moaned, "but they have no idea what we'll be going through. Can you imagine my father being of any help in dismantling the old cast iron furnace?"

I saw Theodore in his white linen jacket, impeccable in the throngs of jostling cab drivers and porters, as he stood at the station to meet the train from Athens. I remembered the time in Greece when Theodore, proving that he was a modern husband, had undertaken to oil the wheels of the stroller. He had covered his hands and face with oil, dripped oil on his best trousers and almost smashed the stroller trying to turn it upside down to get at the wheels. In the end he had left it on end, wheels spinning, and stamped off to fetch the gardener whose job it was to do such things while I, ungraciously, was in fits of laughter. The idea of Theodore doing anything at all with his long useless fingers brought on the same giggles.

Despite the promises of the workmen, and our nonstop efforts, the jobs never seemed to end. We learned the hard way that in working with an old house, one job opens onto another quite unexpected one. By the time Coola and Theodore called to us from New York the house was torn up inside and out; everything started and nothing finished. We were so exhausted from the long hours and anxiety over the whole situation, I at least, felt more like weeping at the sound of their voices than rejoicing. There, at the other end of the phone they could not see our expressions or the chaos around us, and were so pathetically excited at the thought of being with us and seeing the children again we decided we would forget the house and try to meet them joyously. For the two days they stayed in New York to see the sights, we were scraping paint off our hands and laying in supplies of groceries.

For the provisions Kimon had gone into Cleveland to the Mideast grocery, with one of his best friends, Yuksel a Turk, (Greeks and Turks are traditional enemies) where the two of them had spent a glorious day selecting a true feast, what one didn't think of the other did, as the food of both countries is so similar.

When the bags were set out on the kitchen table, it looked as if we were going into the grocery business ourselves.

"Look," Kimon held high a gallon tin of olive oil. "Greek.

The best. And olives, Greek olives, just look." He opened three containers, each with a different type of olive.

"But . . ." I was cut off.

"Halva, I got several, one isn't enough." He quickly pulled out several round tins and put them next to the oil.

"Retsina, oh yes, real retsina, look at the label, I know it seems too good to be true, we should have known of this shop months ago, and look here you'll never guess, you'll never believe I could get it here."

"No," I shook my head, "I'm sure I couldn't believe it, what is it, goat butter?"

My sarcasm was missed. His grin broadened. "You're a wonder, just terrific, that's something I hadn't thought of, me a Greek and I forgot it but you remembered. Well cow's butter will just have to do."

"On our salary we'll be lucky to have any butter," I reminded Kimon, "but go ahead show me the wonder you've found."

"*Dolmades*! Won't we have a banquet, real Greek *dolmades*."

Remember this was in the days before every grocery sold imported olives and pita bread. Our small grocer carried the local staples—Campbell's soup, baked beans, canned corn.

Food taste starts at birth, I thought. Here I've been trying to serve good nourishing meals, roast beef, ham, meat loaf, roast potatoes, fresh buttered vegetables, home made pies and cakes, and all the time my husband was devouring roast beef, he was secretly longing for *dolmades*, no more than a bit of rice wrapped in a grape leaf.

We were fortunate in those days to have a local butcher who sold home cured hams and bacon, real chicken that had been allowed to grow as nature intended, with resulting good flavor, and beef that had never been near a hormone.

"I haven't finished yet, the *pièce de résistance* is still to cone."

"How much did you pay for all this?" I asked tentatively, mentally trying to decide which column of the budget expense account we could borrow from, to pad the grocery column.

"*Baklava* and caviar even *loukoumi*." Kimon burrowed to the bottom of a large bag. "*Loukoumi* I never cared for much." He turned the box of Turkish sweets over in his hand, "but they're so Greek. Now isn't that a sight." Kimon stood back to admire his collection one arm around me, the other waving expansively in the air.

"Yes dear it's just wonderful, but it reminds me ever so much of Campbell's soup."

"Campbell's soup, what on earth do you mean?"

"Don't you remember my story of your mother trying to give me the food I was used to when I was in Greece, how I longed to have Greek cooking? You know maybe your parents would like to take us as they find us. They might enjoy a roast of beef."

"For the first few days anyway they'll find us with a Greek cuisine," Kimon countered completely undaunted.

Even if it turned out that Coola and Theodore were not particularly thrilled with Kimon's Greek delicacies, it was worth everything to see how Kimon had enjoyed the planning. I realized that food can conjure up more associations than anything else, it forms a bond to past memories, childhood memories, the strongest.

It was with mixed feelings that we drove to the station to meet the grandparents, but Kimon had a speech prepared, warning them that we still hadn't moved from the barracks, that our house was in the turmoil of restoration, but they need do nothing but play with the children they had been so longing to see. I was silent, still visualizing what was not. A bright, cheerful house, with the clinging aroma of fresh bread and apple pie (I was good at making both) a colorful bouquet in their bedroom, picked from our own lavish garden, lavender in the drawers and bars of Yardley's soap in the bathroom. There had been no time or energy to replace our faded towels and sheets, so I had carefully made the beds with the tear at the bottom, the towels soaked in clorox, showed very little stain from being snatched from the orphan rabbit box; it was all I could muster from a shattered House and Garden dream of welcome.

The train was an hour late and the children who had been hopping with excitement for days over meeting the grandparents from Greece, whom they did not remember at all, had fallen asleep. It may have been Kimon's effort to make his parents feel at home with Greek food that set the pattern but so much was *déjà vu*. There they were, the scene a repeat of the train platform in Greece. There was Coola directing a mountain of luggage, half hidden behind a huge rectangular box, not looking in the least travel-worn in her beautifully tailored moss green tweed suit set off by a smart hat, brown leather bag, gloves and shoes. She was just as chic as she had been that day she had met me on the dock in Greece. Theodore was no less smart in an English tweed suit, British shoes and Macintosh. Before she could embrace us Coola had to prop her monster box against a wall.

"An oil painting by our best artist," she said before launching into torrents of Greek. At least it's not a lampshade, I thought.

"*Chryso mou, chryso mou, pethakia mou.*" She hugged the children, hugged us, then hugged the children again. When she left off Theodore took over, holding on high first one child then the other, repeating as he had on our first visit, "My darlings, my darlings."

The children were unprepared for such an enthusiastic greeting but sensed that they were very special to these Greek grandparents who laughed and hugged them with complete lack of restraint. Immediately they piped up with their most important news.

"Carol, she lives up the hill, she's in my grade, she's got a new two-wheeler."

"Tom, he's had a two-wheeler for a long time, he found a dead bat yesterday, it was black, but really sleeping with its mouth open. We had a beautiful funeral."

I was thankful Coola missed most of that conversation. A dead bat would not be her idea of a play thing for her grandchildren.

"Yes, yes, my darlings you speak so much you must teach your grandmother who is not so good with English."

During a lull in the usual Greek exuberance of greeting, everyone talking at once and no one listening, I managed to ask, "Is that really a painting in the crate?"

"Yes, very beautiful, I carried it with me, these porters take no care. It must not be damaged."

"Like the lampshade in Greece," I said. "Someday you should travel without encumbrances."

"These things make her trip more exciting and mine unbearable," Theodore commented.

It wasn't until everything had been stowed into the car and city traffic left behind that Kimon finally broke the news about the house. He explained in Greek and English how all our plans had gone wrong, how we had hoped to receive them in style and now instead we would go to our rented quarters until the house was fit to live in. He dwelt too on the state of the house and what a shock it would be to them, they who had just built such a beautiful building in Greece etc.

"How could anything be wrong now that I can hold my darlings?" Coola answered, hugging the children again. "What do I care about inconvenience? Just to see these little things every day is enough. And how they talk, so much better than their grandmother."

When Kimon and I were alone at last that night I sighed with relief. "Do you know your parents are riding so high now I doubt if they see anything or care about anything but those children. They aren't even offended by their nicknames. After all to call a grandmother Coo-Coo is not very flattering, and Theodore's beautiful name cut to Fidor seems insulting."

"I think they like something other than Yaya and Papou and take a nickname as a sign of affection. Wait until tomorrow when we show them our future home," Kimon warned, returning to the house situation. "But it's true, so far, they have taken everything well, even Watson, Theodore seems to love him already."

We had thought that Watson, our young boisterous Boxer, would frighten a couple who knew nothing about dogs, just looking at him was enough to scare off most people. The Boxer breed have certain characteristics which make them at once the most lovable and most provoking of animals. Watson lived up to all the traits of his breed. He was stubborn, so stubborn he didn't care what the consequences were, he would do as he pleased. He was affectionate, but not just quietly affectionate like other dogs, with a wagging tail and caressing tongue. For Watson nothing less than an embrace would do. An embrace by a Boxer, even a pup of forty or fifty pounds, a pup with paws like saucers and a face like an African tribal mask was memorable. In the way animals have of sensing situations he did not knock Coola and Theodore flat on their backs to stand over them to lick their faces. He behaved like a gentleman, stayed on the floor and only trod on feet, arching his back and quivering his stump tail in welcome. When Theodore sat down he came with the dignity of a lion and placed one huge rough paw in Theodore's lap then turned his head to one side, as if to say, "take my paw and with it goes my heart." Theodore who had never had a dog, looked in surprise at this offering and then holding the rough paw in one hand he patted the broad head. The friendship was sealed. From then on Watson could do no wrong and for Theodore he became the third child. The two became devoted friends, Watson even forsaking his bed in our room to sleep near Theodore. There is nothing more flattering than the voluntary friendship of an animal, and animals seem to know when and how to bestow their affections or loyalties. In this case the dog seemed to sense that here was a man who was ripe for friendship, who had never had this blind understanding of an animal and who could be trusted.

The next morning was like Christmas. It had been too late the previous night to unpack all the suitcases so this great treat was saved for morning. I remembered the first visit Coola had made when she had come just as laden as now. Watching her pick out present after present, I thought she had not aged at all, if anything she looked even younger. Perhaps it was her joy at being with her grandchildren. Theodore never took his eyes from his granddaughters who were dancing with delight around their newfound grandparents.

After the presents had been examined and admired, presents for us all, the children, our home, and of course for my parents and brother, we could no longer avoid taking Coola and Theodore to the house. We knew only too well what still lay ahead despite the hours we had put in already. By now we did not see the house as it presented itself to us every day, we only saw it as it would be. Unfortunately, I could also see it as this couple would see it, who themselves had just finished building one of the finest apartment houses in Athens; constructed of reinforced concrete with parquet floors, marble, and wide terraces opening onto a view of the city and acropolis. We had tried to explain the building tradition of the New World where wood was the material of choice, that even the best, grandest houses were constructed of wood. Then Kimon who is always carried away by any idea he loves, played up the historical aspects. "This house," he told his parents, "is a period piece, a part of early Americana, one of the first houses to be built in this community. It is over one hundred and fifty years old."

Coola and Theodore looked at Kimon and laughed. "Yes very old," was Theodore's restrained comment. They must have been thinking how Americanized their son was, that he a Greek, could consider old, a building of a mere one hundred and fifty years.

His parents might have been ignorant underclass sudents, in urgent need of lessons in classical architecture, as in ardent terms he described the beauty of the Greek revival doorway, the grace and simplicity of the structure, the perfect proportions; I felt that he was building them up for an approximation of the Parthenon at least.

"It would be a crime not to restore this house." he went on, "built with such care by the early pioneers who had traveled through hardships, primeval forests, Indian attacks, to settle here. Think of the trees felled, land cleared, daily survival. The only problem is that we have had so many delays." He was launched now into a defense of the entire project. "The real work is only now getting underway. Ignore the superficial confusion, just look at the basic structure."

This last was said just as we drove up to a massive pile of wood which because of a roof looked as if it might at one time have provided shelter. The car stopped—Coola and Theodore looked at each other in bewilderment. When the children sprang out calling, "Come and see our new house," they looked stricken. The children dragged them as if in a trance, on up the plank which served as front steps, between piles of debris; the remains of the old porch and bathroom complete with broken toilet, plaster, slats and odd pipes all tossed together. The property was fenced on one side by what could well have passed for the village dump. Broken bottles, cans, twisted metal chairs, linoleum, coat hangers, newspapers and old clothes, formerly the contents of the cellar and attic. The trash man was one of the delays. On the other side of the property was a neighbor's rotting barn with no windows, sagging roof and a dangerous list in our direction.

Everything had been started both inside and out and nothing finished. The plumber was in the process of installing a new bathroom, the carpenter was still tearing out the old. The furnace man was supposed to be hooking up a new furnace to replace the old coal burner. The painter had come and removed most of the windows for restoring, leaving open holes. The trash man expected for two weeks had promised faithfully to have collected everything two days ago.

It was not necessary for the grandparents to be tactful. They were speechless, and that is something for a Greek. They stared in disbelief. As we took them from room to room they seemed increasingly glum. We had hoped that by showing them the living room first, the least torn up, they would be able to visualize how the rest would be. This room had needed no major alteration so we had redecorated here, really to impress them of what was to come. The walls had been repapered after the old layers had been removed, and the woodwork painted. But the floors were our real pride. Under the layers of linoleum we had found solid wide boards, and after scraping away the old paint found them to be ash. That was all we needed to start sanding, the most filthy grueling job, to be undertaken only once in a life time in the naiveté of youth. In the end with a soft oil finish which brought out the natural grain of the wood, the results were thrilling—for us.

At last Coola spoke. "So much work to do, so much work."

With a far away expression Theodore, described the building in Athens. He told us exactly how the parquet had been laid, piece by piece by expert workmen.

"Well," I said quickly. I didn't want him to linger on comparisons, "when the plumber and furnace man finish we'll have only the fun of decorating. By the way, did you notice the hand hewn timbers in the basement and attic? Houses aren't built like that any more. The trouble is with the workmen, not the house," I went on. "They say they'll come on a certain day at a certain hour, then weeks go by and they never show up."

"Ah, workmen," Theodore ventured, "that is always the trouble even in Greece. I had many difficulties, they do good work, but always there are two who don't get along and the whole day can be wasted while they argue." At last we had found a frame of reference. "The painters are the best, they always sing. All day long they sing; they have the best voices and know all the Greek songs."

The initial shock was over and we had all survived. Coola and Theodore were even resigned, after long explanations on our part about houses, housing, and property. Grudgingly they admitted that we had done the right thing. What else could they say? Then with typical good will they settled down to help. We had suggested that the greatest help would be to look after the children which would free us for work on the house. Oh, yes lovely, of course, but this was not enough, they wanted to work too.

"I have watched the painters paint our whole building," Theodore said, "show me what you want painted and I can do it as it is done in Greece," implying with this remark that nowhere is painting done better.

With reason we were leery of Theodore as a workman. He had done nothing with his hands in his whole life. The first day they were with us, it was evident that Coola had primed him on a man's role in America, he had seized the mop before I could stop him and proudly announced that he had been watching the servant do this in Greece so he could be a help to me, and now it would be his job to mop the floors every day. I didn't bother to say that once a month was more like it. Dressed in English tweeds, hand tailored Egyptian cotton shirt and Italian silk tie, Theodore's uniform, he started swishing the mop with great vigor and immediately upset a lamp. No sooner had that been righted than he knocked over a table which held our favorite vase, smashing it to pieces. Poor Theodore was so upset, he vowed to replace it with one more beautiful and then confessed that although he had watched he had not been able in Greece to practice the skill of mopping. "Someone might have seen me," he explained. We assured Theodore that there was no need for him to mop floors, that I seldom did, and that there were other more manly occupations for him such as taking out garbage and walking Watson. From that day those jobs became his personal contribution to our servantless household, a daily ritual like the opening of his shop in Greece. In cold weather he would put on boots, an extra sweater under his jacket, then a heavy overcoat, scarf, hat and gloves, all to take out the garbage.

Coola said to me, "show me to wash dishes, this I can do."

(In those days automatic dishwashers were rare). Dishwashing became her chore.

Meantime the work progressed all too slowly. It seemed at times that nothing was accomplished unless we did it ourselves. The workmen would come one day, giving us unfounded hope, cut through walls, make holes in floors and then depart. Weeks would go by without seeing them again. Finally Kimon got through to them in some mysterious way; they must have felt some sort of minimal compassion, but every one promised to come the following Saturday, the day we had chosen for the final work of sanding the upstairs floors. The success in the living room had spurred us on.

The sander was rented at dawn from the local hardware where we were by now on intimate terms. The owner, Mr. Irwin, and all the assistants were very much au courant with the restoration and long hours had been spent in consultation over heating, plumbing, tools, in fact everything; they had become a second family. Theodore was to start his Greek painting technique, and Coola had set herself to picking up debris inside and out.

So there we were, Kimon in charge of the large sander, I was trying to control a flighty little machine called an edger and keep it from sailing out the window with me attached, the children were running in and out of the house enjoying the confusion and playing hide and seek behind piles of rubbish, Watson was trying to keep track of everyone.

I was running the machine which besides the rasping noise, had the same effect on the operator as a reducing vibrator, when the plumber arrived with his helper. Kimon had to stop work to tell him all the fixtures had come and were in the basement on a table. The sanding was resumed to be interrupted half an hour later when the carpenter came.

"Yes, that's the lumber in the hall. Nails? Just a minute. Turn off that infernal thing I want to speak to you." Kimon shouted in my ear. "That's better. What about nails?"

"Nails? What nails dear?"

"How do I know? Joe wants to know if the nails came."

"In brown paper bags?"

"In brown paper bags?" Kimon shouts to the carpenter below.

"Yeah, sure, how else?"

"They're all on the kitchen sink then," I answer.

"They're on the kitchen sink," Kimon shouts down.

"O.K. Gottcha.

"The noise and dust keep us company for another half hour.

Next comes the furnace man. He is too meek to shout over the noise of the dragon so tugs at Kimon's sleeve, making him jump. Kimon turns off the motor, none too pleased with the deep gouge plowed in that second's jerk on the handle.

"Just to make sure I'd like to show you what I'm installing. The 9 inch elbow instead of the 12. Now if you'd prefer the 12 I'll do it that way, but most folks go with the 9 inch."

"Whatever you do will be fine with me," Kimon replies still eying the furrow in the floor.

"Just come on down and I'll explain, so's you'll get it right." A good teacher never taking for granted that the student understands. A hands on demonstration.

Half an hour later Kimon's machine starts again, runs for a few minutes before Theodore comes in, hands drenched in paint.

"Where do you keep the turpentine?"

Then Coola appears. "If I can have a box I clear away all plaster."

Another twenty minutes of sanding and the carpenter shows up again. "Them nails is all the wrong size. I'll have to go to town to get the right ones."

And so the day wore on. We couldn't swear at the interruptions as we had been praying for these men to come for weeks; and that one day, hectic as it was saw us over the hump. From then on the work sped along, if speed can be considered having workmen turn up at all.

We had become used to having neighbors and the whole village disturb our work and the guided tours were time consuming but a necessary evil in a small community where a house that hadn't been touched for a hundred years was undergoing such a face lift. We heard several variations from the old timers of the community about the origins of the place and who had lived in it.

"It was Holmans had the best garden," the president of the historical society told me one day. "I approve of all you've done," she confided to me. "It was time this house was taken over, what you've done has helped the whole town." It was satisfying to have town approval.

There were other do-it-yourselfers who gave us detailed accounts of how they had done painting, heating, plumbing, what tools they had used, or how they had solved a problem with drains or leaks. Our renovations were the highlight of the summer and on Sundays a procession of cars would creep by with the passengers craning necks to see what was being done to the old Field place. (A house, until recent memory faded, kept the name of the last occupant). Many would wave and call as we perched on a ladder or were picking up debris which seemed to accumulate outside the front door.

"Never noticed that doorway before, sure is pretty."

"Doing a fine job,"

"What color you going to paint the shutters?"

We were finally able to move in. The painting and decorating finished, the newly found floors gleaming and now at last the house looked as we had wished Coola and Theodore could have seen it when they first arrived. They were as proud of all the work accomplished as we were, more so perhaps.

"It is impossible," Coola said, "I never thought it could be done. Now you must have curtains. I make them." Which she did when the furniture had been moved in. Even though she said she hated sewing, there was no thought of buying ready-made. She found remnants, to offer a greater challenge, turning and piecing, she created the most distinctive curtains for every room, which were the envy of all our friends. When the curtains were finished she started on clothes for the children.

By the time we had moved in the students had returned and Kimon was fully occupied with his courses. The house was comfortable, remarkably so with large airy rooms, large kitchen for everyone to gather and a separate room for Kimon's study.

Now, even with endless odds and ends to be done we decided to call a halt to all disrupting projects. It was time to start living. We had not been anywhere; the Cleveland Art Museum, concerts at Severance Hall, The Play House, even Niagara Falls were included in the new plans.

Coola was now faced with the realities of the modern husband. As long as we were all working on the house and Kimon didn't have classes she seemed to take the American do-it-yourself attitude in stride. Now however, dressed in coat and tie, her son left every morning for a strenuous round of teaching. He returned completely exhausted, a state I had come to know only too well. I had learned to leave him alone at such times and above all, not to be chatty. There were certain domestic occupations which he found relaxing, such as making a soup or pasta sauce. Now Coola made the decisions about what he should or should not do. Throwing a ball for the dog was permissible but picking up a hammer to hang a picture was not, and certainly puttering in the kitchen was out.

"I just don't want to speak," he would say. "After lecturing three hours I'm drained."

Coola would circle Kimon just as he picked up the hammer and in the tone of one addressing an idiot child would tell him to sit quietly and read the paper.

"We are two women in house now," she would say. "You have your work, let the women do theirs."

"But I don't want to read the paper now, I don't want to read anything, I don't ever want to see a printed word again and I don't ever want to speak another word, I just want to hang this picture and I don't care if it is a woman's job, right now, to me, it seems like fun."

"You are tired and work too hard," Coola would say, like a nurse restraining a delicate patient, ignoring his pleas to be allowed to find his own relaxation. "Leave this to us, don't you worry about the house."

"But don't you see Mama, this is the kind of worry that is no worry. Just to do some little thing is restful."

"You have worked so hard you don't know how to rest." Coola never gave up.

The first time Kimon served his own soup, the soup he had made against all orders, he was as pleased as a child over a drawing.

"You have never tasted such a soup even in Greece," he said proudly ladling it out. "And the recipe is a secret. My own concoction. Isn't it superb, it's all in the seasoning."

"But poor boy, you shouldn't have to come home and make soup."

By this time the children had finished theirs and were in a hurry to get out, I was sick of the word soup and was in as much of a hurry to escape. Theodore tasted with the appropriate look of a connoisseur and diplomatically pronounced it the best he had ever had, even in Greece and Coola was grudgingly eating hers.

As I made excuses to leave with the children, I heard Kimon in good Greek style of never letting an argument go, continue his theme. "I don't have to come home and make soup, but sometimes I just feel like making soup and this is my house and if I want to make soup in it I don't see why I can't, and I don't care if I'm the only man in the world who makes soup. While I made this soup I didn't have to think of anything except how to bring out the flavor, which herbs to use and just how much. Sometimes Mama all I want to think about is soup."

"My poor boy you have worked too hard," was the inevitable reply. She seriously thought her son's brain had been affected through his years of study. In a way it had because there were times when he didn't want to use it at all.

Coola was torn between two ways of life. She knew in a servantless household that a husband had to perform some domestic duties, but she could not understand that manual work could be any kind of therapy, especially for an academic. She had coached Theodore on how to be a modern husband, but she could not reconcile herself to seeing her son, a professor, performing household duties. The whole idea of a man pitching in to help his wife she could accept in theory but in practice it was still too new to her.

Despite all the nagging we did settle into a fairly normal routine, school, walks, meeting friends, entertaining them and being entertained in turn; some of these friends visited the grandparents years later when they travelled in Greece. Coola and Theodore loved going about the countryside in the car, most especially during the spectacular Ohio autumn foliage, a sight not to be matched in Greece. There were visits from my parents and my brother, a dashing man of great wit with an unconventional attitude toward the world. For Theodore he was the epitome of the British officer, and for Theodore there could be no higher praise. In those far distant days of bribery and chaos in Smyrna, it seems the British had been the only refuge of order and impartial justice. My mother delighted in teasing both Coola and Theodore, and sending the entire household into fits of laughter. My father, ever remote, polite, gracious, with his biblical and literary aphorisms, won over Theodore by his "correctness." Most especially they delighted in their grandchildren. Their sayings were repeated, gestures commented on, their beauty and perfection were an every day subject; they could do no wrong. This bias continued through adolescence when it is hard for parents to find any good in their offspring. Perhaps that is why we need grandparents.

Some aspects of American life they could not adjust to. "Where do you go to watch the people?" was a constant refrain. At that hectic time of my life I couldn't think when I would ever have time to watch anyone, but I accepted the fact that without the coffee house, pub or cafe we were a deprived lot.

In Greece, Theodore had been holder of the keys and every door and drawer had a lock. Every night he made the rounds locking up everything and every morning he unlocked, not just the doors but the drawers in the kitchen holding cutlery, the pantry with linens and utensils, even the bedroom drawers. I had been told this was because the maids would steal everything. Now Theodore was uncomfortable when we all got in the car for an outing without locking the house, or even took a walk without locking. In our small college town no one locked doors, our house didn't even have a key.

"Look at the papers." Coola said. "We do not have such crimes in Greece. Murders, every day, and you do not lock."

"It is not like the big city here," I tried to explain.

"In Athens we do not have such murders. We only have crime of passion, or honor. That must be. But what I read here!"

It took decades for Athens even to have theft to report, and still they are far behind us. But Hiram? In those days it was idyllic. One Sunday morning Coola came into the kitchen to find a small boy serving himself corn flakes and milk, Watson at his feet waiting for a hand out. "Hi," the small boy said, mouth full of food, "Mom and Dad aren't up yet so I came for breakfast."

There was the incident with our two girls. Three houses away lived a senior professor, very correct with his very correct wife. If she went off for the day she left her husband's lunch ready for him on the kitchen table, according to the custom of those days, when men were not considered capable of opening a can. On this occasion she had left the tuna sandwich wrapped in wax paper set on a China plate, next to it a jello salad topped with cottage cheese, and a small plate of homemade ice box cookies. Our girls had gone for a visit but finding no one home, the door open and lunch set, had like Goldilocks sat down to enjoy the spread, dividing it between them and leaving the wax paper neatly folded next to the empty plate.

Children were safe anywhere, everyone knew them, where they lived and where they were supposed to be at any time. There were fields, woods, ponds to explore, brambles for hideaways, vines to swing from, small animals to discover, alive or dead and eventually a horse to care for and ride into the countryside, without fear.

Finally the visit was over, it was time for the grandparents to return, they wanted to pick up in Athens the routine they loved; Coola especially needed more of a challenge than we could offer, she needed to be running a business, not our lives. We desperately needed to live without discussing at length the minutiae of everyday life, and Kimon the only son, needed to be left alone. Only Theodore could have settled in happily with books, Watson to walk, the children to spoil.

There had been times, during their stay, when I doubted that any of us would speak to the other again but the final success of the tense beginning was expressed in Coola's parting words.

"For the good of all you must come to us in Athens next year! Until then, Be Happy!"

I was much too self absorbed at that stage of my life to realize what that expression meant to Coola. I knew the facts of her own life struggles, struggles for survival, but I was too slow to put this into the context of our lives. I had listened to her stories of fortitude and ingenuity in keeping a family alive but the words had not transposed for me until years later, into the scars she bore and her desperation for us, not to have to repeat her life.

My parents.
Grumps and Patie.

Grumps and Patie

G RUMPS NAMED HERSELF as a joke and it stuck, Len called his father the Pater, corrupted to Patie. And that stuck; as much Coola, nicknamed Coo-Coo, and Theodore, called Fidor by small children, were in our lives long distance or long stays, my parents were in our lives through visits to wherever they were living. Letters were vital for both sides of the family and I was the letter writer. This was long before email or cell phones; still at a time when my father considered a long distance call an emergency and raised his voice to be heard so far away.

When we were first married we were frequently at the farm in Michigan, then it was the farm on the Eastern shore of Maryland, and finally, Florida.

The farm in Maryland my father had bought on another romantic impulse. Remote, a mile and half drive from the main road; waterfront, a mile of beach on Chesapeake Bay; land, two hundred acres of pine and scrub. He loved it. My mother loathed it. On these two hundred acres he put two Black Angus cows, male and female. His idea was that with no effort on his part the two would eventually become many and multiply biblically. What they did do was range beyond the two hundred acres to be found or rounded up miles away, always at the most inopportune time. My mother coaxed them to stay close, by feeding them corn cobs twice a day which did help.

"There's Bullion," she would say when the bull stared into the kitchen window blowing hot breath on the glass. "He is always around now. Just wants a little attention. Why doesn't someone give him a good grooming?" She was sympathetic to animals anywhere but not to these forbidding surroundings.

"Just listen to the wind in the pines." My father

"No lights, no laughter, nothing."

"How can you say that, every time I come down the drive I see fox or deer, and listen to all the wildfowl."

"And what about all the hunters shooting everything in sight, the noise of guns."

"Only for a few days a year."

"The rest of the time we are eaten by mosquitoes and if a hippopotamus rose out of the pond it wouldn't surprise me."

"Yes, the pond is wonderful right next to the house, you see in the early days they needed the fresh water pond." My father loved the remote, bleak setting. At the time the tidewater colonial was built all transportation was by boat and the road to the highway merely a track.

Our visits were usually at Christmas. We drove from Hiram in a station wagon through the mountains, no turnpike yet, with children and food, warm clothes and presents. The mosquito season was over, the waterfowl had moved in, the oysters were plentiful and walks endless. There was confusion in the inadequately heated house.

"Nothing more than a windbreak," my mother repeated. And confusion in the inadequate kitchen.

"You all go on your way rejoicing and come back to a banged up dinner," said my father trying to help.

His banged up dinner was either corned beef with cabbage, or Campbell's beef stew with potatoes. Amazingly we all tucked in with relish. The sea air must have given us good appetites.

Len turned up on occasion and as usual put otherwise impossible activities into motion, such as exploring the bay by boat with a dubious outboard.

"I got it from a guy who doesn't know anything about motors. All it needs is a little adjustment." Which he did, then loaded as many as the rotting row boat could hold to test the motor out on the frigid waters of the bay, never staying close to shore which I pleaded for. In the end we always returned safely, the children delighted with the adventure of the motor stopping, Len endlessly trying to start it, the drift taking us ever farther out, then the miracle of the cough and put, put to return us to safety. Everything with Uncle Len was fun and an exciting adventure.

There was the Christmas when Roger, too excited to sleep, crept down to the Christmas tree in the dark and opened every present. By the time the rest of us arrived we did a guessing game as to who was the most likely candidate for the tumble of socks, gloves, scarfs, books, etc. It turned out to be a free for all, each claiming the article we fancied. Thank you notes were all the same: 'thank you so much for the beautiful present. It is just what I wanted.'

On one occasion we had agreed with friends to a New Year's party at our house in Hiram before leaving for Maryland. "If we are not back early afternoon just go ahead with whatever you think we should have," I had said to everyone. Of course we were held up by trucks in the mountains where there was no passing, snow in Pennsylvania and Ohio and the inevitable late start. By the time we came into Hiram the children were asleep but our house was glowing, music pounding out the open front door; it seemed the entire faculty was coming and going, some with platters of food, others with bottles.

"It's time you arrived! You'll find drinks in the kitchen and food on the dining room table." This is definitely the way to give a party I thought.

We put groggy children to bed. If it hadn't been for the music and laughter downstairs I would have gone to bed myself, but the pinata had been saved for our arrival. The party continued with parents taking turns to check on children a few houses away, the pinata was broken at midnight, a few more drinks were consumed as even those without children all lived within walking distance. The childless couples lingered until the wee hours, it took me weeks to clean up the confetti from the pinata, but what fun we had at a party we had nothing to do with except leave the door unlocked. That was Hiram!

Florida was a longer trek with station wagon overflowing with children climbing back and forth, mixed with blankets pillows, shoes, dog, and on one occasion Helen's pet crow, Bandit.

All these trips were done before throughways so we drove up and over mountains, through Tennessee with chenille bedspreads decorating cabin yards, every gas station offering a deal on fireworks, and small towns where the light never seemed to change and where there was never anything fit to eat. If we stopped for the night it was at 'Tourist Cabins'. There were no motels and it was never considered that children, dog or crow would not be accepted. Breakfast was the best meal on the road, and one we usually stopped for grits, scrambled egg, toast. If we ever did stop for lunch we avoided the hot beef sandwich, the fried chicken, ham or meat loaf, all served with canned green beans, mashed potatoes with gravy puddle and jello salad. Our order was grilled cheese sandwich, (American cheese it was called) with Campbell's tomato soup. Often these problems were solved by driving through the night. It was for me the best part of the trip; everyone asleep or at least quiet, the roads and towns deserted, and the countryside: hills, or red dog earth, sorghum canes, pecan groves, tobacco fields and drying sheds, one room shacks on stilts surrounded by decaying machinery, all at peace for this instant while I passed.

In St. Augustine there was the excitement of reunion with grandparents and the urgent question, "when can we go to the beach?" Grumps often had a cocktail party planned for the afternoon, where we met the new residents, the snow birds or the art club. The children passed the sandwiches, the dogs, ours and my mother's current dog, frisked underfoot, the Pater told the ladies, no matter how old, that they 'looked like the breath of spring.' Roger aided those breath of spring ladies to their car, handing over the cane, the handbag, the wrap and continuing his grandfather's gracious words with, "It was a delight to see you again Mrs. Twamly."

St. Augustine was life on the beach, no matter what the weather, to be diluted spasmodically with meanderings downtown to visit the fort, the wax museum, or along the boat dock, (not a proper marina then) and critique the carriage horses. As the house at Inlet Drive was on Davis Shores, across the bridge, it was thrilling for our girls, led by Roger as guide, to watch the bridge come up for the shrimp boats and talk to the bridge keeper who was ever ready to tell grim stories to an eager audience. In this way they could pass the morning or the entire afternoon. If I expressed concern for them my father said, "Jove, they are lucky to have Roger. He knows the whole town." This was based on the fact that Roger was enrolled at the convent on the other side of the bridge and as neither of his grandparents had ever heard of driving a child to school—he walked—across the bridge. My mother's big chocolate standard poodle Ozzie made the same walk to visit another chocolate poodle, a street urchin my mother called her. We all wondered how Ozzie knew when or how to find her, but he did and in due time the irresponsible owner (my mother's words) called to say that there were two brown pups. One of those pups taken home at a few weeks became Roger's devoted fun loving companion, Zoe. She started following on walks, progressed to surfing, fishing, sailing and finally motorcycling. Zoe knew every survival technique. Never on a leash, able to jump into or out of anything, cooling in the sprinklers set out everywhere, jumping waves on the beach, she learned to balance on a surf board, and the seat of a motorcycle or beat the motorcycle by cutting corners across yards. On one occasion Roger was caught out in his boat after dark. After frantic searches he was discovered on the beach but because of high tide he couldn't get out nor could we get in. At least we knew where he was and next day when the tide turned he returned with Zoe to say that they had had a wonderful night on the beach, under the boat, listening to the waves. With Zoe he was never alone.

The stories from the bridge keeper were so grim they were repeated with awe to the adults at dinner, Roger who could take on any accent imitating the voice.

"It war back home when lil' Sally Lou fell in the sorghum pot. Jus fell otta the winner an thar she was right in. The screams was sumpin turrble."

"Just like those twelve year old boys playing on the railway bridge," my father would interrupt. "Did poor Sally live?"

"She was fished out and died in her mother's arms," one of the girls would answer.

"Jove it's iniquitous, a child scalded to death."

"Back then," Roger continued the accent, "there war twelve of us young'uns when Pa one day looks to me and sez, Curly y'all be gone by sunup. Cain't feed ya no mo. An I wuz gon never did go home. Lived off'n the land, fish'n, hunt'n. Came natr'l cause I don't lack but lill'bit o bein' a thoroughbred Indian."

"The Indians all knew how to hunt, even make their own bows and arrows." My father loved to reminisce about his youth on the Six Nation Indian Reserve in Brantford Canada.

"Tell us the scalp story," someone would plead. That would be the start for endless Kanyengeh, the parsonage where he grew up, stories the children couldn't get enough of, no matter how many times they had heard them. Stories of pranks played by the vicar's children on visiting friends, and visiting dignitaries. The dignitaries were Bishops from England, unapproachable in black coats and gaiters, to be called "My Lord" when spoken to; in all their formality ripe for children's tricks of runaway horses or Indians behind every tree.

"As long as you are going to sit and listen all of you sit together so I can make a sketch." My mother would pull out pencil and sketch pad and invariably make a record of the evening.

Sunday "early morning service" was inescapable. During our first visits punctuality was required and my father insisted on sitting in the first row of pews. Later as revisions of the prayer book were tried, my father who for too many years had recited the same forms in the same order rebelled at any change.

"Patie we are going to be late." Roger would say.

"Yes, Patie we are all ready to leave," Alice.

"We are late as a protest," Grumps.

"It is just iniquitous. Like burning Cranmer and Ridley and Latimer at the stake again." This referring to changes in the Book of Common Prayer.

At the church we crept down the aisle during the opening prayers, led by Patie who lowered the kneelers with a clatter and recited his own prayers which he had been saying since he could speak, at his own pace and in a loud voice. The rest of us, except for my mother, were trying to sink below the pews and out of sight.

After the service my father, gracious and smiling, would congratulate the vicar on a beautiful service. For him it had been, as against the rest of the congregation, he had continued the familiar ritual of a lifetime.

From Fellowship
to Fellowship

IN THOSE DAYS an unusual faculty had been assembled at Hiram College, whether by chance or deliberate care, I don't know but there was a humane and intellectual excitement rare I think on any campus, and extraordinary in such a small college. It was Hiram's liberal leave-of-absence policy which, through the years, allowed us so much time off campus, and we were not the only beneficiaries. There were those like Kimon who sought grants, others who set up foreign study programs (a new concept then), or established special gardens. There was the Shakespeare garden John Shaw created for the English house, the garden Roland Layton cut out of tangled shrubbery behind the history house, the purple beech garden Grace Gruenler insisted on when there was talk of cutting down a magnificent tree for a parking lot, the historical garden a treasure of heritage plants salvaged from cemeteries, roadsides and abandoned farm houses by Jim Barrow the biology professor. Through Jim a biology station was created on the edge of town, with ponds and viewing rooms to watch migrating birds, and other areas to monitor animal behavior, especially fowl.

Our family settled in to surfing the waves of Kimon's brilliance; washing up first in Madison for a year at the University of Wisconsin, where Kimon was guest lecturer, then in Brussels, Belgium, on a Belgian-American grant, a few years later in Washington D.C. with a grant to study at Dumbarton Oaks, and finally a year in Greece on a grant at the Gannadius Library. Along with these yearlong stays, for twenty years we spent all but a few summers in Greece, where Coola planned our visits "for the good of all."

Kimon was brilliant. Not smart, as so many pseudo-intellectuals are today with heads full of facts and figures, but intelligent. As a graduate of Athens College, he had an excellent background in languages, literature, philosophy and history, even science, as he had started out to become a chemist. What set him apart was his ability to judge, analyze and synthesize the facts and events of the Middle Ages in a fresh and exciting way. His lectures were never dull, laced with references to classical and modern, tying in literature, architecture, societies; even with supreme logic presenting the philosophy of medieval writers he had studied in manuscript form, and enticing students into discussions. He was a scholar and thinker, ever deep in thought and the epitome of the absent-minded professor. He could pass his own children on the street and never recognize them, he mislaid the most necessary things, wallet, lectures, letters, books. Io and Alice teased him by telling outrageous stories just to watch his reaction. Such as, "we had so much fun today when the toilet overflowed all over the bathroom floor," or "Mummy fell off a ladder and they took her off in an ambulance." Deep in thoughts of the interpretation of a line of philosophy, the usual reply was, "That's nice dear," which would send his children, into fits of laughter.

By the time we returned to Madison for a year to replace Kimon's major professor while he was on sabbatical, we had another daughter, born in Ohio: Helen, so much younger than her sisters was treated like a living doll and spoiled by everyone, especially her father.

For me, the years bumbled along with the usual routines of a non-career housewife. (Looking back I could say non-thinking). It was always nature that gave me the joy and spiritual nourishment I unconsciously craved in the circumscribed life of house and small children. The relentless daily routine and mindless tasks didn't allow for introspection; there was always someone who needed or wanted something so that I was panting to accomplish the round of meals, children's outings, laundry, cleaning and all the mundane tasks with which housewives of my era were saddled. So head down I carried on, fulfilling what I like to call the worm phase of my life.

We had already gone through three Wisconsin winters during student days at the Cabin Camp but with school age children, a proper job and a proper house, we enjoyed the city in a new way. It was fun just to walk the campus in winter to watch the ski jumpers sail off onto the frozen lake or cheer on the ice boats as they whined past at unbelievable speeds. We would walk to the end of Picnic Point, our favorite walk winter or summer, and onto the frozen lake to the ice fishermen's huts. We enjoyed those bitter cold sunny days. Wisconsin winters were not something to hide from indoors but to relish for all the fun they offered.

We lived on the edge of the school district so the walk to school for our two elementary children was a mile. (Helen was too small to attend school). In those days in Madison, the school thought it best for children to return home for lunch (taking for granted stay-at-home mothers), so there was another walk home and then back to school again. The children seemed to thrive on the walks and even in the bitterest cold there were no parents who drove children to school. They dressed for the weather. After school they couldn't wait to be off to the nearest rink to skate until dinnertime when it was all I could do to fill them up. It is sad that children in these days are deprived of walking to school, one of the healthiest releases for youthful energy and imagination. They have the chance to meet friends, giggle, fight, tease, and work out a pecking order of their own. The clothing today is of Everest protection and yet children are not allowed out in cold or wet, as if they might melt, so protected they never feel the bite of wind, the catch of breath from the first step outside on a cold morning, the joy of sun on the walk home, the sparkle of frost, the sullenness of wet days, or the caress of rain on the face. At the time, children are probably not aware of all this but it is part of our animal heritage, our primitive contacts with nature which feed the soul all through life. Walking, running, hopping, skipping, dawdling, roller skating to school formed an important part of the day for our children in Madison. They certainly did not trouble teachers or parents with hyperactivity after their mile walk to school and back four times a day. We were the beneficiaries of a good school system guided by sensible parents.

Those days in Madison Kimon worked endlessly on lectures, so time for entertainment was rare: an evening snatched for a film at the university, a dinner with friends when I could practice upgrading my cooking with the help of Julia Child, weekend forays to Aldo Leopold's Sand Counties, the usual walks to Picnic Point and of course in winter, walks across the lake or children's skating races at the local rink. It was an unexciting, confining, repetitive life and perhaps because of that, easy. With three small children one doesn't crave excitement for one's self, it is just a blessing to end the day alive and more or less sane. It was Madison which saved us.

Family Outing

A T THE END of the year we were not to return to Hiram, except briefly to drop off and pick up clothes for the stint in Brussels, where Kimon had won a Belgian-American grant to the Bibliotheque Nationale.

The plan was to start in June in Germany where Kimon had arranged to buy a new car, a Borgward, in Hamburg, drive through Europe to Greece where we would spend the summer, then return a different route through Europe to Belgium.

This plan brought Coola from Greece, to the very edge of the wharf where we landed in Hamburg. There she was standing out from the dockside confusion, elegant and aloof, in an amethyst blue rain coat, ready for the trip through Europe from one medieval town to another.

The dollar was strong against all European currencies; there was even a book, *Europe on five Dollars a Day*, which was the bible, not only for backpackers, but for all of us traveling modestly. Car rental was not what it is now, available at every airport, station and town; it was unavailable, so buying a car, using the car for the stay then shipping it home as a used car was a popular and practical scheme. Our itinerary, out-of-the-way medieval villages, towns and churches, would have been difficult using only public transportation, good as it was. With the car we had the luxury of flexibility to see Kimon's medieval monuments.

What amazes me now was my persistent naiveté that these "for the good of all" plans could be—not fun—not even I expected that, but even possible. It wasn't as if I didn't know better. Ever the optimist, and still in my worm faze, I somehow clung to the thought that this time it would work. No matter how much one loves each child individually, or husband, or mother-in-law, they are not to be tolerated collectively within the confines of a small car, by any normal person. Baggage was stowed for the most part on top, behind the back seat suitcases were laid flat to make space for Helen. This was well before the days of seat belts so of course there was much climbing back and forth, and the usual squabbling.

"Ouch you stepped on my hand."

"Then why didn't you move?"

"I don't know why we're doing all this, I'd rather be out riding."

"Val look at the map and find out if we go past Rottenburg on this road."

"Always Kimon he thinks of the past."

"I'm not getting out of the car if I see a swan."

"Why don't we see who can count the most horses?"

"It's just cows, there aren't any horses."

"Well count cows then."

"I'm stopping here to let everyone out."

"Kimon we never get to Greece like this."

"Don't you see Mama, we'll never get to Greece if I go crazy."

No matter how picturesque the medieval villages might be, this "holiday" with a two year old, a ten and a twelve year old, husband and husband's mother who argued all the time about everything, is not a recipe to promote kind thoughts about anyone, rather a direct route to insanity, or suicide or murder.

But there we were in the new car, Kimon polishing off every speck of dust on the unblemished paint or spot on the pristine interior, smelling delightfully for all of one day of that new-car smell. If he had known then of what was to become of this perfect paint job he might have let up. That was later: now with a strong dollar at our back, Europe stretched before us on almost deserted roads. The car was called a station wagon but was smaller than today's compacts; the space we squeezed out for six people and luggage was made possible by the rack on top, where our modest luggage was strapped. I still had control over what the children wore so I could pack a minimal wardrobe for them; kilt skirts, one white blouse each, a twin set, a coat, one trouser, underwear, socks, knee and ankle. This meant washing every night and hoping everything would be dry by morning. Coola was an old hand at looking stylish from a small suitcase, quite a contrast to me who didn't have much luggage and showed it by always looking rumpled or stained.

In the diary I kept of that adventure no squabbles were mentioned, nor comments on the claustrophobia of long distance automobile travel. There is mention of stomach upsets, ear aches, restless children waiting endlessly for meals, feeding ducks and being chased by swans, relief at putting everyone to bed, of unremitting rain and cold.

Translated that meant vomiting, diarrhea, visits to doctors who spoke no English, long waits in rigid German restaurants for meals which often turned out to be far from what we imagined with strange sausages and thin soups, hard even for the adults to adjust to, endless walks in parks and castle grounds to release the pent up energy of small children where, if we were not chased by swans, we were constantly scolded for "trespassing" on the grass, (this in a grass growing climate) of trying to slip out at night on our own for one moment of adult conversation and of feeling warm only under a duvet. With few exceptions, the views we planned our route to see, were obliterated by cotton wool fog or lashing rain.

There was the other side, as there always is. The villages which we could see when the rain did stop were certainly picturesque with houses covered in flowers and on the rare occasions when the sun came out the effect was flamboyant: ivy geraniums trailing from every window, fountains and village wells circled with blooms and every patch of soil either filled with flowers or more practically with potatoes, lettuces, cabbage, leeks. There were Gasthofs with welcoming hosts who went out of their way to make us all comfortable, with the best rooms and food. Of course there were very few travelers in those days so there was time for welcomes and questions.

When Coola announced that she must go to Switzerland to pick up the special fabrics for her business in Athens, she wanted Kimon to go with her. They were to be gone only overnight but it seemed to me at the time, like being let out of school. For one day, there would be no bickering, no explanations about anything. The Greek argumentative nature is amusing to watch as a spectator, when a discussion between a cab driver and a motorist he has bumped turns into street drama with pedestrians or motorists nearby taking sides. Voluble insults, threats and menacing gestures which anyone watching would expect to erupt in blows, invariably end with mutters, shrugged shoulders and final curses as the original antagonists part. But to live this intensely every day, with every move questioned and discussed left me exhausted. So now I had the day all to myself with only the children who were so easily amused if they were allowed the outdoors.

Almost as if those Gods of mythology were interfering for me the children met friends in the village, and were invited by the mother for lunch. After many thanks and the children's excitement I felt free to take off through the woods for a long solitary, restorative walk. By the time I returned to pick up the children they were fast friends with Joanna and Heini, even to inviting them to visit in Greece. Over omelet and fried potatoes in the wood paneled Gasthof I heard about the day.

"They have rabbits."

"But we couldn't hold them."

"Do people eat rabbits?" This from Helen.

"Of course they do silly, didn't you hear Heini say that's why they keep them?"

"I'm not going to eat rabbits."

"You will if that's all there is."

"No I won't."

This was disintegrating into the bickering I wanted to avoid. "It is a good thing you didn't come with me because I crossed the bridge where the trolls live all overhung with trees and vines so that you couldn't see under to make sure the trolls were away when you crossed."

"How did you know?"

"I didn't but here I am back."

Next day the Austrian children turned up again and I had another walk before Coola and Kimon returned, Coola very pleased with her fabrics and Kimon with views of mountains and the organization of the Swiss.

We never made reservations in those days, and never have since. How could we know where to stop when Kimon might have to see the cathedral so little out of the way from our tentative route? And ever since, reservations have seemed constricting. Travel, may turn out to be just what was expected or it can be unusual or even grim. On one trip through Yugoslavia, we could not find the hotel we were looking for and asked directions from a man on the street.

"Not good," he said. "Let me show you very nice place. Hotel school, where young men are trained to run our new tourist hotels."

We ended up in what had once been a very grand hotel but now was indeed a hotel school where supposedly staff and management were being introduced to the idea that tourists were to be treated kindly. What we found was a bathroom so filthy I wouldn't allow anyone to use it—we took long walks in the surrounding pine grove. Our dinner, we were the only diners, was on a terrace overlooking the city, decorated with strings of lights with few bulbs still working. Our waiter approached us most formally with pencil and pad in hand. He took our varying orders repeating after us in English—green peas, fried potatoes, tomato salad, snitzel one—biftek two, omelet two with cheese. Carefully he wrote, or pretended to write, the orders. When they came they were all exactly the same. We all got snitzel, fried potatoes and peas. It seems that he could pronounce English after us as if in a classroom, but didn't understand what he heard. It was all done with so many smiles and such effort to be gracious—"Everything good? Very good. Thank you—" (more basic words) We felt obliged to accept with equal graciousness what was brought. We left hoping that for the sake of the new tourist industry training would include the basics of cleanliness.

There was the former palazzo in some town in Italy where we stayed on one occasion when Coola was with us. It was supposed to be a pension. To find our rooms we were led along corridors, past closed doors, through one empty reception room to another, and everywhere there were cobwebs hanging from paintings and statues. To me it was romantically mysterious and the children quickly caught the spirit by peopling it with ghosts and witches, while Coola who likes everything new and spotless couldn't wait to get out. Just as she was turning to leave a door was flung open and there was the most beautiful bedroom, of an opulence certainly never seen by any of us; imposing carved bed with brocade bed curtains, dressing table, cheval glass, and huge windows opening onto what could only be called a *jardino segreto*. With the flourish of a magician our landlady opened two more doors to show equally elegant rooms, one with two beds covered with a field of flowers to match the flowered curtains. Coola was won over, but we never did know the story of this strange "hotel."

There was another hotel in Rotterdam, not found by chance but sought out—from some guide book of the moment. It had been very difficult to find, tucked away in the labyrinth of docks which make Rotterdam what it is. This strange hotel, had been built for seamen but was open to anyone. We were shown with great courtesy, to immaculate rooms overlooking all the shipping, cranes, and dockside commotion. In true Dutch tradition wherever there was a patch of land; a strip at the edge of a warehouse, a bare wall, an entrance, it was covered with flowers. These patches of color and care, sprinkled amongst the huge machines, buildings and loading pads moved me almost to tears. It is one thing to garden in garden surroundings, in space set aside for a garden, and another in a wasteland tended and appreciated by rough laborers. Our dinner and breakfast were served in a dining room overlooking the port with views of ships from all over the world entering, docking or leaving. Certainly it had been worth the trouble to find this memorable hotel.

On one occasion, on our trek to Greece, in a small German town, after walking the ramparts and surrounding fields after dinner, and settling everyone in bed, Kimon and I went into the local Bierstube. We had no sooner ordered when one of the locals from a group at another table, came over to tell us that the beer would be on him. That was the start of a long evening with many beers, none of which we were allowed to pay for. Between my school German and the unpredictable English of the German host, we had laughs and lively conversation. Foreigners were still a novelty. When we told them that we were on our way to Greece, one of the group stated quietly that he had been there once. Of course we knew when. If it had been an American he would have openly said, "I was there in the service." The atrocities of war were still too fresh for us not to wonder who we were drinking with. Had this pleasant companion murdered Greek villagers? Had he been one of the officers who took the furniture, paintings and piano from the house in Volos? How do we overcome this suspicion of the past? It has not been until the end of Apartheid in South Africa that a sane solution has been found, through the Truth and Reconciliation Commission, to punish murderers and torturers. The crimes are made public, as is the criminal. There are no secrets. The unfortunate individual can no longer hide as a law abiding citizen, but must live amongst his compatriots with his crimes revealed. But that evening of pleasant talking and laughing ended in firm handshakes.

Taking winding roads,(no motor ways in those days) we had finally come into Austria on our way to Graz. The country was not spectacular but the sun had come out and in late afternoon even the skimpy villages we passed through looked less miserable in a golden light. We had stopped to wait for a lumbering hay cart to cross the road, my attention fixed on the heavy team. There was a sudden crash and we were all thrown violently forward, our car crushed from behind into the car ahead. The shock was all the more violent because so unexpected: we were immobilized by the only three cars on the otherwise empty road.

The car behind us had been hit by a car behind him that had come on without braking, so we were all mashed together. Except for the shock, none of us seemed to be hurt but I remember, standing on the road in a semi-daze holding Helen, who had been thrown out of her nest at the back, and watching a local with motor bike produce a can to catch the fuel pouring from our broken gas tank, then mount his bike and take off without a word or offer of help. The village, more farm than village, was a collection of yards, manure piles, cows, chickens and ducks. The natives in this rural backwater were unhelpful and surly, and of course no one spoke English, even their German was a thick dialect. My German may have taken us cheerfully through beer drinking sessions but was not up to the vocabulary necessary for a car accident: insurance, gas tank, towing, fenders, bumpers etc. We had pushed the car off the road ourselves and were wondering what to do next when a young man came forward and said, "speak English, come." Which we did only too willingly. We followed him to an old house fronting the street, through a side door and up dark stairs. Here he told us with gestures to wait. In a moment he returned all smiles and said again "speak English," opening wide a black oak door.

There we were on the threshold of a small room which had absorbed the elegance of a past age; walls tiered with paintings of bucolic landscapes and castles, portraits of men in stiff uniform and ladies in jewels and silk. The atmosphere was gloomy despite the dominant deep red of the Turkish carpets, sofa, chairs, walls, even the rich red paisley shawl with trailing fringes covering the piano. The light from the small windows at the far end was not enough to break the shadows where we stood, only enough to play fitfully on gilt mirrors and silver photograph frames layered on every table, even the piano. It was such an unreal atmosphere in such an unlikely place that if it had not been for all of us standing, mouths open, I would have thought that the accident had given me an out-of-body experience.

A woman's voice, firm and quiet spoke from the depths of a chair next to the window. "Come in. I hear that you have had an accident and need someone who can speak English," She spoke beautifully articulated English with only the slightest accent.

A shaft of light from the window stroked the thin skin of an elderly woman of porcelain beauty, fair and fragile. It was not the fragility however or even the erect posture that was arresting, but the startling eyes of a penetrating blue. We were caught by them as she studied us, then she allowed herself a faint smile, a crinkle of these blue eyes and a twitch of the mouth. Had we passed muster? Here was a woman both quick-witted and strong and despite her age, still very much in control.

Everything: room, decor, the half lit figure of our unknown benefactress, the sheen of her silk gown, the trinkets on nearby tables and in the dark recesses of the room, all seemed to have been assembled as a set for an artist, Vermeer perhaps. She did not rise to greet us but waited for us to approach, mentioned her name, barely understood, but with a von somewhere, then held out a veined hand, the long fingers sparkling with gems. The children awed by the atmosphere, shook hands, smiled sweetly and stepped back.

"There will be no difficulty," she said. "Just a few telephone calls, which I shall make. Tomorrow come to see me again and all will be settled. You will be comfortable at the inn, I shall make arrangements." It seemed that we were dismissed.

Over our dinner of potatoes and omelet augmented with flour we each had different theories about our aristocratic lady how she ended up in one room in this primitive village, what her life had been, her age—everything.

"She's a princess," Alice said.

"No she isn't, she's a duchess and I bet she owned dozens of horses and rode them all the time," was Io's assessment.

"She's a relic of the Austro-Hungarian Empire when the aristocrats . . ." Kimon launched into a history lesson.

"It is just as in Greece," Coola pronounced. "It was the war. All men gone and killed, she now left with memories. Ach, always the same. She lost her husband and her sons."

"These eggs taste funny," Helen brought us down to the present.

If we had not been preoccupied with our fantasies we would have been more upset with the miserable meal.

Next day Kimon and I returned alone to the Vermeer setting.

Everything was the same. The light still poured over the proud figure. The velvet ribbon and cameo were still in place round her graceful neck, the same pearls trailed over the same fitted brocade dress. While Kimon got on with the car business I surreptitiously peeked at the photos ranged on the piano. She caught me. "All so long ago," she said waving a hand, dismissing it seemed, the past in all contradiction to her surroundings, "we used to own it all. Now you find me here." She continued with the instructions for towing the car and again we were dismissed.

This meeting with the mysterious noble woman (we had all decided that our lady, if not a princess, was of noble birth), in some way mitigated the inconvenience of the accident. She was a source of fascination for all of us and the children used her for endless stories.

As if by intuition a tow truck arrived to take our car to the closest city—Graz, certainly arranged by our noble woman. The insurance officials agreed not only to pay for repairs to the car but to put us up at the best hotel while this was being done. As the days strung out for repairs to be finished there was nothing for it but to make the best of our situation which started, now the spell of rain and cold had broken, with breakfast served outside in a deep bower of roses which trailed their fragrance over our plates while we planned walks to explore the fertile countryside. Country outings were not for Coola, she could not wait for the car to be repaired to return to Athens with her Swiss fabrics and resume business. "For the good of all" she made the decision to go on ahead by train with Io and Alice leaving us with Helen. Again, once the decision to leave had been made, Coola would not wait for the comfort of the wagon-lit which was on only twice a week, but booked tickets for the following day. We bought books, paper, pencils, crayons, buns, cheese, salamis and saw them off on the Orient Express which was neither oriental nor express. The trip was long, starting in Graz at 5:00 A.M. arriving in Athens 10:00 P.M. the following night, but the children not knowing what they were in for, climbed aboard excited over a real train ride.

We were not to hear the grim realities of that trip until we were all reunited again in Athens.

Yugoslavia

A T LAST THE car was ready. We had explored all the sites; castles, museums, and parks within a day's range, Kimon often carrying Helen on his shoulders, and we were more than ready for a change. On the tenth day after the accident we set out with the usual picnic supplies, bread, cheese, fruit. Yugoslavia then, was very much under Tito, very much a repressive communist state, open to foreigners only that year, with the hangover of officialdom and no sense of service. The only hotels open to tourists were new, state run, and already shabby. The bathrooms were filthy and employees rude, if not outright hostile. Frequently however, we met strangers who took us in hand and at inconvenience to themselves directed, translated and advised. They were anxious for us to enjoy our visit and to see the best their country had to offer.

On the recommendation of one middle aged man who had attached himself to us in Zagreb, guiding us to restaurants and hotels, we decided to take the route along the coast, instead of the old road down the center of Yugoslavia to northern Greece. The new road he told us, was open and waiting for tourists, with new hotels and beautiful scenery. It was not his fault that there was more propaganda than truth in his recommendation; even the tourist offices encouraged us.

With a full gas tank, the back seats down to accommodate Helen, we set out for one of the beauty spots of the Mediterranean, the Adriatic coast of Yugoslavia and the medieval towns of Rijeka, Trojir, Split and Dubrovnik. This road which was to bring tourists flooding to the paradise of the Adriatic had been touted as an alternate route to Greece with beautiful scenery and historic sites along the way. So anxious was the government to have these tourists that they neglected to mention that the road was not finished, which meant that most of it was a cart track of stones or deep dust, with cliffs plunging to the sea on one side and wall of desolate rock on the other. For today's four-wheel-drive cars it would have been a test. This unspoiled scenery was magnificent, if one had the courage to look; sheer cliffs uncontaminated by condominiums or hotels, a few fishing shacks nestled into coves, and ink-blue water swirling below.

The first view of the navy blue water of the Mediterranean was such a welcome the three of us jumped out of the car to admire the view and I even took a photo. I felt like one of the army of the Ten Thousand who cried *thalassa, thalassa,* when the Black Sea came into view after their grim march through Turkey.

My optimism was to be put to the test in the next few days. Crawling in second gear there was time to see small urchins, tending a pig or goat amongst the karst outcroppings. When we stopped these tots surrounded us, rising from the rocks like children in a fairy tale who have been turned to stone by the wicked ogress and are now awakened. Where fields should have been, rocks were piled like cairns to clear a space large enough to grow a stunted olive tree or vine. It was worse than desert because no irrigation could bring this rock to life.

After a night in the best (only) hotel in Rijeka, where our "private" bath was lined with a gray scum embedded with black hairs, and staff were not only indifferent but hostile, we were ready to give up the drive and enjoy the scenery from the deck of one of the cruise ships which were in and out of the Yugoslav ports all summer. But no one seemed to have any information or schedule. Anxious not to have to spend another night at our new and disgusting tourist hotel where we were told Tito and cronies were expected (I wondered if the baths would be cleaned for them), we decided to continue by car to Trojir.

Not on the road more than ten minutes, a dust cloud rose in front of us, and out of the cloud a line of black cars came at us, full speed down the center, like a line of tanks determined to wipe us out. It was Tito and the party members, we were told later by a shepherd who appeared out of the rocks. He and Kimon smoked together, while he in broken German told war stories of the partisans fighting in the mountains.

In Trojir, the booking agents seemed to be at odds with each other and us, one agent contradicting the other. No one could tell us about a boat to Greece, even though we were on the cruise boat path at the height of the season. Again we drove on, this time to Split where agents in Trojir, after consulting dog-eared schedules, had assured us we could catch a boat.

The drive to Split was the worst yet. The car churned through dust like fine talc that seeped into every crevice and all our pores. Kimon told Helen not to talk. "Just keep your mouth closed, so you won't choke," he told her, and she did. We had no food but it would have been impossible to eat anyway without devouring dust. In Split, tired, hungry, covered in dust and irritable from the frustration of getting no information, we searched the quay and shipping offices, where again we were passed from one to the other. Walking out of one office we noticed what we had missed in our hurry to find an agent who would help—a beautiful luxury yacht, tied up in front of us—all white and shining with a friendly Italian name on the prow. But it wasn't a private yacht, it was an Italian cruise ship.

Kimon called out to an officer on the bridge, "Where are you going?"

"Piraeus," was the answer.

In the end it was only by negotiating directly with the captain that we were waved aboard. Maybe it was because we looked like refugees or maybe because we had a small, by now filthy, much subdued child, the captain smiled widely, the first smile we had seen in days, and gave orders for the car to be loaded. I remembered Theodore's story of escaping Smyrna and was thankful that we didn't have to swim after the ship to prove a point.

Washed, changed, sitting at a table covered in crisp white linen for our first dinner on board, waiters hovering to tend our slightest request, the memory of those lonely children rising from the rocks—only ten minutes away, destroyed any appetite for the gourmet food. The contrast was too sudden and too great. I couldn't help thinking that but for a chance of birth those struggling children could be my own.

We tied up in a new port every day with time to explore walled cities, most especially Dubrovnik, swim and satisfy my need for exercise. We also met friends, an Australian mother and daughter, whom we saw much of once in Athens and kept in touch with for years. Following the coast with us was a yacht of the same size, only private. Aristotle Onassis was entertaining Winston Churchill that summer, cruising to Greece.

Coola, elegant even donkey back.

Kimon's Parents.
Coola and Theodore.

Sun and Sea

LANDING IN GREECE brought us back to reality. The noise and confusion of Piraeus had not changed much since my first visit to Greece, only there were more trucks and cars now displacing the forlorn animals. Despite the calm order of Germany and the postcard picturesqueness of Austria, this was like coming home. Instead of mindlessly obeying the rules, for the Greeks, it was a matter of honor to ignore them.

There was a great reunion in Athens with grandparents and children. Before we could tell anyone about our fabulous cruise, we had to hear the horrors of the train trip through Yugoslavia and Greece, to Athens, told by the children with breathless descriptions of unusable bathrooms, aisles jammed with people, men, women and children, no air (the usual fear of a draught), no food, all tumbling out with the excitement of an adventure we had somehow missed out on.

On this visit our base was not Volos but the beautiful new flat in Kolonaiki. Coola had had the foresight to buy the bit of rock she had showed me with such pride on my first visit, where with tremendous effort, loans and the supervision of Theodore the building with five flats had been completed. Now along with their building, other apartments had already crowded in and were occupied, with concierge at the doors. Mitso and his wife Keti had been hired by Theodore, part of their payment being the garden flat. Mitso was general factotum, helping with everything, even parking the car on the slope in front of the building. Keti did jobs in the house and became through the years champion for Io and Alice when they were teen-agers, and wanted to meet young men who had not passed inspection by father and grandfather. She monitored the outside stairs to the roof and would arrange rendezvous especially for the young man who lived on the first floor and his many friends who were eager to meet the American girls.

After the long trip the apartment was a haven. Large airy rooms furnished by Coola with well made Greek pieces or furniture she had brought from Europe on one of her many buying trips. Local Greek art hung on the walls, mementos of Coola's visits to galleries and art openings. Yes, it did have parquet floors, marble bathrooms, and floor to ceiling windows front and back to take in, on the street side, the rock of Lycabettos, and on the other the Acropolis. I lived again the embarrassment I felt when this couple had arrived in Hiram during the renovation of our derelict wooden house, when they had just finished this earthquake proof apartment.

That summer, as if we had not done enough touring, we explored a good bit of Greece, including the Peloponnese: Nauplion, Mystra, Mycaenae, Olympia. We did it all in a leisurely way with swims, hikes, stays in small hotels or private rooms. It was all very inexpensive, and fun, with no pressure to get anywhere. In Athens, we celebrated Helen's third birthday by taking her to the very new pay beach of Vouliagmeni, instead of swimming off the rocks. At home Coola ordered cake and ice cream from Dolce, the chic shop at the foot of the stairs (many streets in Kolonaiki end in stairs) and I, always needing flowers, added gladiolas the only survivors in Athens' July heat, and my least favorite.

It was at this time in Greece that the hotel building boom was taking place, in anticipation of the increasing tourist trade. There was the Grand Bretagne in Athens and small hotels in provincial towns but nothing at the ancient sites, as it had been the custom prewar to camp or stay in the local village. The government had led with the Xenia hotels, models in good taste and sensitive location. Each had its own character depending on the site; they could be built into a mountain top, nestled into an orange grove, or along a stretch of beach. They were intimate, beautifully and individually appointed, most featuring local crafts, and run with personal service.

That summer when we returned to Pelion I saw many changes from my first visit, the most obvious being the new road—paved but still frightening—to the Aegean side of the mountain which I had first visited with Coola. We stayed in Tsangarada, a village on the side of the mountain, which sprawled over two ravines, with two sets of plateas each dominated by an enormous plane tree. The winding mule path was still the only way to go down to Aiyous Yioannis, but ruined houses were being repaired and just off the road was a new hotel.

"Private, I hear good," Coola remarked. "Not luxe, like Xenia, but we can have meals anywhere in village." For Coola the Xenia were the standard for comparison.

What was happening with the private hotels was typically Greek. Anyone who thought that a hotel would be a moneymaker would build one, seldom with enough money to finish the project or to build well. Codes were nonexistent or ignored as, to a Greek, any law is meant to be broken. Again in Greek style, these little hotels would be run either by the builder or a relative, keeping all profits within the family, which meant that the hotel was being managed by someone who had no idea how to run a hotel: someone who had probably never even stayed in a hotel themselves.

Coola had booked us into such a hotel that summer. It had just opened so there were many flaws mitigated by unending goodwill. The rooms, each with a balcony, were on the two top floors with the modern convenience of two bathrooms to a floor. The mirrors the builder had installed in the bathrooms were so high it was impossible to see into them. The electricity in the village was nonexistent, so our hotel had its own generator, to offer demanding tourists light after dark. Imagine lights at night while dining on the terrace! Imagine also reading in bed, coming to the best part of your novel, when suddenly the lights are out, pitch dark, it could be any time between ten and one in the morning—quite arbitrary.

There were about twenty rooms, three occupied by us, four by Greeks from Volos. One overworked waiter, Mitsos, (pronounced MeetSAW when he was being called) was on hand day and night to fetch and carry. He was small, with the round eyes of a marmoset and the same nervous movements, never sure how he would be accepted: apologetic it seemed for his very existence. He was like a dog wagging its tail for approval and then piddling on the floor. Everything he did was wrong; spilled, late, presented to the wrong person in the wrong place—on the terrace instead of the dining room, upstairs instead of on the terrace. He had been brought in from the village with no idea of what to do or how to do it. He was screamed at by the Greek ladies all week, roared at by their husbands on weekends, and scolded by the owner, Kyria Triandaphyllo, (Thirtypetals, meaning rose petals). The only other help was an arthritic geriatric who came in the morning and left after five.

As I am an early riser I would be up and out for a walk before the rest of the hotel was up, even Mitso. The awakening of a Greek village was to me a symphony of the senses: the first crow of the rooster, followed by bleating sheep, goats, braying donkey, and the human sounds, a woman's voice, tin pails on stone, swish of brooms, water being poured, and the smell of a wood fire, the dry smell of fodder, the lingering fragrance of jasmine or the ripe peaches hanging on a tree in a door yard. From a certain promontory, where the land fell away on all sides, and where on this tiny bit of flat surface I could look straight down into the depths of the ink-blue water of the Aegean, I could watch the sunrise spread across the water and cloudless sky. As it turned out I needed these contemplative mornings.

By the time I returned to the hotel Mitso would be struggling in the chaotic kitchen to bring breakfast to the rooms of the Greek ladies and their children. An overwhelming task for Mitso. He would climb the stairs first with the double coffee on the tray and nothing else, then be screamed at for not bringing the rest of the breakfast. Up he would go with the slab of white goat butter covered with fragrant honey, but forget the bread. Down again and up with the bread, but forgetting the yogurt. And so it went for every room. I was in the kitchen trying to make our tea and was exhausted watching him. After the first day I couldn't stand by to see him wither.

In my broken Greek I tried to explain that he needed planning.

"How many rooms?" I asked

"Four."

"Good, now four trays."

He set out four trays.

"Number of room? 14. What does 14 take?"

"Diplocafe, bread, honey, yogurt, two eggs for children."

"The eggs—how?"

"Hard."

"That's easy. Now put on tray 14 all that will be needed except the food—the knives, coffee cup of correct size, not the single coffee size, the spoons, extra plates for the children and when you put the food on remember that the children will also eat bread and honey. Now you see," I told him, "you take one tray up once and they have everything." This miracle of organization was repeated for every tray. Mitso scurried through the performance repeating to himself what I had told him.

"Spoon, knife, nescafe—must have big cup etc."

He was almost panting by the time the four trays were set up.

In the meantime I was still trying to boil water for tea in this small room overflowing with the dirty dishes cleared from the tables the night before. A bucket on the floor was filled with watermelon rinds to be given to a villager who collected them for his goats. The usual two burner ring held the scummy pasta pots. It was a complete mess.

It was my turn to feel helpless. The geriatric wouldn't be in for hours and I didn't dare distract Mitso from his tray setting. I scoured a pot to boil water without tainting it, cleared space on the gas ring and had enough hot water left over to wash dishes for our own breakfast which I served on the terrace surrounded by chestnut trees.

"It seems quiet this morning," Kimon said sipping his English tea we had brought from Athens.

"Why?" I asked.

"I guess no one is yelling—no one yelling at Mitso. Is he here?"

"He's here. Just learned how to be more efficient."

Mitso found the setting out of the trays such a brilliant idea he carried it over into other activities; he began to anticipate requests, not only to serve what was ordered, but even add the utensils to eat with. Kyria Triandaphyllo scolded less but the demanding ladies, even with fewer complaints, still remained peevish. He was so grateful for my suggestions that when he heard that we might be interested in buying a property he showed us a beautiful site at the end of a kalderimi which he said his uncle would sell to us because we were such good people. Wistfully we looked at this land knowing that we were in no position to buy anything even though it would have been a shrewd investment. It would be some years later that a property on Mount Pelion was to come.

For long treks we had a donkey for Helen and mules for everyone except Kimon and me. We visited and swam and ate at the still almost deserted beach of Ayios Yiannes. The small hotel and turquoise waters had not changed since I had first visited. In Tsangarada, the children had the entire village, the mountain, the kalderimi paths between villages, the cafes where they could order their own *tiropita*, *vanilla* or *granitas*. Meals were monotonous. As usual in those times, the minimal was brought in and even tourists like ourselves were given what was locally available: beans, stuffed tomatoes and peppers, salads of tomato, feta and olives soaked in oil. For entertainment, if we were lucky, the Karayosos show would come to the delight of everyone. This shadow puppet show was a remnant of the Turkish occupation and dealt with themes of good and evil, the good always being the poor, evil being brought down usually with blows from a stick, to the tremendous delight of the audience.

At last it was time to leave for Belgium, this time taking the ferry to Italy and avoiding Yugoslavia. Just as we were starting this trip I came down with a severe case of dysentery, and I knew what had caused it.

We had been on an island, and foolishly I drank the water from a carafe put on the table. Many islands in Greece have a very limited supply of water and to augment it during the tourist season water is brought in by boat from Piraeus. I remember Kimon asking the waiter what it was that was wriggling in the water of the carafe, (this was not until I had already had a glass or two).

"Is O.K.," he answered, putting a not too clean thumb into the water and pulling out the offender, "no problem, it is of the water." Of course we should have been ordering bottled water, and I paid for this neglect.

Belgium

THE TRIP TO Belgium started with me in a misery of cramps, vomiting and diarrhea which I seemed to have given to Helen. I remember sitting on the balcony of our hotel room in Igoumenitsa, waiting for the boat to Italy, holding Helen in my arms watching a full moon rise, both of us miserable, whispering stories and singing until we finally fell asleep with the dawn. The doctor we took Helen to next day prescribed the wondrous Endovioforme of those days. She recovered immediately but I kept my bugs for months.

On the way up that long boot of Italy we stopped at the historic cities of Ravenna, Bologna and others I can't remember. The mosaics of Ravenna and ochre arcades of Bologna, became trials in concentration at not being sick all over someone, or fear of not finding the toilet soon enough. I don't know why we persisted in viewing history when I couldn't see a thing. By the time we reached Brussels, passing through the beauty spots of Lakes Como and Maggiore, I was ready for a doctor.

The Foundation provided us with a pension while we looked for more permanent accommodations. It was Madame at the pension who insisted that I see a doctor and fortunately whatever the doctor gave me worked, as finding a flat took a lot of stamina. In those days Brussels had been the one European capital with adequate housing—until the influx of refugees from the Congo, in the throes of civil war, filled every flat and sent prices soaring. It would be our bad luck that these large white colonial families had come in the same year we arrived. Our search system was to drive around and look for *A Louer* signs pasted on the windows of flats. Then we would "address ourselves" to the given number. We soon learned that most landlords did not want children. "The last had eight. You know *Monsieur-Dame*—from the Congo. *C'est de trop.*" After this lesson we told the children to stay out of sight around the corner until we had viewed the flat and made the deal.

In the end we settled for a two-room unfurnished flat with central heating—a big plus. My grocer however told me repeatedly that the *chauffage central* was not *sain* and predicted that we would all fall deathly sick because of it. In fact we only survived the bone chilling cold because of it. For furniture we decided that camp equipment which could be folded and taken with us at the end of the year would be the answer. So we invested in folding camp chairs, a folding camp table (dining table), even camp kitchen utensils. Through the Foundation we were given, on loan, a sofa bed and a crib for Helen. The rack on the car was installed in the one sleeping room along with a camp lounge chair. On both of these we laid inflated air mattresses—beds for Io and Alice. I brightened the walls with evocative travel posters from the tourist offices, and *voilà*—we were installed.

The school was nearby, Helen attending only half day. She was belligerent toward the other children and refused to speak a word of French. It wasn't until playing on the beach in Greece the following summer that we heard her speak fluent French to a child who could speak only French and no English.

In Belgium and in France the home is private; the easy, drop-in-anytime of the States did not exist, at least not then. The children's friends said good-bye at the door—either theirs or ours. Adults met at the cafe not the home, except with rare exceptions. The friends we did meet were not through our children as one would expect, but through introductions and these friends were not Belgian but Dutch, English and Canadian.

Our Dutch friends came to visit from Eindhoven where Henk was a professor of mathematics. They stayed with us on several occasions sleeping on the floor, which they said reminded them of camping in Greece where they slept on the warm marble of the temples. The children adored them. Henk could whistle anything and had the most incredible musical memory so that in the morning he whistled us awake with a Bach prelude or Handel aria. We visited Waterloo with Henk and his wife Anna, where after we studied the battle ground, we all came away depressed at the stupidity of war. Of course we strolled through the Grand Place, the flower and bird market. The children took Henk by the hand to look at the birds and listen to them sing. The Belgians specialize in singing canaries; they are even classified according to song and some we were told could be taught specific melodies.

It was all done with Anna's help; she took us away to look at the flowers and while she involved us in the purchase of a bouquet, Henk and the children arrived giggling with a canary, cage and food.

The canary gave us great cheer through the gloomy winter and at the end of our stay it moved to the landlady's flat. Other than buying canaries, what do you do with children who have no friends and are not fluent in the language? We explored every part of Belgium, visited Henk and Anna in Eindhoven, and never missed a mystery play with elaborate medieval costumes, banners, music, all in the street, better than any fourth of July parade.

Io and Alice who very much missed Watson, our Boxer who was spending the year with my brother, found another Boxer to walk. Almost every day after school they would call at the flat of the owner to walk Nero in the *Bois de la Cambre*. It was a perfect arrangement for all concerned.

We never seemed to have an extra cent so when it came time to find a place to spend Christmas I wrote to five countries, to inns, hotels and gasthofs and came up with the least expensive, a pension in a small village in the Schwartzwald. We drove down from Belgium on snowy roads, slid into a cabbage field once and ended quite gently against a tree another time, but arrived to a welcoming couple and immaculate rooms in a typical chalet. Kimon and I looked at each other the minute we walked in the door but never said a word until out of earshot of the children.

"It is animal smell isn't it?" I asked.

"I remember this odor from village houses in Greece," Kimon answered. "It is one way to heat the house."

The children visited the animals which wintered in the stable on the ground floor and reported with delight.

"You will never believe it. Downstairs there are three cows, a calf and a pig. Right here in the house!"

With fresh bread and strong coffee for breakfast every morning and stalwart dinner at night we had no complaints. After my brother's divorce, my mother had taken over the upbringing of his son Roger, who was between Io and Alice in age. With her incurable wanderlust and spirit of adventure mother could not resist a Christmas visit to Germany and of course Roger came with her. Her cavalier attitude toward school I well remembered. There was snow, the children sledded on curved-runner wooden sleds, we took excursions, ate cream-filled tortes and drank hot chocolate.

At the pension the landlady was all smiles to serve us a traditional German Christmas dinner. We wore our only best clothes and filled the table in her spotless dining room. The children sat in perfect German silence in awe of the occasion and waited for the Christmas dinner to be brought in. With great pride she brought an enormous platter and set it down before Kimon, but it was not a goose or turkey he was to carve. It was the traditional white Christmas carp complete with whiskers. For a moment the children said nothing, then they started:

"What is it?"

"Are we supposed to eat that?"

"Yuck. Where's the turkey?"

"I'm not eating any."

All this said in English while our landlady was out of the room because even if she did not understand English she would certainly have understood the expressions of disgust.

Before she came in again I had time to explain, in as firm a voice as I could manage, trying not to burst into giggles, that this was a Christmas treat here and disgusting as it was we were not to show any disapproval and all of us would eat it and smile.

"Remember the banana brandy," I reminded. That had been a similar incident in Greece where a poor farmer had brought out home made banana brandy, his most special treat, for the children—for all of us—absolutely disgusting and sickly sweet. Then it was possible to empty our glasses into handy plants. Now adults and children did valiantly with the carp, only refusing second helpings and even that was difficult with the landlady standing at Kimon's elbow to make sure he was serving enough. There were carp stories ever after, even to the whiskers wiggling.

We brought in the new year at the local *Bierstube*, where we were the only foreigners, by dancing with the sooty chimney sweep, who went from table to table with his piglet to touch for good luck. No one seemed to mind when the dear little pig wet the table. My mother who didn't know a word of German had the attention of the only elegantly dressed gentleman in a room of farmers. We watched as they glided around the crowded floor. Grandmother she may have been, but she was more than a match for the erect unknown gentleman in his loden jacket with silver buttons. As tall and erect as her partner her long, graceful tweed skirt, was short enough to reveal neat ankles and nimble feet. The tempo of the waltz quickened, one by one the other couples stood back, my mother's silk scarf flew behind her as she kept up with the increasingly intricate twirls, until at last the music stopped. Everyone applauded, when the gentleman bowed formally to kiss her hand she broke tradition by kissing him on both cheeks, bringing on more applause.

Ever wanting to be independent, my mother had one day gone into the nearest town and bought a VW beetle for herself with the ease of buying a new hat. In this she left with Roger for England to catch up with people we had never heard of but whom she insisted were looking forward to seeing her again "after so many years."

We returned to Brussels. Coola, of course, visited in the spring giving Kimon and me a chance to go to Paris where I wandered the streets in a nostalgic trance. While we were gone there were riots in our neighborhood over the language war (Flemish versus French). We were given a description when we returned of how the mounted guards arrived when they were walking Nero and their horses jumped over the hedge to chase some rioters, and the horses were wonderful and we should have seen how good they were with all the people and how well they jumped.

Coola and Helen in Greece.

Skopolos summer.

Islands

A T THE END of the year, like Bedouin nomads, we folded our camp equipment, replaced the rack on the car, and deflated the mattresses, to make another trek to Greece, through Italy, for another summer of sun and sea and excursions planned of course by Coola.

How could I forget the trip down the long leg of Italy? The scant two lanes of the former Roman road bordered on each side by lines of trees, enhancing the classic symmetry which could have been a film set had we seen only the lumbering ox carts. But no, this road running the length of Italy was jammed along with the beautiful oxen, with modern vehicles; motorcycles, overloaded trucks with nerve-shattering air horns, minute Fiats, as well as Ferraris, in numbers to rival rush hour in the city, and each desperate to drive fast—otherwise why have a motor vehicle? The casualties were everywhere; mangled against a tree, bits which had somehow missed a tree strewn into adjacent fields, and even bodies covered by sheets waiting for removal. By the time we reached Brindisi and the ferry boat I was wiped out.

Greece at last! We drove off the ferry after dark, impatient to arrive in Athens, we decided to drive on instead of spending another night in a hotel.

In those days in Greece there were few private cars on the roads but many trucks which usually pulled in at night. The villages on the other hand came alive at night, which in rural Greece of that time, meant going through dimly lit clusters of houses—the roads went directly through with no by-pass—to come suddenly upon a group of black figures sitting at cafe tables right in the road, the one unshaded light of the cafe only visible to those inside. It was only through the grace of God that we didn't, on several occasions, plough right through them. The men, unaware that they had had a reprieve from death would wave cheerily. Then there was the matter of car lights. We would see an oncoming car driving with bright lights, then as it approached change to parking lights, and at the moment we were passing, no lights at all. Very unsettling to say the least. Some drivers had all lights out from the moment they saw ours, which meant that we were passing speeding cars in the dark not knowing where they were until they could be seen in the rear view with all lights on. There were no speed limits in those days and any Greek worth his salt who owned a car was going to drive as fast as he or the car could go.

Somehow we survived all this and arrived in Athens to the joy of the grandparents, late as it was. Exhausted, I drifted off that night to the familiar wailing of Greek cat fights, now I was truly back in Greece, I was home.

Coola announced next morning, "You must visit some of our islands. I have tickets for us to Mykenos, is most unusual, all white. You must see." Our summer was already well planned.

Theodore who enjoyed the comforts of home had dug his heels in and refused to come.

Coola had booked our tickets on one of the new ferry boats built for the islands.

"You must see for yourselves, so modern, so fast these boats, like Italian. I book bedroom for us, otherwise too far to go without sleep. My darlings sleep with me, you and Kimon have another room." It sounded perfect.

Then in Greece it was quite common for hotels, trains, theater, anyone, anywhere to overbook and for no reason. It cushioned the odds perhaps. So when we arrived on board in Piraeus and Coola presented our tickets to the purser, she was told abruptly with no apology, that those rooms were not available. Poor man should have known better than to cross a Greek mother.

"What do you mean? These tickets are from two weeks in Athens. Look," she said turning to us standing tongue tied, "my son and his family back to Greece from America. Is this how you are going to welcome him back under the Greek sky?"

By now as always happens in Greek arguments, a circle of onlookers had gathered. The women were questioning Coola who gave up talking to the purser so she could bring them up to date. They took up her cause immediately turning on the purser in piercing Greek female voices, pointing first to Kimon with, *"kalo yerisete,"* (welcome home) then to me and the children, changing expression as they did so from shrew when addressing the official, to adoring mothers when they turned to us, where we stood as if watching a tennis match, they even pinched Helen's cheeks, a habit she loathed. No professional actresses could have done better.

"Do you not have a mother?" one asked. "Is this how you would treat her? Shame on you. Do you not see how this mother loves her son—her only son—(always a tragedy in Greece), and all his family?"

The purser I had thought at first was ready to capitulate, but this onslaught of women and bystanders stiffened his Greek male image. He no longer spoke or argued but stood behind his desk defiant with the upward toss of the head and the single "tst," Greek for no. He was not to be bullied.

Nor was Coola to be outdone. "I see my only son go off to America, never see him here, now he comes with this beautiful family to enjoy his country and he finds Greece does not want him." There was silence from the onlookers. It was just the kind of mother-son story they all love.

"Po, po, po, crima, crima," too bad, was the exclamation.

"Tst," another upward sweep of the head. I had to admire the official, he was hard to break. Here was Greek drama being played out before us. Coola the protagonist, fighting officialdom and the chorus of onlookers providing the moral reinforcement. The chorus had advanced script as to the outcome, they had played similar roles many times and they were in it to the end.

Coola, then changing the drama from tragedy to comedy, gathered her tickets from the desk and without hesitation tore them in front of everyone. "This is all the modern Greece is worth and this is all these tickets mean—nothing—*tipota*."

What a dramatic touch! I had to admire her.

"Bravo, bravo," from the chorus.

Now our official, still unbending and formal, making no apologies, turned to Kimon and abruptly asked for his passport, after examining it he asked for mine. Then he called a steward over and ordered him to show us to cabins he would provide, as if from the goodness of his heart. Of course the passport was not necessary but it helped him to save face.

"*Endaxi*," all right, was the choral antiphony before moving off stage.

Mykenos was beautiful, sculptural, and welcoming—that was in the days before hordes of tourists. We took a small boat every day to a beautiful beach where Helen finally learned to keep afloat by doing the dog paddle.

A wind had come up on the day we were to leave and our ferry boat could not dock in the little port. The *meltemi*, we were told. The winds of the Aegean are sudden and very strong and visitors to the islands must realize that they cannot always arrive or depart just as they please. Our ship however was the same new one we had had on the trip out and large enough to sail even in stormy waters. The problem was to reach the ship through the rough waves. A fisherman volunteered his small boat and about ten of us piled in, most under the canvas tarp covering the front half of the boat. The rugged fisherman wearing one of the hand knit sweaters, now so popular with tourists, faded trousers rolled to the knee, balanced through instinct, clung to the high stern with leathery bare feet and held the tiller fast against each wave which threatened to wrench it from him. Every time the boat crashed down sending spray over us the women in the boat crossed themselves and screamed. I could see the fisherman, rugged and knowing, holding the huge rudder, silhouetted against a white sky lit by a full moon, a perfect model for a Winslow Homer. The children were becoming frightened, not from the waves but from the screams of the women endlessly crossing themselves. "Look," I told them, "at the beautiful sky and our strong fisherman. You can tell that he would never let us come to harm. Just remember this beautiful picture."

"Anyway I can swim," Helen piped up.

That seemed to calm our family at least and of course we made it safely to our big ship, where, this time, cabins had been held.

We hadn't been in Athens more than a week when Coola announced. "Is good Kimon is teacher and he has long summer." (Kimon in reality never had "long summer" as he was always studying and writing). "I have house ready for us on Skopelos for one month. Better than always in hotel. Theodore does not want to come. He always prefer to stay at home where he say he have everything. This is chance for all of us to see something else. Toola will come with us. She cook very good Greek food." I had no idea where Skopelos was, or why this island had been selected from hundreds but it didn't matter the house had been rented and plans were already in motion.

Skopelos had traditionally been the summer retreat of the Voloiotes and a few knowing Athenians which meant that it was not crowded or touristic. The town occupies a perfect setting, whitewashed houses clinging to a hill circling a perfect bay. I stepped onto the quay into a stage set atmosphere of white houses, bright fishing boats, a line of sleeping donkeys, and tables from the restaurants and cafes set invitingly under the trees, and best of all no sounds of motors. The children danced along the quay, Coola and I followed with the bundles she had insisted we bring; sheets, blankets, towels, Kimon loaded with his briefcase and suitcases of books, Toola the cook, clattering her pots and pans brought from Athens tied together with string, even her own jugs of oil as she trusted nothing in what she considered an outpost. Coola soon had everything loaded onto one of the donkeys and strode ahead with the key to the house.

It was perfect. On a corner, at the end of the town promenade, which meant that there were no steps to climb. Bedrooms upstairs with balcony overlooking the sea, downstairs a large room which was both dining and living, and a kitchen of sorts—Toola had been right to bring her own utensils.

Outside the door a large wooden boat was stored, evidently awaiting repairs. Io discovered immediately as if they were a personal present, three mewing kittens cowering under the gunwale. Coola refused to have them brought into the house and even I, seeing their runny eyes and emaciated bodies convinced the girls that they could be better cared for in the boat which, I explained, was like a giant cradle. They would be safe there.

The kitten story lasted the summer. The morning after our arrival an old woman came to the boat with yogurt for the kittens. In explanations to Kimon she said that she had found the kittens put out to die and had rescued them and put them in a safe place until they were strong.

In Greece in those days, we were not too far from the memory of putting girl children on the mountain to die. Coola in fact, had stories of an old woman whose job it was to do this. "She hate this," Coola had said, "but she know that there is not enough food for all and what to do with a girl? So she feel that she helping many to live while letting one die."

It was the same with dogs and cats. The unwanted would not be killed; they would die either through starvation, accident or disease or be left somewhere to die. It often happened, as with these kittens, that some old woman would rescue them long enough for them to succumb in another way.

When Kimon explained that his daughter was concerned about the kittens and would feed them, she embraced Kimon and Io and told him in her squeaky voice that he was fortunate to have such a daughter. She continued to monitor the kittens' progress, and embraced Io every time she saw her, as if she were her own daughter. It wasn't long before the kittens were climbing out of the boat and crawling into the road, one of the main mule tracks of the island, so now the mule drivers took an interest in the kittens even to picking them up to put out of the traffic.

Eventually, as was inevitable, two died from unknown causes and the one left was taken by Io as her special challenge. That year she had a full skirt with large patch pockets and it was into one of these pockets that the surviving kitten spent the summer. Everywhere we went, the cafe, exploring the village, even the beach, the kitten rode in a pocket to be allowed out on safe supervised outings—and it thrived. In the end when we left, it was given to another child who had fallen in love with it and promised equal attention.

Skopelos gave us a wonderful summer. The only motor vehicle on the island was an old army jeep fitted with a canvas top which took us on a dusty road five miles to the beach each day. The turquoise and navy blue waters, opened to us a new underwater world, through snorkeling. It became a passion with all of us. We swam to rocks where we studied fish going about their lives in their own environment, some lazy, others in frenetic darts. At other times we could swim through a whole school of fish flashing like silver tinsel in the sunlight pouring down from above.

In the village, nothing with wheels could work as the maze of lanes and paths started or ended in stairs. Whitewash outlined the risers, essential on dark nights, otherwise the polished stone gave footholds to the mules by adding an upright at the point where a mule could catch his foot. We loved to wander the town day or night, after all there was little else for recreation. Io and Alice would run the paths to see if they could find us again without being lost, it was a bit of a memory game with land marks of flower pots, numbers of steps, roof tiles, even the communal water pumps. Doors and window-frames were painted bright blue, whitewashed oil tins stood grouped on steps or at entrances filled with brilliant geraniums, grapes vines rose from stone to travel over walls and into courtyards where they unfurled a dense shade, and always following us through those immaculate streets the fragrance of jasmine, as much Greece to me as the yowling cats.

There was a tranquility about that summer, with our one taxi the army truck. Children had the entire island to themselves; no harm could come to them. After our morning swim we ate moussaka or *imam baildi,* stuffed peppers and tomatoes, green beans and tomatoes, all beautifully prepared by Toola and baked in the local oven. In the afternoon, beginning about six, the cafe took over. The children roamed, adults met friends to talk and watch the people, locals augmented by summer regulars.

There were two special outings with our new friends Boko and Mitsi, (Greek women often have nicknames which sound more like names for pet dogs, and yet Boko's poodle was named "Black"). One was by foot, with help from three mules and one donkey, to the other side of the island via the *kalderimi,* the other by caique to the nearby island of Aloynossos.

We had met at the cafe where Boko and Mitsi had oohed and aahed over Io's kitten, and in turn we had oohed and aahed over Black. In those days it was unusual for a Greek to be seen with a pet dog. These two were lively and adventurous and keen to augment the summer of swimming with something more strenuous. Our friends were remarkable women, as I came to think all women were in Greece, perhaps formed by that school of survival passed down through the genes. It was the women who bore the children, or suffered the shame of not bearing them, or the anguish of putting a girl child to die; it was the women who were left to forage, to find something for their families to eat when men were away fighting or at sea on one of the many Greek steamships or tankers, or in America to make a fortune; it was the women who tended the sick, wounded, the dying, even the fields when men were not around.

Boko and Mitsi had come from well-to-do families and both had lived most of their lives abroad—Boko in France, where she had earned her degree in French literature, and taught at a French *lycée*, Mitsi in England where she had studied Byzantine art and gained a position at one of the more prestigious English universities. Neither had married and today I would have picked up on their close relationship. Both had retired and returned to Greece to live. They had stories, endless stories, of childhoods in France or England with nannies, animals and gardens; moving into war, train trips through Europe, the family fear for fathers marked by the Nazis, hiding, shootings, killings. It seemed to me an all too familiar theme.

"Is always same," Coola said. "too much suffer. That is why," she spoke directly to our friends, "children must be happy." Children meant Kimon and me. It made me feel as if I must play the court jester.

Mitsi was tall, angular with huge Byzantine eyes, a mobile face and endless energy. Boko was her complement, round, easy going and fun loving. Whenever we met, at the cafe or on the beach, Mitsi and Kimon would be involved in discussions of Byzantine history, the fall of Constantinople and endless advice as to the churches to visit.

"Have you visited the church of Aiyos Dimitri in Thessaloniki? No? po,po,po. You must." Here she would lean forward, her long face suddenly longer when she raised her eyebrows. "Of all the Byzantine churches, I would say Aiyos Dimitri is the most interesting."

"The frescoes then are intact?" Kimon would ask.

"What do you ask? These are the most important in mainland Greece." Her hands struck out in front of her, and her eyes were by turn half closed and wide open as if in shock. Her face was so expressive her words so dynamic I found that I was watching a performance instead of gathering the sense of her words.

Meanwhile Boko would wander off with the children to feed the fish if we were at the cafe, or the cats. Then she would tell them of the pets she had had as a child, the monkey a relative had brought back from the East, the parrot: then she would repeat the French obscenities the parrot had taught her and which our children can still repeat; she would tell of gardens filled with roses, rivers overhung with willows, ponds with frogs. I can see them now three children dancing around this humpty-dumpty figure, Helen clinging to her skirts, strolling the quay, all three waiting for the next story or vying to be the first to spot the fish.

Coola planned our outings together with Mitsi and Boko, the first by donkey and mule to the other side of the island. The mules were for the three women, the donkey to be shared by our girls but mainly for Helen, Kimon and I were to walk. The picnic supplied mainly by Toola, included bread, tomatoes, dolmades, feta, olives and hard boiled eggs. With the animals came the owners as no one would loan an animal to unknown tourists. We followed the *kalderimia* through the pine groves which make Skopelos "the green island." These pines provide a livelihood, not for their wood but for the resin which is tapped for turpentine. It was through this aromatic pitch that we walked—the scent of pine held in by the heat. At intervals a plane tree would stretch out over the path where we knew there would be water, and where there was water there was always the fountain. These fountains were designed for man and animals, with the water trickling from the spring directly into a small stone basin which in turn spilled into a larger basin below for the animals. In those days no one would have thought of carrying around a plastic bottle filled with water. We put up with tremendous thirst until we came to a spring then drank in great gulps, luxuriously pouring water over our heads and splashing our faces. When we finally arrived at the pebbly beach we couldn't wait to plunge into turquoise waters to swim and snorkel. (The snorkels came with us everywhere). When appetites were at their peak the picnic was laid out on bright hand woven cloths, red, blue, yellow stripes splashed over the brown fragrant pine needles. Our mule drivers never went near the sea, ate only bread and feta pulled from their colorful wool bags, then stretched on the ground using rocks for pillows, while the rest of us dozed under the pines which came to the water's edge. There it was possible to laze, looking up into pine branches, dry as driftwood, inhale the unusual mix of sea and resin to the sound of gentle lap-lapping of the water and the not so gentle snores of the mule drivers.

The walk back was muted from a surfeit of sun and sea, children no longer ran ahead but took turns riding the mule, deference given to their grandmother, as well as Boko and Mitsi. We arrived back in town in time for the evening promenade, our favorite pastime in a summer of no amusements.

We were so pleased with the success of the expedition that soon another was planned, this time by sea.

A large *caique* was making the rounds of nearby islands, carrying passengers, mail and cargo. Boko made the arrangements for us to embark at seven in the morning, for the trip to Alonyssos where we would spend the day at the beach then pick up our same vessel for the return in the late afternoon. This would give us an outing not too far, in deference to me, on the water, then the day on a new island with of course swimming. It was the same group, our family, plus Boko, Mitsi and the poodle Black. We had our usual picnic in case there wasn't any food on the island, so often the case, and of course swimming gear and snorkels. It was a perfect day, calm waters, essential for me, and shade under a canvas out of the fierce sun. We chatted and exchanged stories.

When we reached Aloynossos, where for some reason I now forget, we were not able to dock at the quay.

"O.K. don't worry," our captain announced. "Everyone who wants can go ashore. No problem. We have life boats to take you." He snapped his fingers at two small boys, "*grigora pedia,* these passengers want to go ashore."

The small boys ran to the two life boats fastened on each side of the stern deck. After unleashing knots on one boat, one lad jumped in while the other lowered it to the water. Immediately there were shouts.

"I can't swim," the child shouted as water filled the life boat.

We all peered over the edge to see the life boat—that boat which was there only to save lives, very quickly drowning one.

"The ladder," shouted the captain as he stripped and jumped into the water to save not only the cabin boy but his reputation.

The ladder was put over and captain and boy climbed to safety to cheers from the onlookers. But now that tragedy had been averted, the passengers all twenty of us, clamored to go ashore, but even worse the Greeks, now that the boy was safe, honed in on the captain.

Another drama followed with Greeks shouting, wanting to go ashore, accusing the captain of everything from murder to incompetence.

"You can loose your license for this," someone yelled.

"What would you do in a storm?"

"Do you never think there might be an emergency?"

The captain had had enough. He pulled himself to full height, in his wet clothes, he looked a Figaro figure, pathetic and comic.

"Why?" he asked, "do you think that I have not checked the boats recently?" No answer. "It is because my boat is so safe. I know the winds, the rocks, the hazardous ports, always I guide my boat in safely. Never have I had an accident, never lost a boat, never lost a life." He paused to let this sink in.

"This life boat will swell now it is in water and you may all go ashore safely. You can trust me."

We looked over the side at the life boat which had been sinking an hour earlier and was now bobbing, a bit low perhaps, but quite high enough to take a few at a time to shore.

I decided to swim with Io and Alice, Kimon was to dog paddle alongside Helen who would not hear of taking the boat, Coola, Boko and Mitsi would wait to be rowed ashore.

For some reason the passengers accepted the captain's explanation of faulty life boats, accepted his assessment of competency, and his twist on safety.

When we were reunited ashore we found a delightful beach where the ubiquitous shade of palm fronds had been put up to protect a makeshift kitchen, with extension for two tables. Instead of our picnic we had fish caught that morning, cooked over the grill with lemon and olive oil, fried potatoes cooked on a two burner gas ring, and salad of tomatoes, olives and feta soaked in a fine olive oil. Without drama, one of the lads rowed us to the boat for the return trip to Skopolos.

For long treks we had a donkey for Helen.

"This person is not good," Coo-Coo commented about the captain when we were back on Skopelos at our cafe. "He think he can talk his way around this sinking boat. Not a good captain. Make sure Kimon that when you travel you look at papers of pilots. Do not fly with bad pilots. Better you take Italian ship to America. I hear they very good. Greeks good too but always something not right."

I had visions of asking for the credentials of every boat captain, airline pilot, train engineer, then gave up exhausted; my imagination stumped. It was hard enough to be happy.

That was the order when we left Athens for the trip home, through Italy, (this time with no stomach upsets) through the Alps, France, to view various cathedrals and finally Cherbourg where we caught our boat.

It was good to be home again, back in familiar surroundings and routine, to be reunited with Watson and my brother who had taken him for the year, to weed the garden, fuss in the house and settle in to watch the fast maturing girls, all to be broken the following year by another stint away.

Dumbarton Oaks

DUMBARTON OAKS WAS a scholar's paradise, the first and only ivory tower Kimon had experienced. The Fellows were given their private study in the library of the awe inspiring quiet and refinement of the house, filled with art treasures collected by Mildred and Robert Bliss. An attendant was on hand to fetch books from the Library of Congress to save the scholars that bother. Fellows were also provided housing according to their needs. For us, a pleasant house near excellent schools, within minutes of beautiful walks. The children were settled into schools, Io and Alice, high school, Helen within walking distance of the elementary.

Dumbarton Oaks had been bought by the Blisses' in 1920 and turned over to Harvard, which still administers it, twenty years later. During those twenty years additions were made to the house to accommodate the Bliss collections of Byzantine art, and new facilities had been built on the grounds for a pre-Columbian museum and a landscape history library.

For me the gardens created by Beatrix Farrand with the close involvement of Mildred Bliss, were the equivalent of any luxuries given the Fellows. Of the original fifty-three acres ten have been retained for the gardens, which reflect elements of French, English and Italian gardens the Blisses' had visited abroad. As the land descends from the house the gardens become less formal in plantings and garden features. Plants were selected for winter beauty as well as summer bloom and in the climate of Washington D.C., it is the spring flowering trees and shrubs which steal the show. Farrand however never used the flamboyant azaleas or flowering trees with a heavy hand. There is always a delicacy and restraint and no garish colors.

The gardens were open to the public during the day but after four, the gates were closed and the Fellows and families had the gardens and most especially the pool to themselves. The pool, seemingly lifted from an Italian villa, not visible from the rest of the grounds, was intimate and sublimely elegant. It was backed by a lacy flowering cherry and over hung by a willow, a typical Farrand touch, to relieve the formality of the space.

The pool was our focal point, as in the humid heat of Washington it was longed for as much as the sea in Greece. It was where those with families could socialize and in a relaxed atmosphere meet those without children. So every afternoon in hot weather, I would drive to D.O. as it was affectionately called, to join others at the pool. One of the Fellows, Robert Townsend, lived with his family just down the street from us. It was the husband Robert who had the grant, but his wife Elizabeth was as much a scholar, it was just that her period—Elizabethan England—did not fit into any D. O. category. Like us, the Tounsends' had three daughters, the elder two at the same high school as Io and Alice and the youngest, Martha, in fourth grade with Helen. We saw each other frequently and I especially enjoyed the company of Elizabeth who was a caricature of the female intellectual, unable to cope with everyday life, which put her ever in a crisis be it losing her keys, or losing her way, forgetting appointments, or burning the applesauce; for her the mundane seemed to bring on disaster. Paradoxically when she set out to make a gourmet dinner, she could beat Julia Child at her own game. She was blessed with wit and endless good nature and humor. She spoke with a drawl, New England drawl, (there is such a thing) which made even simple accounts droll. We took turns driving everyone to the pool, but it was a real adventure when Elizabeth drove. She never changed gear so that no matter the speed or the incline the old car had to struggle on its own. Nor could she turn left so if that maneuver was required she went round the block and in those picturesque residential districts of Washington with winding streets it could mean a long detour. The hood of the car was tied down with rope to keep it from flying open, "Like the ships of the Armada. They held them together with rope, did you know that?"

One of the most charming of the Fellows that year was Ivan from Czechoslovakia, tall thin and gangling, not quite coordinated. He reminded me of Monsieur Hulot and evoked the same sympathy. He was on his own as the government did not allow his wife to join him for fear they would never return. This would be bad enough but his wife was expecting their first child after ten years of marriage, so poor Ivan was a nervous wreck most of the time. He was a delight nonetheless, witty and fun loving and it was he who introduced us to Slivovitz. He also introduced those at the pool, to the male European bathing costume which was no more than a colorful G-string.

"My dear I don't know whether I should look or turn away when Ivan dives in, really it is too fascinating—and then there is the problem when he lounges at the side—even riskier, one can hardly talk thinking that it might all fall out at any moment, and then one cannot help thinking that it really wouldn't matter but there you are we are all so conventional, would it really matter?" This was Elizabeth voicing all our thoughts.

We lived through Ivan's anguish at not being present for the new baby and his utter, overwhelming joy when he could announce a little girl. He was bubbling, grinning, hopping, aimlessly flapping his arms, very much like a nervous wading bird, embracing everyone, kissing on both cheeks, in the delight of his most special good fortune. Mother and child both doing well! We all learned the power of Slivovitz on that occasion.

Our girls each had different experiences in Washington.

The teen-agers attended a huge high school where they reported no one could feel strange because everyone was from somewhere. They played this up by reporting in broken English that they were from French Canada. This put them into remedial English class which they paid for when it turned out not to be much fun. They made good friends, went to parties, had boy friends, and even learned something.

Helen walked to her elementary school with her friend Martha Townsend, and was in battle with her teacher most of the year. Mrs. Draker was one of those teachers none of us will forget. For me it was constant parent teacher conferences, and endless struggles to get Helen off to school, for Helen it was almost every day detention after school. The one bright spot was the weekly writings which for some reason Helen liked. This assignment involved writing, anything, no corrections involved, just writing, and this assignment turned out to be the most formative. It made her think, form sentences, and consider at any time, wherever we happened to be, of a good subject for the weekly writings. Ironically after a year of personality clashes it was to Mrs. Draker that Helen insisted on sending post cards through all our travels.

For Io and Alice, even boys and school were overshadowed by a friend's offer to exercise their two horses boarded at the police stables in Rock Creek park. For two teen-agers mad about riding and very competent, it brought a bit of home into a new situation. Leaving Hiram had been traumatic because Duchess, our steady old mare, had to be left behind. It wasn't until a friend had offered to take her for the year and they had tutored Melissa in the daily care of this old horse, that we were able to leave on a peaceful note. It was strange to hear the words passed on that I had used when I bought the mare—"No matter how tired you are or how sick you feel, you have to take care of Duchess. In winter when it is cold she still needs a clean stall, food and water."

I had said that there would be no riding, the passion of their life, as we would have other activities, we would have to adapt to a new situation—one without horses, so this offer so unexpected, gave the year in Washington an unexpected glow. It was for the two girls a welcome change from the way we usually spent weekends when away from home, in exploring the surroundings; plantation houses, Gunston Hall, Mt. Vernon, Ash Lawn, among others and of course Jefferson's Monticello and the University of Virginia. Frequently Ivan was with us, thrilled to be able to cross the "frontiers" so easily. (Driving from one state to another, impossible not to do).

After school in cool weather, I would drive to the stables, drop off Io and Alice to ride through the park, often in the company of the mounted policemen, while Helen and I would return to D.O. where I could wander, analyze and wonder at one of the most sophisticated gardens in the U.S. I had no idea then that gardens would become the focus of my life and a flourishing business.

We had with us a standard poodle Bodo, Watson's successor, named for a medieval French peasant. He was large, magnificent and very intelligent. He loved to perform the many tricks the girls had taught him, but never for free. One of our favorite walks was down M Street to window shop and every so often treat ourselves to some of the delicacies to be found in the food shops there; in particular a gourmet cheese store. Bodo would walk in with the sophisticated air of a New York model, sit up in front of the counter, and bark once. This brought the owner Anton from behind the glass cases with a handful of cheese, then with a smile and nod he would tell any customers who happened to be in the shop to watch this dog. No one seemed to be in a hurry or if they were they were transfixed while Anton took Bodo through his repertoire with the flair of a circus animal trainer. Bodo worked with hand signals as well as voice and at times even I was impressed as the dog seemed to go from one trick to the other seemingly without any command—roll over, crawl, speak, shake hands, dead dog, stand on hind legs and dance, balance cheese on nose to flip and catch, pray with head on paws, and all the time Anton and Bodo smiling at each other. It always ended with applause and a huge piece of special cheese for me, compliments of the house.

When the year was over Bodo came with us to Greece.

Athens

THE YEAR FOLLOWING Dumbarton Oaks we left for a year in Greece where Kimon had a fellowship at the Gennadius Library in Athens. The trip was made as usual by ship, this time from New York to Piraeus, complete with Bodo, and Plymouth Valiant station wagon. The ship had a dog deck and kennels where we spent most of our time on the crossing, with Bodo and the two other dog owners. We were all glad to disembark in Piraeus, have the car unloaded and drive right to the door of the apartment where Mitso was on hand to help with the luggage. There was no lounging in bed next day, despite the cat fights which went on most of the night. The Greek sun is too insistent. From the balcony on the street side, vendors still shouted or rather sang their wares, some in a quaint archaic language; the shoe repairmen, the knife sharpeners, the vegetable and fruit sellers, even Gypsies with drums and bears. Theodore was still in charge of provisioning the house, and as usual he went his rounds very early to have delivered the precise number of fruit and vegetables he thought we would consume that day. He didn't reckon on teen age appetites so the two kilos of peaches were eaten long before the midday meal and another two had to be brought in; it was impossible to keep up with the delicious ripe summer fruits.

The balcony on the opposite side of the house which looked over the whole of Athens, became a necessary refuge as cars increased with the size of the city. From our balcony we could look down an everyone, no other buildings blocked our view. Here we were remote, like the hermits of old, spared the frenzy of the streets below. Always dominating the view was the Acropolis, whether in morning pink, noonday white or blood red of sunset, it was a focus of our lives and constantly brought us to the balcony, just to see how it was at that moment, rather like visiting a favorite painting in a museum.

Coola, "For the good of all" had arranged for us to rent a house in Kifissia, a beautiful suburb of Athens which she thought would be to our liking with gracious houses set in sprawling gardens, pine trees everywhere and a very lively center with shops and cafes. It was the nineteenth century summer retreat for Athenians.

The house she found was perfect, just the right size with spacious terrace where we lived most of the time, and a large garden enclosed by a ten foot fence as is the custom. As well as the pine trees near the house there were fruit trees, apricot and cherry, as well as an aviary filled with budgies of startling colors which the landlord tended. We were near the bus stop, where the girls picked up their respective school buses every morning, but off the main road. Bodo had the run of the garden, the car could be brought into the foot of the garden every night, and the few conveniences we lacked Coola quickly made up for. She even insisted that I have a maid several times a week, so housekeeping standards were kept high.

We settled in easily, the children off to school, Kimon to Athens and the library and me to my own devices. I learned to shop at the irresistible markets, hauling home kilos of fruit and vegetables and listening to the cries, songs of the vendors relating their wares to politics of the moment . . . "These apples would sweeten the words even of" . . . (name of a particularly caustic politician). "With the new taxes you don't have to eat meat, try my lentils—they keep." "You can trust these berries from Attica, unlike our double-tongued" . . . (again name of politician).

It was like reading the newspaper, all the immediate causes were sung out in the market.

If I hesitated in finding the correct coins, I would pour them all into my palm and the vendor would pick out each one saying its value, looking at me, then, at the end, "*endaxi?*" with a big grin. The Greek housewives were at constant odds with the merchants, always trying to outwit them. "That is not a kilo," one might say, which brought on a huge argument as to the fundamental honesty and honor of the merchant. If I, on the other hand, remarked that he had gone over the weight, without a word three extra would be popped into my bag.

Greece had been going through a period of social unrest with strikes, demonstrations and riots. Four colonels put their heads together and seized power without firing a shot. They arrested all generals and politicians they considered a threat and in one night took over the government. George Papadopoulous appointed himself as Prime Minister and regent, the others had appropriate high ranks. Elections were suspended and martial law imposed. One of the great protesters was Eleni Vlachou, owner of several respected newspapers. She refused to censor her papers, instead shut them down. She was put under house arrest where she wrote to the foreign press and gave interviews to foreign journalists. She was slated to be tried before a military tribunal but fled in disguise to London where she remained a voice against the colonels until they were ousted in 1974. What has rankled the Greeks ever since is that this coup was done, if not with the help of the CIA, at least with their blessing. Certainly the CIA was involved with the Turkish invasion of Cyprus, a situation which continues to fester.

It was not a very happy time in Greece just then during the Junta, with so many restrictions so contrary to the Greek way of life; no large meetings, curfew for youth, no breaking of glasses after parties, and on and on. That of course was the least. More serious were the communists exiled to an island, and almost anyone the Colonels considered suspicious could be jailed or exiled. Theodorakis, the composer and film director, was another popular protester: despite imprisonment and exile he continued to compose patriotic songs, promptly banned, which made them all the more popular. His songs became a symbol of free Greece. Our own girls reported proudly when they had daringly sung his songs at parties, after making sure no one would report them.

Even with this undercurrent of spying, Greece was a wonderful place for teenagers as there was really very little they could do that was illegal. Despite curfews, they felt less inhibited by the state than by their own father. In Greece parents are expected to control their children, and Kimon was no exception. Drinking was never the problem it is here perhaps because wine or beer are a natural accompaniment to a meal. It is not the man at the kiosk or waiter at the cafe, who impose age limits for drinking, most certainly not the government. The result is that all the fun is taken away from what is here, illicit. If their behavior becomes in any way unseemly there will always be a Greek to tick them off in very graphic terms, and best of all there is public transportation so that they can come and go on their own without demands on parents. There are endless places to meet, to hang out—to loiter, which I found later with grandchildren in this country, is anathema almost a crime in itself.

We were to find out first hand of the arbitrary measures the Colonels used to keep their order, with restrictions so foreign to the Greek way. It happened that Io and Alice with two boy friends were strolling to the cafe in Kifissia one Saturday evening when they found themselves followed by two men. Io picked up a stone and threw it which is what one does in Greece to get rid of stray dogs, cats or boys, or men. These men however turned out to be the secret police who promptly arrested them and took them to the local police station. It was from there that they made the phone call. Kimon answered. At least they were allowed a phone call. I can imagine what parents or relatives go through when police or army make arrests without notifying next of kin. I can imagine the desperation when a child vanishes but I cannot imagine why such cruelty must be inflicted. It certainly cannot make anyone feel more secure. When I heard that my children were held in a Greek jail I was beside myself, ready to call the American consul, and go myself to the station to drag them home by force and take on the secret police if necessary. Fortunately Kimon was able to persuade me to remain at home while he went to get to the bottom of the case. I was so angry that I am sure I would have made matters worse.

As it turned out the girls were released immediately but their boy friends, both Greek, were held all night and harassed, for what reason we never did know. The police never had to answer why they were not in uniform, why they were spying on teenagers or what they expected to gain from their arrest. We had had a sobering lesson of eroded civil rights, of how easy it is to find any excuse, at this time in Greece it was to restore order, for those rights to be swept away. It happens slowly and insidiously, most of the population lulled into thinking that things would be better.

This episode caused even more heated discussions at Coola and Theodore's dining table. Coo-Coo was for whatever it took to rid the country of endless strikes and street protests, (law and order) Fidor hated the Colonels and all they stood for and was deeply disappointed that America, represented by the CIA should be supporting them. The CIA involvement was as usual hinted at abroad, but general knowledge in Greece. Our meals at the apartment, were always political forums with Keti hovering near to add her opinions. Theodore expressed total disgust when the girls told him their story. His reaction was as mine; the insanity of it all and the continuing prospect of equally unwarranted, perhaps not such benign arrests. Of course Eleni Vlachou's name came up and even Coola admitted that she was courageous.

"More," Theodore answered. "She has principles. She can be an example to all Greeks."

"Greeks always ready to argue, everyone wants for himself," Coola countered. "How to run a country with such people."

Coola could run down the country and all Greeks in one breath, and in the next defend every aspect of Greek character and life.

At this point Keti set down the platter of *barbouni* she was passing the better to use both hands to present a passionate defense of "the people." Greek servants are never subservient.

"Vlachou is right. She speaks for the people who have nothing." Theodore was more of a socialist than he would admit. "Look at those ship owners who register under foreign flags so they never have to pay taxes. Why do they think they owe nothing to their country? They have no principles, no shame."

As I had free time I decided to volunteer to teach English at an orphanage on the other side of the mountain, by the sea near Raffina, about an hour away. It was a beautiful drive which I took twice a week. The orphanage was in a convent in pleasant pine covered grounds with the sea close enough to smell. It was the smell of the boiled cabbage however which was difficult to overcome—all-pervasive the moment I walked in the door. Mother Superior greeted me at the door and led me down the polished floors familiar to all convents, to a pleasant room where four teenage girls were gathered. After introductions Mother Superior left and I was on my own. Through our lessons we had fun and laughter, which I suspect they had not come upon frequently. Several weekends they came for the day for lunch and dinner and a walk through Kifissia. The eldest of the girls was so clever, I asked Mother Superior about her prospects for a university education.

"She has a father," I was told. "He cannot care for her because he is lame and cannot work so she is to stay here until she is old enough to marry, then she will care for her father and husband."

That ended my fantasy of sponsoring her for a college education in the States.

That year Professor and Mrs. Kitto were in Athens where he was lecturing. He had recently retired and came with the aura of the great scholar he was. His definitive work *The Greeks*, interprets for scholar or lay person the Greek character, mainly through literature, in an easy, clear style. Short and round he might have been passed by on the street, but never in conversation. He was the epitome of the English scholar; eloquent, learned in many subjects, with a great sense of humor and endless store of anecdotes. Mrs. Kitto, frail as a sparrow, was an accomplished pianist now unfortunately handicapped by severe arthritis. Through British Council, that marvelous cultural outlet and lifeline for

English speakers which the British established wherever they set foot, she had scheduled a concert. Not only that, she was keen to work up a chorus and needed volunteers. After one of those evenings at the taverna with good food, too much wine and endless anecdotes she made me think that I could join her group.

"Nonsense to say you can't sing," she had countered when I told her that I couldn't carry a tune, "anyone can sing."

Next day in my misery of realizing what I had committed to, I encouraged a friend to join me. Eddie and I had met at the laundromat of the American club and hit it off right away: she had married Tasso, a Greek, also a graduate of Athens College, our children were about the same age, but her three girls and one son attended Greek schools. The two of us joined Mrs. Kitto's choir along with a few other stragglers—some students and three Brits who sang in the choir of the Anglican church.

Rehearsals were three times a week, at six, in a small British Council room of just off the corner of Kolonaiki Square.

Eddie had fitted beautifully into Greek life because the bureaucracy never bothered her. For instance to get stamps meant all morning at the post office, which even more than the French post office took care of many non-stamp related activities; old age pensions, licenses of all sorts, electric and heating bills, rents, even more. Eddie, instead of becoming frustrated took her book along and settled in. She would tell me of the novels she had read at the post office or the bank—same story—or the dentist or doctor. She had so adapted to Greek ways that she herself had no sense of time, and I soon realized that when meeting Eddie there would usually be a long wait.

"It will be fun to sing with Mrs. Kitto," she had told me. Eddie had sung in church choirs as a girl. "I can drive us down." In those days it was very easy to drive into Athens from Kifissia and even to park when we got there. However Eddie's family car was an ancient Austin. It still ran, but fitfully. I sensed that if we were to participate in anything with Mrs. Kitto we would have to be on time.

"We can't be late," I warned.

"No, it would be very rude," Eddie agreed easily as if that were the last thing she would ever be.

And so the two of us would start out with what seemed like hours to spare and arrive barely on time, after a coughing spasm or worse, on the part of the car. On one occasion when turning a corner abruptly the steering wheel came off in her hand.

"Not again?" she laughed. "It happened the other day with Tasso. It was supposed to be fixed."

All this was said without slowing the car, while she calmly pushed the wheel back on the stem.

"I don't know why it does this," she mused, as if it were nothing more than a puzzle to be solved, not a death threat. We were always the last to arrive, barely in time for the warm up breathing exercises. We must have rehearsed several pieces but the only one I remember is—do-o-na no-o-bis, do-na no-bis etc.

Eventually we put on our little British Council concert. The British are so tolerant of amateur theatricals or amateur performances of any kind. It always comes as a surprise even today, how kind the remarks are of some very poor theatricals I have attended with discriminating English friends. Mrs. Kitto's own concert was agony as there were constant stumbles and restarts, all taken in stride by her and the audience, by everyone it seemed but me, who worried through every note. Eddie and I have remained fast friends through the years and still keep up with our respective children and grandchildren.

Crete

WE ARRIVED IN Heracleon a few days before Easter. In Greece Easter is the big celebration of the year, much more so than Christmas which has been taken up, American style, only recently. Easter coincides with the abundance and fertility of spring, but before the celebration there are forty days of fasting. In those days, travelling outside Athens, during Lent, it was difficult to find anything to eat in the villages, as fasting meant more than giving up meat, which villagers had only once or twice a year anyway. Of course there was no meat, or fish, even if near the sea, no yogurt, no oil, no eggs. We could get bread, feta, spaghetti with no sauce and that was about all.

On one occasion I was innocent enough to ask for yogurt. "Yogurt?" was the horrified response. "Aren't you Christian?" Even though it is the time of new lambs and kids, of much milk, of fresh greens (*horta*) picked from the mountains, of prolific egg-laying; during Lent the plenty of milk would go into cheese, and the eggs hard boiled until the days of baking came—the special the Easter bread yellow with eggs.

Crete is a large island, an overnight ferry boat trip from Athens so we had saved going there until Easter holidays when we would have time to explore.

Another family outing! It was with great expectations that we boarded in Piraeus; car, Bodo, two teenagers and a ten year old.

No one who loves animals or who thinks that meat comes from little packages without the sacrifice of a living creature should ever visit a Greek island at Easter. The flocks fill roads and hill sides, lambs bleating, ewes calling. To us it all seemed so picturesque until Helen who had not read the bible verses of the lambs marked for slaughter asked, "why do some sheep have red on them?" Impossible not to tell her.

"It is Easter and a big feast day. Everyone eats lamb at Easter, even if they haven't eaten meat all year. The lambs marked with red will be eaten."

"I'm not eating a lamb," she stated flatly. What should have been joy in the biblical rebirth of nature, turned sour at the thought of killing the sheep. From that moment the trip fell flat, even with all the associations of Arthur Evans, the Minotaur and labyrinth, pottery of bull gymnastics, dolphins, flowers and the more recent heroics of the fierce fighting during World War 11 when the Germans, on May 20 1941, launched the first airborne invasion in history.

We visited the palace at Knossos first uncovered by Arthur Evans in 1899, and where he worked until his death in 1941. It is a huge complex, some 40 acres, with sections restored under great controversy, but most intriguing is that the palace was unfortified, nor did the paintings or any of the art works glorify the warrior. There is still no explanation for why the Minoans, alone among archaic civilizations, showed no warring tendencies. Their art is pure delight in beauty and movement. The teenagers loved the palace and dutifully went through the museum before announcing that they wanted to return to Athens. Obviously they had only come this far to placate misguided parents who thought a family outing in the car through primitive villages was a holiday. So we saw them off on the ferry to Piraeus and Athens where the excitement was, with friends and boys, even if under the watchful eye of Coo-Coo and Fidor.

Of particular delight in the museum, were the small terra cotta heads, each one a portrait. Sitting at the cafe in the evening we saw the same faces all around us; with the same imperfections of chin, nose, mouth, it was as if all those terra cotta figures had come out of the museum for a round at the cafe.

We had heard many stories from Coola and Theodore of the occupation and guerilla war of Crete, of the escapes to Egypt and the indomitable spirit if the Cretans who risked their lives and the safety of their villages to hide and save stranded British soldiers.

A New Zealand friend Ann, who had made her home in Greece as an archaeological artist had many stories to tell of the ANZACS as the Australian and New Zealand forces were called. The ANZACS along with the British had formed the main defense of Crete, and had fought hand to hand with the villagers against the German invaders. During the occupation, stragglers were hidden in caves often for months, and given food already at subsistence level for the locals. When an organized resistance had been formed, a stream of soldiers were evacuated by submarine to Egypt from the south coast.

"I remember a Maori telling me of how a villager had saved his life; of hiding in a cave, eating bread shared with the family, sometimes honey, of this villager inspiring hope for rescue and neither speaking the other's language, of his obsession of one day returning to thank the whole village for what they had done." This was one of Ann's stories.

Years later visiting Ann in Athens, sitting at her favorite ouzeria she picked up on the ANZAC story.

"You remember the Maori who thought of nothing but returning to Crete? Well he did finally. I was working at a dig nearby so he sought me out to join him in a party the village was giving for him. Wild horses couldn't have kept me away. I had spent enough time on Crete to know what their parties were like. They brought out all the wine, the sheep were on the spit, the women had been cooking for days, the food was laid on tables under the grape arbor in front of the door. I'll never forget the dizzy excitement of that night; dancing until dawn, bouzouki, fiddle, all ages, babies sleeping, grannies smiling, men embracing, tears staining dry furrowed cheeks. My Maori, Jimmy, danced higher and longer than anyone else. It was to show his thanks. And they understood. As the music wound up, faster and faster, the intensity increasing, as it does in those dances, Costa and Jimmy broke from the line and grabbed each other in a smothering embrace, the big black flat-faced man enveloping the twisted wiry mountaineer.

There they were from opposite sides of the world, each with generations of survival in his genes, tears running down their faces; the music continued its frenzy to tease the young men into the athletic leaps Cretan dances are famous for, more wine was poured and in the end the two old survivors, Costa and Jimmy, fell asleep under the fig tree in the yard. I made my own way back to the digs but I tell you I couldn't do any drawing that day." Ann lit a cigarette and sipped her ouzo, a slow smile spread over her face. "If you want to have a party come with me to Crete."

In the end it was our daughter Helen who visited Crete with Ann.

Our Cretan war stories came from the adventures of Patrick Leigh Fermor, the British travel writer and war hero. After reading his books 'Roumeli', of travels in northern Greece and 'Mani', of travels in southern Greece, I was taken with the heroics of his war years in Greece, when he had been parachuted into Crete during the German occupation of the island to organize resistance. Disguised as a shepherd he lived in the mountains for two years with the partisans. His most famous adventure was the kidnapping and capture of the commanding German general Heinrich Kreige in 1944, a story of daring and panache. Most moving was the change in attitude between captive and captor after Kreige looking out on the Mt. Ida dawn quoted lines from an ode of Horace. Picking up the quote Leigh Fermor finished the ode in Latin. As the story goes the German turned to his captor and said, "Ach so, Herr Major." Fermor replied "Ja, Herr General." This implied, in Fermor's words, that they had both drunk at the same fountain. From that moment the relationship between the two men changed.

We had all these stories and those of Theodore who described the Cretans as the bravest of all Greece. Even today he had told us, the Cretans keep their own dress and still carry a knife in their sash. It was

Theodore who told us of the rescues of English soldiers through the Samaria gorge.

We left with Bodo and Helen for the other side of the island to the village of Sfakia, the home we were told of the fiercest of all the fierce fighters of Crete. They had held off invaders for centuries: Saracen Arabs, Venetians and Turks and had sent 300 men to the defense of Constantinople. From Sfakia we could visit the base of the Samaria gorge through which so many soldiers had been led to safety during the war.

Roads in those days were primitive, no highways; just tracks, paved roads only from one main point to another and these paved roads so narrow, especially on hairpin mountain turns, two cars could not pass. Kimon driving, was able to comment on the scenery as we wound around mountains so steep I would have gnawed my nails even if I had been on foot. As it was I did all the driving and more, never daring to lift my eyes to the spectacular scenery of rugged mountains, only nodding at Kimon's comments, not even daring to speak. Adding to the hazards were flocks filling the road, shepherds waving, smiling, in a ritual to separate the animals marked for slaughter.

We picked up a fierce looking, black mustachioed villager, dressed as Theodore had told us, in the traditional tall black boots, baggy trousers, even the wide sash holding, yes, holding a sheathed knife. A homespun wool jacket topped it all. After the usual courtesies he asked if we could take him to his cousin who was a cheese maker, not far off the road. He pointed to a path, it looked like a foot path, which wound uphill through an olive grove.

"I can't take the car up there." Kimon said.

"No problem, my cousin go all the time," was the reply.

Kimon, not to be outdone, assessed the path again and decided that if we went slowly enough we might avoid a broken axle.

"Bravo," our passenger said as Kimon manipulated around a huge rock to come in sight of a shed circled by sheep pens. He was out in a second kissing the cousin and waving in our direction. "Come must see."

We were taken in by the cousin who seemed pleased to show us around. Several small boys were standing by obviously waiting for orders. A huge kettle hung over a fire where a young man was combing through thick curds with what looked like a small wooden rake.

It was all explained to us. "Now sheep with new lambs—we milk day and night—twenty-four hours. Milk goes into cheese. Cheese here—must be turned every three days," he waved to racks of rounds of cloth wrapped cheese lining the shed, curing, row upon row. The highest shelf held thick blankets and was evidently the sleeping shelf. "To make money government teach us to make gruyere, sells better in Athens. Always before only feta, so we have more sheep now to make better cheese. In summer when milk is little we still make feta." It seemed to be an all male preserve, away from the village, where the shepherds lived with their flocks which roamed the mountains, at this time of year to be brought into the pens to be milked twice a day. Of course we bought a round of aged gruyere to take back to Athens. Even after giving away quantities, it kept us going for months.

We left the shepherd and his cheeses to wind our way back through the stony track, but our companion now had a lamb with him tied by the legs—a black lamb.

"My cousin save me Easter lamb," he said proudly.

It was disaster for us with Helen. The lamb as the symbol of innocence is not misplaced. There is nothing more appealing; soft, vulnerable, gentle, everything a child's stuffed animal imitates. Somehow that this gentle animal, flung carelessly on the floor of the car, was black, made it worse and then knowing its fate, was more than we had counted on when picking up a hitchhiker. In vain I tried to explain that any meat we eat comes from a living animal, that here it is only that we can see the animal.

"These are poor people," I tried to explain, "many have meat only once a year at Easter, they plan for it."

"We could give him money for the lamb and we could take it home. There is room in the garden," Helen pleaded.

Fortunately, lamb and hitchhiker did not go far with us. We let him off at another track where he slung the lamb around his neck and strode off leaving Helen in sobs. Neither she nor I ate any lamb that Easter and she became a dedicated vegetarian, an example I was soon to follow.

That was not the last of the Easter lamb story. We arrived at Sfakia on the coast on Easter eve. In those days we never made reservations travelling in Greece or anywhere else so it was a surprise to be told that there were no rooms available. There was no hotel, but not even a room to be had to rent; not that they were flooded with tourists for the holiday—they never had tourists. No one came who was not related to a villager, something we didn't know.

After walking into the one cafe and stating that we had come for Easter, in Greek fashion, about a dozen men came forward to say that we were welcome and a room would be found.

"*Ela*, come," one young man said and strode from the cafe down the street a few paces, took a large key from his pocket and opened the door to what seemed a warehouse. Following him we went upstairs to a huge loft room with large doors at the end which he swung open to a view looking onto the small rocky harbor with a few fishing caiques swinging at anchor. It was a view millionaires would envy. This room, quickly to be furnished with cots and heavy blankets was offered to us, view included, as guests of the village. Of course there was no running water but the cafe had fresh water and the surrounding rocks and woods would do for our ablutions. We expressed our gratitude which was brushed off—"welcome to our village, you guests now." We bought bread at the cafe and sliced off hunks of our gruyere cheese, (it was still Lent and fasting in order) and took a walk along the shore until it was time for the Easter celebration.

The church, no more than a chapel, was set into the hillside high above the village in a grove of Cyprus trees, a stream rushed beside it; another example of the perfect settings selected by Greek monasteries and churches. On that night a trail of lights wavered up the stony path, broken in places where shrubs or rocks blocked the glow of candles held by every villager. We joined the procession with our own candles. The familiar aroma of incense and beeswax met us on the path to guide us up to the church. Candle light spilled from the open door onto the stone threshold. The church was so small it barely held the crush of bodies. We were pushed in to circle the priest under the dome, as guests, not to be left out. The intoned chants which we had heard on the way up continued with responses given by the informed, always men. Women crossed themselves and pushed to the iconostasis to kiss the icons. The priest, a thin, bearded young man had the voice of a monk from Solemne, and the same huge eyes of suffering represented in the pantocrator above us in the dome. It was as if the resurrected Christ was before us—that he had indeed arisen, or more likely dropped down from the dome above. The sarcophagus of Christ at the entrance was covered with flowers gathered by the women, wild lilies, anemones whatever the mountain offered; the most intensely fragrant bouquets.

If the soaring cathedrals of France represented a spiritual search for God, this simple tableau was close to creating a reunion with the divine. The slow candlelit march up the path, the exotic fragrances, the modal chants, the crush of bodies, the Christlike priest, transported me into a dizzy trance. I seemed no longer a part of the group. All those stories of saints and mystics who collapse with visions now rang true. When the service was over and the red eggs came out, one cracking the egg of another with a joyous, *"Christos anesti,"* and the response, *"Alithos anesti,"* Kimon and I, and even Helen were too much subdued by the service to participate. It was so unlike our bunny rabbit Easter; we descended the track in silence, awed by the scene we had left.

In the very early morning I heard bleating outside our windows—then cats meowing. Helen and Kimon were still asleep. Silently I went to the open window and looked down. Just as I thought. One sheep was being skinned and gutted, two others were tethered nearby waiting their fate. If they are slaughtering sheep right under us, I wondered, how am I going to keep Helen from seeing it all? I lay in bed until Helen woke up then with great excitement I told her to dress quickly, that we were going on a special walk to explore the whole cove, and maybe find the path to the gorge. Praying that we wouldn't pass the slaughtered sheep I enticed her in the opposite direction and on to a very long walk with time to play in the sea, search for shells and special stones but most especially time to have all signs of the slaughter removed and the sheep already on the spit before our return. It worked. Somehow once on the spit the act of killing lost immediacy and the live animal became meat—not that we were going to eat it!

That morning everyone had a red egg. With children in the street running to crack each others eggs, we felt that we could participate with eggs given to us from the cafe. "*Christos anesti,*" "*alithos anesti,*" We stayed in the village for the feast, most of which we couldn't bring ourselves to eat, but in joy it was almost up to Ann's description for the war heroes; wine, Easter bread with a red egg baked into it, Easter cookies and of course *kokoretsi* which the men were making, stuffing the intestines with the various organs. The resurrection soup made with the head of the sheep along with various other parts was not something any of us even wanted to look at.

I remembered the story of a Greek woman who had lived abroad for years, and returned to Athens at Easter to stay at the Grande Bretagne Hotel. There, in the elegant dining room, she ordered soup forgetting that it was Easter. When she lifted the silver cover to the tureen a sheep's head stared up at her complete with eyes and teeth. She screamed and dropped the cover on the marble floor, unsettling everyone in the dining room.

"But Kyria, it is *mayiritsa,* for Easter," the waiter said.

"I had forgotten," she told me, "even though I am Greek I cannot eat *mayiritsa,* so I don't blame you for not being able to eat it."

Easter is the time when all over Greece there is the smell of the lamb on the spit; it is the time to eat meat, and all traditional dishes are a way of celebrating every part of the animal so that nothing is wasted. The head made into soup, the vital organs into *kokoretsi*, but the real treat comes when the men chop the roasted meat into hunks, no such thing as slicing, to serve around.

We ate the bread, the carrot and cabbage salad, gorged on sweet tomatoes and cheese and drank wine. Kimon to uphold the honor of the family, accepted the roast lamb and to everyone's delight said it was the best he had ever eaten. I was proud of how gracefully we had eased through the day.

Next day we set off to walk the gorge. The gorge of Samaria is by many accounts the longest in Europe, starting in the rugged White Mountains in western Crete. Today the gorge and surroundings are a national park and crowded with tourists and their guides, way stations and regulations. In those days it was known to hikers with a sense of adventure or those who wished to see the gorge escape route or the refuge it had provided for centuries.

From our village of Sfakia we took a small boat to the mouth of the gorge where we were left on the rocks to investigate. We knew that with Helen we would never be able to climb the gorge, and anyway we were attacking it from the wrong end—climbing up instead of down from Omalos on the plateau. We did hike from the "Gates" at the sea for a few hours, awed by the height and narrowness of the gorge. The entrance is 3 meters wide. This "entrance" is so narrow and high that it is no wonder no occupying force was ever able to conquer it. Kimon told us one of many stories of fights with the Turks; on one occasion 4000 women and children took refuge there, defended by 200 men who blockaded the gorge taking in with them supplies and ammunition. Then of course there were the escapes during the German occupation of Crete when British soldiers were led through the gorge by partisans to be met by submarines off the coast. This was the escape route for Leigh Fermor and his kidnapped German general. Years later I was reminded of Samaria and the defensibility of a gorge when hiking down the gorge to Petra. But the entrance to the Nabatean city was only rock, no greenery other than an occasional oleander where light permitted, unlike the fragrant sides of the Cretan gorge.

When we left Sfakia after such a short stay, it was like leaving family; half the village waved to see us off, laughing at Helen and Bodo sharing the back seat and calling 'kalo taxidi.'

For the entire trip we had Bodo with us, quite a curiosity in the villages. We were frequently asked what kind of animal he was. A large standard poodle was after all a strange creature to see in rural Crete, long before the Greeks had taken to pet dogs. He was in a fairly long coat as I had not had time to clip him before leaving so he looked twice his size. When the women asked what he was and we answered a dog, there were exclamations of approval. How useful to have a dog that gives wool. Had I made anything with it? How much did the wool sell for? When I answered that I had never made anything from it nor sold it I was asked why. "*Po,po, po,* leave him with us and we will send you a garment."

We struck those formidable roads again, this time heading for the cave of Zeus. Legend has it that Zeus was born on Crete, in a cave, and it was one site we wanted to see with Helen. It is in dispute whether he was reared in the cave of Dikteon or Ideon on Mt. Ida, but it was Dikteon we visited. We left the car at a cluster of souvenir shops, where the road stopped. From there a steep path wound up—straight up—through olive trees to a wide shelf. Once up we could catch our breath, and take in the magnificent views of the plateau to the rear, and ahead to rugged mountains but still with no sign of a cave. Another tourist couple loitered under a tree, diverted from climbing the last path to the cave by a bright eyed boy of about twelve, who it seemed was guardian of the entrance. There were no signs, no entrance fees, or any tourist information other than one sign written in Greek and English, CAVE OF ZEUS. I am not much for caves as I find them too claustrophobic but the self-appointed guide was all smiles and with a ready English vocabulary. There was no way I could stand aside, no matter how forbidding I imagined the cave to be.

"Good morning, me very good guide. I know Greek history and history of Zeus. Follow me and watch steps." He climbed the stony trail which ended in the gaping maw of the entrance.

"Wait until I come," he ordered.

In a few minutes he had returned. "I light candles in cave," he explained. "Now safe. Watch steps and hold rail."

Helen followed first, close on his heels. He held a flashlight for us to navigate the steps, waiting until we were assembled on the brink of, to me a terrifying gap, before continuing down into the depths. The flickering candles stuck at intervals into the rock confirmed my fear of caves. It wasn't until my eyes became more accustomed to the dark and I could make out the beauty of the stalactites, that beauty overcame fear. Slowly I continued down to trickling water, pools and beautiful stalagmites, all catching mysterious light from the candles, all creating the effect of a holy chapel. It was the perfect setting for the myth of Zeus.

Our guide was at his best waving the light around the dark interior. "Zeus grow up here," he said. "Brought because mother Rhea want him to live. Father Kronos want to eat him. Father afraid son will become king and kill father." That was certainly a simplification of the myth.

"What about the goat?" Helen asked.

"Yes." Our guide laughed. "You know story. Sacred goat Amalthia, feed baby Zeus and five *kuretis* make noise so father not hear baby cry."

Slowly we climbed into sunlight, the boy again monitoring our steps. Outside he stood there smiling. "You like visit to cave?"

"You are a good guide," Helen told him, while Kimon found an ample tip.

There was no begging for payment. We had found this so frequently when travelling in Greece in those days when even the poorest peasant would not beg. There was the shepherd who asked the time. When Kimon told him and then offered a cigarette, he refused but took a half from his own pocket and allowed Kimon to light it for him.

Helen grabbed my arm. "Look those tourists are just walking away, not giving him anything."

It was true. Our fellow visitors had never even recognized the boy in all his earnestness to please. They had not seen the bare feet, the clean white shirt, the mended shorts, the scrawny frame. They had not sensed the continuing scrabble of life here on Crete.

Back in Athens we heard that everyone had had a good time but we felt that in Sfakia, with no amenities, we had found the perfect place to celebrate Greek Easter and rebirth.

Spring in Greece

S PRING IN GREECE is a miracle. The countryside awakens to a biblical renewal. The very rocks bloom. Within a few days the dry olive terraces are Irish green, and a mossy fuzz covers the land. In Ohio it is the awakening trees which catch the eye, tinting the woods with a pastel version of the autumn flamboyance. Flowers are hidden under leaves or grasses unsure of themselves, but in Greece flowers splash over the land and sprout from every crevice; it seems in defiance of what I, as a gardener, consider essential—soil. Red poppies and anemones, white anthemis, blue iris, muscari and campanula, to mention only a few of the dozens of small flowers which drift through the hillsides, roadsides and fields. Frolicking in this abundance are new lambs and goats. In the garden of our rented house the cherry, and apricot trees bloomed and Bodo found an escape from the garden to pursue his own spring amours. I am sure that long after we left there were poodle crosses on the streets of Kifissia; that was before designer dogs were popular. Greece is a botanists paradise. There are over 6,000 species of flora and new discoveries still to be made. Pre-glacial species exist because Greece was largely shielded from the ice age and in isolated parts of Greece endemic plants have survived which have become extinct elsewhere. In anticipation of the flowering miracle of a Greek spring, I found a wildflower guide which I read with the same avidity with which I read garden catalogues in Ohio. The list of wildflowers reads like the pages of Whiteflower Farm, wild peonies and gladiola, acanthus and of course all my favorite herbs: nepeta, thyme, chamomile. I find the favorites which I have struggled so hard to grow in my Hudson garden, thrive here in the wild. There are all the delicate species bulbs: tulips, crocus, hyacinth, scilla. Listed as wild are iris, campanula, euphorbia, anthemis, poppies, silene, anemone, roses and the list goes on and on. Of course not all are to be seen everywhere. Each has its range, its locale, and for the plant hunter this makes for daring explorations into mountain fastness or heights, remote valleys, secluded islands.

If I was not examining flowering plants on our weekend excursions, I was buying local produce at the market where seasonal bounty exploded onto stalls. The Greeks are not only seasonal, but regional eaters.

This was the season for *horta,* the wild greens gathered even by sophisticated Athenians. Women could be seen scattered over hills and mountains, bottoms up like ducks, filling sacks of wild greens. Cars were parked anyway, anywhere, if it was thought *horta* could be picked. It is said that a good housewife can pick a bag of *horta* while her husband changes a tire. Sometimes old men would be selling their gleanings by the roadside, from the more inaccessible high mountains and we could never resist buying from them, knowing what climbing, bending, stooping and of course knowledge was put into a small bag of aromatic greens. Knowledge is what it takes, as there are at least 80 different plants which are picked and every one has its own flavor and season. Now we were into the spring abundance, but after the drought of summer the first rains of autumn bring forth many favorite *horta* and the ritual begins again. Dandelions, kale, sorrel, black mustard, fennel, chicory, mallow, wild leeks, hoary mustard are just a few. It is important to a discerning picker not to include too much of any one plant, to balance the flavors, the bitter with the mild, the piquant with the bland, like the mesclun lettuce mixes which are commonplace in today's markets.

The best Sunday outing for a Greek is to pile as many people as possible into a car and head at top speed for a predetermined village. The travelling speed does not indicate a necessity to arrive quickly. On the contrary, the best outings are those which involve the most stops, and these are always to buy or to eat some local specialty, and there seems to be hardly a hamlet which cannot produce its own. In the most forlorn village a row of cars will be seen parked in front of a restaurant which looks hardly capable of feeding a cat. Word will have passed that this is where a certain soup is made best, or a *meze* or a sweet. Rarely will a Greek be seen travelling without a bag of something which is more special where it comes from than where it is going, even if it is only be apples and the trip only ten miles.

We spent many week ends exploring some of the least exploited ancient or Byzantine sites of Attica. One memorable excursion was to Perachora on the Gulf of Corinth.

Perachora had been excavated by the British in 1929 under Humfry Payne, specific excavations taking place at the Heraion during the seasons of 1930-33, where rich finds were uncovered. The event and subsequent lifelong love of Greece is evocatively written in Dilys Powell's book, "An Affair of the Heart." At the time we visited en famille, I had not read the book but the place has remained in my memory.

Kimon had warned that the site was remote, no village nearby for food, so for this family outing picnics were in order, bread, cheese, tomatoes, fruit, and water. It was a balmy spring day with heat from the Greek sun already strong. Kimon at the wheel took this time in the car to explain the site, as he knew from experience that once outside, the children's attention could never be caught.

He told us we were to visit, a jewel of a site, secluded and quiet, a beautiful spot where a temple had been built to the goddess Hera. They were enough up on mythology to know that Hera was the wife of Zeus. I reminded them of Rhea who secretly hid her son Zeus, in the cave of Diktaeon we had visited on Crete, to save him from his father Kronos.

"Well," I said, "Hera was the daughter of Kronos.

"Why didn't Kronos want to eat Hera?" was the question.

"The oracle said that it would be a son who would grow up to kill his father and become king in his place."

"So Hera ended up marrying her brother," Io correctly assessed.

"Weird."

"Well if I had a brother I wouldn't want to marry him."

"It was only myths, stupid."

The parking was no more than a barren area, space for about three cars, no shops no stalls, and there was no one else there on that day. An obvious path led down but there were no signs to indicate where we were or what we might be coming for in this desolate place.

Perachora is indeed a jewel. That day the jewel we looked down on was set in a protected box of turquoise sea on one hand, backed by rocks skimmed with green, padded by hills tufted in aromatic pines, and lidded under the clearest blue sky. It was one of those rare experiences of feeling that one is now, at this moment, the first human for centuries to lay eyes on this perfection of sea, rock and land. It was as if we had just discovered the broken columns and strewn masonry, on a small scale much like what we had seen in other ancient sites, but on this day we were the discoverers, the explorers.

The children rushed down the path, impatient to reach the water, Bodo at their heels.

"There are ancient cisterns around here somewhere," Kimon said casually.

It was enough for me to panic, all the poetry of the place gone in an instant. My father's story of little Bobby lost down the well haunted me. It was on the Indian Reserve of the Six Nation Indians where my father and three surviving siblings were raised. Four had died in childhood, little Bobby being one. He had gone to fetch the eggs but not returned. In the search, his hat was found floating in the well. For years after, my grandmother would call out into the surrounding woods for Bobby.

"Bobby where are you?" She would call repeatedly.

"Bobby come home."

This story of Little Bobby and a mother's inconsolable grief I had heard for years. It affected me much more than little Daisy dying of diphtheria, of little Valerie dying of typhoid, or the infant Mathew, who was given a Christian burial even though he lived such a short life. These other deaths took place when it was not unusual for children to die; Little Bobby it seemed to me, did not have to die, he only went to fetch the eggs and probably showed too much curiosity looking down the well he no doubt had been warned not to go near.

Now I gathered my brood and reminded them of the story which they had heard so often from their grandfather.

"For God's sake don't try any daredevil tricks here. If you go down you'll never come up. If you find a hole somewhere just back away. Anyway they are probably filled with scorpions and snakes." I left them with that thought.

I needn't have worried. The only thing they wanted was to dash into the water. It was still early for swimming but that clear water was so tempting that we all thought it a good idea. All except Kimon.

"We never swim so early in Greece," he stated flatly as if that were a rule.

"I'm going in." Helen was the first to start undressing.

The others followed quickly but lost speed when feet touched the water.

"You're right Dad it's cold."

"Freezing."

"Just a little. You get used to it."

As cold water never bothered me, I dared everyone to jump in after me, which they did, all squeals.

I stumbled out on the stony shore after a very few minutes, but Kimon was by now looking over the edge of the stone jetty to analyze the foundation.

In one version of the story told years later, Helen had not yet gone in so when Kimon fell over in his eagerness to see the huge rocks it was she who gave him a hand to crawl out, soaking wet, clothes, wallet, guide book everything. In another version, Alice had asked Kimon for help climbing out onto the rocks, as she didn't want to put her foot onto sea urchins which covered the bottom. In helping her he lost balance and fell in with her. Whatever the version Kimon did fall in with all his clothes which took forever to dry, while the rest of us dried instantly under the strong sun and put on dry clothes. Whatever the version the day at Perachora has remained a family tale of Kimon falling in the sea but no one falling down one of the many cisterns which we did discover.

Mani was an area I was determined to visit, perhaps even more after listening to the negative stories of Coola and Theodore who could do nothing to dispel my fascination with Leigh Fermor's account of the history and remoteness of this part of Greece.

The Mani is the central peninsula of the Peloponese and at Cape Matapan, the entrance to Hades, the southernmost point of mainland Greece. The Taygetus Mountains, 8,000 feet at the center, historically blocked, except for the most determined, entrance from the north. These wild mountains run south, 75 miles on the west, forty five miles on the east allowing a bare scrabble of livelihood for the refugees who for centuries have dared the crags and heights to find asylum; from the second century B.C. when Spartans fled their tyrant to later Slav tribes, then when the thirteenth century conquest by the Franks created more refugees from Byzantine Sparta, to the fall of Byzantium, and onslaught of Turks. It was resistance to the Turks which created the reputation of wild and unconquerable people as it was here that many guerilla heroes were born and kept Mani free from Turkish occupation. With arable land almost nonexistent any influx of newcomers created strife and vendettas between villages and clans. After independence the Mani continued with and confirmed strict codes of social behavior and honor (vendettas). It was only now with electrification and new roads built or proposed, that this rock outpost of Greece was about to change.

"Why you go to such place?" Coola had asked. "Not beautiful like some islands and people know nothing. And where you stay, no food, no hotel, *tipota*."

"The people are brave but crude." Theodore took over. "They have blood feuds like the Sicilians. These can go on for generations. That is why they build the tower houses for protection from their neighbors." He laughed. "Can you imagine protecting against the house down the street? Worse than the occupation."

What made the decision for us however, was talk of a new road which would go right down the length of the peninsula. In defiance of the warnings we decided to make the trip, taking Helen with us, leaving Io and Alice in Athens with grandparents and boys. A Greek couple, Maria and Yanni friends of Kimon, were keen to join this expedition to a part of Greece reserved until recently only for adventurers, backpackers, Helenophiles.

It was perfect weather for an outing, the countryside in bloom, the Greek sun spreading warmth, the sky clear. We were all in festive mood and drove in our car out of Athens to Corinth where we stopped to ramble the ancient acropolis. The columns stood white against the bluest of skies. Poppies, anemones, and all the abundance of spring growth pushed through cracks, through stones, or sprouted from broken columns.

The entrance into the Mani was through Gythion a faded port town with a long waterfront, where we strolled and lunched at a cafe looking out onto wine dark water. The Greeks of the party were so into their own discussion that they never asked about the road south, taking for granted information from the tourist office Theodore had consulted was correct.

Immediately we found that the new road was no more than a road bed of newly laid stone. Where fruit trees bloomed in the rest of the Peloponnese, here rocks decorated with prickly pear cactus seemed to be the only crop, even the ubiquitous olive was rare. Kimon drove the car cautiously over the sharp rock, in vain trying to avoid damage to car and tires. The first tire change took place with cheer from the men who were sure that the road would soon change to a paved surface. After the second puncture we all stood by the roadside in dismay. Not only was paving no more than hope, after a walk down the deserted road we found that even this rock bed stalled at mule tracks through the rock.

"If we can't drive, we can walk," I encouraged. "I see a tower over there, let's find the village."

It was an excuse to enter into the most magical of Greek spring landscapes. A green skim splashed over the rock and soil, and onto this wash blood red anemones refused to acknowledge the grim place of their birth, dazzling the eye with a flamboyance out of tune with the realities of surrounding human life. An ancient olive stretched a tortured limb over the ground to the delight of young goats endlessly climbing and pushing to become masters of the height. The contrast between the rocks, accented with unfriendly prickly pear, and this carefree exuberance of renewal, exaggerated both the poverty and the beauty of the place.

We had not been walking long before a lean boy came up to greet us with shy smiles. Where were we from? How long will we stay? How long did it take to come from Athens? Where were we going? When I said that I was from America there was po, po, po, he had an uncle in America. Maybe he would go there some day.

We had come with presents for the children we had been forewarned lacked everything. Instead of sweets we brought pencils, pens and paper. Now with the offer of a pen and paper to our friend Costa, he took the presents but not for himself he assured us, for his little sister. Then as mysteriously as he had appeared he disappeared.

It wasn't long before he called to us again. "My mother sends you a gift and thanks you." He held out his hand to give us, laid on a cactus leaf, a lump of feta.

We all thanked him and gave yet another pen and pad for any other siblings but he stayed, watching.

"We are supposed to eat the feta now," Kimon said, breaking off a piece for himself and the others.

I bit into mine and almost gagged. This was feta preserved in brine, this was feta made for hard times, feta that would last the drought of summer when the goats went dry. It was comparable to the salt cod I remembered from childhood when fish was cured in salt kegs. But then the cod was soaked. Now I was expected to eat this offering and smile—which of course we all did, even Helen.

We headed back to Gytheion that day after changing the second tire, praying there would be no more punctures. We had come with two spares at the insistence of Theodore who liked to be prepared for any eventuality. While the two tires were being repaired we sat subdued over dinner at a waterfront restaurant. We had not penetrated the Mani any more than the Turks, we had not seen the tower house villages, but we had experienced the code of hospitality, the pride even of the boy who accepted gifts only for his sister, although they may never have been given over to her, and the mother who reciprocated with the only thing she had to give—last year's feta.

Despite aborting the trip I felt that we had met the Mani. It was not until years later when I visited Helen, who was living in Greece as an established photographer, that I finally made the whole round of Mani on paved roads.

End of the Year

T HE YEAR WAS ending. Io had graduated from the American high school and decided that she wanted to spend the following year in England at an equestrian school where she could not only learn horsemanship but earn a certificate as a qualified riding teacher. Alice would finish her last year of high school back in the States and Helen would, we hoped, enter sixth grade.

I had been corresponding with every school of horsemanship in England and after many family consultations we had decided that Talland in Cirencester seemed best. We had been warned that some of these schools used the students as skivvies and taught them almost nothing other than how to handle a pitch fork.

The year in Athens had been memorable for the ease with which we took on our new country and enjoyed the adventures Greece always gives. From the cat fights, the uncertain political situation, outings to everywhere and nowhere; sometimes remote classical sites, sometimes remote swimming beaches. The living Christmas pageant driving to Raffina Christmas Day, hearing the shepherd's flute wavering over the fields; the shepherd himself, as he moved slowly up a rock slope, like a two legged sheep, covered in the traditional tent-like cloak made from the wool of his own flock, removed us that year from commercial Christmas. This was before the Greeks had found how to make money from the tradition of giving.

The girls had entered into their schools with mixed emotions. Io and Alice in the high school did best in small classes which were often conducted outside around a picnic table under pine trees with chickens scratching nearby. They had field trips to classical sites with teachers passionate about their subject. Whatever was lost in traditional high school requirements was made up for in discussions, not only of ancient Athenian democracy, but the lack of democracy now under the Colonels. Helen's school year was not as rebellious as had been her last. She developed a Greek entrepreneurship which delighted her grandparents. At the kiosk just down the road she bought bubble gum, then sold it on the way to school for twice the price. When I brought up the question of honesty I was cut down by the grandparents who stated flatly that no one forced the children to buy the gum, that it was their own money evidently given to them by their parents. "Elenaiki does not need our money," they laughed, "she knows already how to earn it." I remember standing at the rail of an island boat, listening to tourists complaining about how much they had paid for a trinket when a friend had paid half for the same thing. A Greek woman hearing the conversation had interrupted with, "but if you think it too much you don't have to pay. No one is forcing you." It was logical but did not satisfy the complaining tourist. And now my own daughter was doing the same with the encouragement of grandparents.

There was the unexpected then in Greece which made life so interesting. Would the bus run? Would the boat be overbooked? Would the telephone work? Would it be possible to buy stamps today at the post office? Would the bank be open?

One thing sure was the delight of the local markets. The shouts, the produce; glistening bundles of spinach, orange tangerines with slick green leaves attached, shining purple eggplants, the whitest cauliflower sharing space with yellow lemons, fragrant bouquets of dill, dried herbs or fresh horta, potatoes and in season all the fruits, strawberries, plums, peaches, apricots, cherries each with an aroma more enticing than any perfumery. The exchange of quips, merchants vying with housewives, the energy from buyer and seller, crowded stalls, arguments, made grocery shopping something like a film spectacle.

There were the outings with Coola and Theodore, the theater with Coola, movies and meals with them in Athens, and long taverna dinners with friends. There were wonderful island or remote beach trips with Eddie and Tasso her husband and an accomplished spear fisherman. He would set off with snorkel and spear while whichever children had joined us, usually only Helen, swam, climbed or explored sea and rocks, while Eddie arranged with the proprietor of the thatched roof nearby to make mayonnaise, and boil a few potatoes. Tasso always returned with enough fish for us to hand over to the owners of the roof to grill while Eddie whipped a mayonnaise together with egg and drizzled oil. A salad of some sort, fresh that day was added by someone, bottles of retsina flowed until the stars came out and we could pluck them from the sky. The drive home was always gay with Tasso driving the old Austin, the steering still not reliably repaired, Eddie leading in all the old American songs: I've Been Working on the Railroad, Camptown Races, Swanee River.

At the end of it all we sadly loaded the car, with Bodo, Alice and Helen, but not Io who stayed on in Greece for the summer to start in September at Talland in England. This time we gave up all thoughts of scenic routes to follow the main highway through the backbone of Yugoslavia. My most vivid memory was the August heat. We were not on our way to swim off the rocks, or to an island with cooling beaches where past August trips had taken us, we were driving into the heart of the Balkans at the wrong season; we were driving through Greece to the Yugoslav border. Air conditioning in those days was to have the windows down but the air that came in carried dust and heat from the Sahara, the Notus, hot wind of late summer. Plastic water bottles, as we know them now, were non existent, although we did carry a water jug for Bodo. Our eyes hurt, swallowing was painful, lips cracked and skin turned to parchment. There was no relief and no prospect of relief. There was nothing to do but drive on and hope that with sunset the worst would be over. The temperature did drop with the sun but it remained stifling all through that long drive through Yugoslavia. Crossing the border into Italy was a triumph; it was like being released from prison, not just the heat; the constraints, like suffocating bands, were gone. Trieste the first Italian town we came into, seemed frivolous, with crowded streets, busy shops and flamboyant gestures. We unloaded at the first hotel, looking much the worse for two suffocating days on the road with miserable accommodations and poor food: even Bodo wouldn't eat. The hotel staff cooed over dog and children, talking and smiling, asking questions we couldn't answer but it was a treat after the indifference of the Yugoslav tourist hotels available along that road. The porter after carrying our luggage to our room filled the bidet for Bodo's drink. We luxuriated in the cheerful, atmosphere of hotel and town. Pasta dinner was a hit with Helen and Alice, Bodo had a special bowl of meat brought to the table and when we felt that our reward for the grueling drive from Greece had been fulfilled, the restaurant owner came to offer a special digestif for us and any flavor gelato for the girls. He joined us long enough to hear the story of our trek and as if he had not done enough already presented me with a painted ceramic photo frame. All trials forgotten, we strolled back to the hotel, laughing now at getting gas in Yugoslavia, which at the time had not been funny. No attendant, pump locked, signs in a language we couldn't read, then at last a surly man who would open the lock and push the pump into Kimon's hand as if helping were beneath him.

Off the next day for Milan and Switzerland, France, Holland where we had booked on the Holland America line ship Rotterdam.

It was another run through Europe with resuscitating stay in the Swiss Alps. We climbed out of the humidity of Italy up into the Swiss Alps on a twisting road bordered on one side by a roaring stream of clear green water, on the other by pastures fresh with dainty wildflowers. Sturdy cows slung huge bells which resounded over the valleys. Our windows were down again, this time to suck in the clear mountain air and listen to the mesmerizing cow bells. Kimon pulled to the side, the doors opened and with the timing of a circus act, we spilled as one onto that mountain green, tumbling, rolling, running up and down. We shed socks and shoes and took off after Bodo who ran us in circles barking, delighted to feel frisky again. Out of breath we fell laughing into the flowers, Bodo panting at us with a big grin. At the local Gasthof we enjoyed a fondue eaten slowly with a bottle of wine and view onto snow capped peaks, our hostess chatting to encourage finishing what we thought a huge portion. That night we slept under duvets, windows wide open.

Up through France, taking in a medieval church here and there, with the usual wanderings in remote towns and villages, picnics beside streams and skinny dipping where possible.

Finally Rotterdam. This was the most difficult bit of any trip we had so far taken. The plan was to visit Talland the equestrian center Io was to go to for a year, but we could not go to England with a dog—so Holland America had provided us with the name of a kennel, a good one, where we could leave Bodo for the week we would be in England. The kennel would put Bodo on the ship in Rotterdam which we would then join in Southampton. It was all very Dutch efficient except for my feelings at leaving our best friend alone in a strange kennel for a week. Would he be put on the ship? The right ship? What would we do if he was not there in Southampton? In the end, of course we did put him in the kennel, which spoiled every minute of the visit to England for me, even though Talland measured up in every way. He was on the ship in Southampton, in a frenzy of delight at having found his family again. With the connivance of the steward Helen befriended he did not spend much time on the kennel deck. He seemed to delight in being smuggled into the cabin every night to sleep with Helen, never barking at sounds he would normally not have put up with.

The lazy days on the ship did much to absorb the transition from Greece to every day life in the U.S. which we were all in our own way nervous about.

Life Continues

W E SETTLED IN. Not in our 'brown house' in Hiram but a large house in Hudson, where we thought Helen could enter a better school. Although it meant a half hour commute for Kimon we felt it necessary as the old system had changed in Hiram, for efficiency we were told, and various schools such as the Hiram local school were consolidated into one huge school district. We had lost the intimacy and connection to the school through excellent teachers, that had made Hiram elementary special. Alice finished high school by taking courses at Hiram college as her credits, every year in a different school, didn't match the local school requirements.

We all plodded on. I took a teaching job at Western Reserve Academy, where Helen attended, Kimon joined a car pool for the commute with colleagues, John Shaw, Francis Scalzi and Brainard Stranahan. Then Alice spent a year abroad with the Hiram program, Io returned from England and found a teaching job at Red Raider Camp near Cleveland, bought her own car and became quite independent.

The house we moved into from Hiram was two blocks from the Academy where I taught and where Helen attended high school, best of all there was a large barn for the two horses we brought with us.

Duchess the old mare we had had for several years, bought to be steady and safe, the wise aunt of the family; Glory, the opposite: skittish, and unpredictable but a good ride, the glamour girl. The barn was soon filled with an assortment of creatures, chickens (fresh eggs), rabbits, and strays which came and went.

Helen in some way found a neglected standard poodle and persuaded the owners to give him up. He was smuggled into the barn loft, installed, before anyone could refuse him. The trouble was that when Kimon went to look for the hammer, Oliver barked. Even from the kitchen I could hear Kimon screaming Helen's name, in a frantic way, as if he might have hit his thumb with a hammer. We all ran to the barn, expecting an accident. What we saw was Helen holding something that looked like an orphaned lamb.

"Don't get mad," she said, "I knew if you saw him you would feel like me."

She carefully placed the fleeceless sheep skin on the ground. It tottered. "I was afraid at first they wouldn't let me have him," she went on, "but they gave him to me free. I didn't have to pay anything."

"Good God," her father said, repressing words and emotions.

"He's a pure bred standard poodle, I can get his papers."

"Real bargain," said Io.

No one wanted another dog. We already had one standard poodle. Kimon didn't want any pets at all and I felt that I had enough with one dog, two cats, two horses, six hens, a rooster, a husband, and three children. Even Helen didn't want him; she just felt sorry for him.

The outcast wavered at our feet, buckling and pulling himself up like someone who is falling asleep, or drunk. Then he looked up at me. His tail wagged, trembled more than wagged. It was as if he had smiled. The effort must have been too much because he sagged to the ground and lay there stretched out, not even panting. I knew from that moment that this wreck we named Oliver would stay with us. My will had crumbled before that half-dead, raw-skinned, reeking cur that passed as a dog.

I was furious with my weakness, but determined not to show it, and so snapped at Helen, "I'll try to save him. If he pulls through you can find a home for him. That's the condition."

Helen threw her arms around me. "I knew once you saw him you wouldn't be able to resist him."

"In the meantime, keep him out of my sight, and do what your mother says about a home. I won't have another dog. Take this and buy him some meat." Kimon gave her a dollar bill.

"Don't let him near the horses, he'll give them a disease," warned Io who was deep into Pony Club that summer.

That started our life with Oliver. Helen told me about his sad childhood, and how he had not been sold while still cute and how the kennel had changed hands and how he had ended in a cage living in his own mess and how, never clipped, he was rotting away and that was the reason for the smell. The bald patches on his skin were urine burns, the tumors at his elbows were from lying on concrete, the bleeding scabs were from worms and the sagging hind quarters from malnutrition.

After two weeks of daily visits to the vet, Oliver decided to live. Helen and I tried to keep the bills a secret from her father. No one again mentioned finding him a home; it was too late, Oliver had found us—or rather Helen.

He became Helen's appendage and she his therapist. Our home was his rehabilitation center. No matter how he tried to compensate for the inadequacies of life in a cage, everything he did went wrong, and everyone became irritated with him, despite his bumbling good nature. The cat scratched him because he kept stepping on it, sort of tripping over it. The horse kicked him for following too close, he wasn't even nipping. Our other dog snapped at him for bad manners; he fell around in the car, unable to balance himself, and pushed to be first in or out of any door, habits which no well brought up dog could be expected to overlook. Oliver accepted the discipline, wagging his tail through it all, never understanding what had gone amiss. That first wan smile of a wag had become a grin; he even wagged his tail while eating dinner.

Oliver was afraid of everything. In time he overcame his phobias through the greater fear of losing Helen if she was out of his sight for a moment. The bare floors sent him on an obstacle course which, after a frantic leap, left him marooned between the carpets, just where he didn't want to be. As for stairs, it was only the thought of never seeing Helen again that made him attempt them at all. After the whining indecision at the bottom he would give a jump which took him half way up, scrabbling for a foothold. There he would cling, digging his fore paws into the tread above, hind legs dangling uselessly, evidently unable to control four legs at a time. On the descent he acted with more abandon, ignored the stairs, and trusted to the law of gravity. There would be a prolonged bumping, as if some maniac were throwing the beds around, which brought curses from Helen's father who repeated that all he wanted in life was a little peace and was it too much to expect to have it in his own home.

"Don't worry Dad," Helen would soothe him, "It's just that Oliver is a slow learner."

From my point of view, his most gauche social drawback was the unpredictable way he turned up his leg in the house.

"He is marking his territory Mum," Helen would tell me when I called for the ammonia water and sponge. "It shows he feels wanted." Helen interpreted all Oliver's misdemeanors as psychological failures.

The only formal education Helen gave him were the commands, "stay" and "come." Everything else he learned by following her around. He even went to class until his habit of letting off overpowering fumes proved too much of a disruption.

"No one knows who's done it," she reported with glee. Oliver learned to swim by following Helen on horseback into a pond. In summer when she retreated to her tree house, Oliver went too, pulled up in a basket, his now wooly head hanging out one side and his tail wagging out the other.

"It shows how dumb he is," Helen's sister said, "any bright dog would try to get away."

Once up, he was more confined than in his former cage, but now it was freedom. In winter he made the fourth on the toboggan, rolling off with the others in a heap at the bottom. He followed Helen through adolescence: he waited outside shops while she did errands, he hovered over baby rabbits and naked birds, he spent hours in the dark room waiting for the results, of his own pictures, and when the day came to go on dates, Oliver made the third.

Except for knowing Helen, what did the most for Oliver's ego was turning on the German shepherd that had been trying to kill him for months. This bully had so intimidated him that he ran from any dog in town. Helen defended this cowardly behavior by saying that Oliver was insecure, but she was embarrassed to be seen with a dog that looked like a lamb running for its mother. One day, the black wolf-like brute caught up with Oliver. (He still couldn't run very fast because of his hips and back legs which sagged from his early confinement). Oliver prudently turned upside down, and the Shepherd having some sense of fair play, stood over him showing a set of white fangs, but not using them. Maybe it was seeing those teeth that gave Oliver the idea. Whatever it was, he snapped. The Shepherd was so startled that he backed off, which allowed Oliver to get to his feet. Again he snapped, but the big guy had lost interest in Oliver. He turned, lifted his leg on a tuft of grass, and disdainfully walked home. This experience did a lot for Oliver's confidence. He never again ran from other dogs and even bare floors lost their terrors.

They say that no one is without his unique contribution to society, and it must be true because even Oliver had a talent. He found tennis balls. He found them almost the way a French pig finds truffles. I say almost, because although I have never seen a French pig finding truffles, I imagine that they do a lot of snuffling and rooting, but Oliver didn't find tennis balls that way at all. He sensed them. He could be walking at heel along the sidewalk when, hardly missing a pace, he would put his head into a hedge and come out with a tennis ball. Around the ivy of the tennis courts, where the best ball hunting ground is, he would walk quietly into the center of the ivy patch, muse for a moment rather like a medium making contact with the other side, move off a few paces, bury his head in the ivy at his feet and matter-of-factly pick up a tennis ball.

Once found, they were carried home to be added to a sizable collection. Oliver never did learn to retrieve or play with balls like other dogs, but there was nothing that gave him more sporting pleasure than to settle down to the slow destruction of a tennis ball. He would rip away the outer fluff as if he were stripping the skin from a wild animal. I am sure that tennis balls offered Oliver all the satisfaction other dogs get from the chase and the kill.

When the day came for Helen to leave for college I was all Oliver was left with. It was then that I found that the real trouble with Oliver was that he had no hobbies—that is other than tennis balls. If he were a person, everyone would be trying to interest him in weaving or even whittling. It was most trying, I found, to live with someone who has no hobbies. Oliver was like those men whose whole life is their work and who have nervous breakdowns when they retire. Oliver's life work was us—first Helen and then me—and I was the one who was having the nervous breakdown. His devotion made me so nervous, Kimon thought I was going through the change of life.

It bothered me that Oliver didn't really enjoy anything. In the car for instance, he took no interest in the scenery, or in where he was going. He sat behind me staring at the back of my head. I could feel his eyes on me all the time I was driving and I couldn't stand it. I would forget what I had set out to do. If on a walk, he saw a rabbit or squirrel, he froze like a good hunting dog, but then wagged his tail, probably remembering those nights when he and Helen filled the eye dropper to feed orphans. He never chased wild animals, even for fun, not even cats. On the beach he took no interest in setting gulls to flight or in teasing crabs, and he swam only because I swam, not because he really liked it.

When he lay down, he lay facing me, or the door I closed in his face, like a Muslem facing Mecca. I didn't like the feeling of being worshiped, as my role in life had been more that of slave than deity. Every time I moved an arm or leg when I was reading, Oliver wagged his tail. No one in my family had ever treated me that way—the equivalent of approval and gratitude at every move I made. Quite the opposite, they are usually curling their lips. I started to suffer from a stiff back from sitting so long without moving, so Oliver wouldn't have to wag his tail at me.

The other awkward thing was that he decided to guard me. When I told Helen on a visit home from college, that Oliver had bitten Mrs. Rush our neighbor, while she was standing on the front steps waiting for me to open the door, Helen was delighted.

"It's really wonderful how Oliver continues to develop. He feels secure now. He knows he has you and a home to defend. Just think how long it has taken for him to reach such stability."

"He just nicked Mrs. Rush and she was very good about it, but the postman says he won't deliver letters anymore. Still I expect one thing cancels the other—do you know he doesn't lift his leg in the house now?"

"He never did in my room," Helen answered.

"Now he is safe anywhere, even in the living room with the velvet sofa."

"Well Mum, it makes me feel great to hear all this. Now when I go back to college I can think of you and Oliver here at home together. The house must be terrible with me gone. With Oliver you'll never be alone, or bored."

"No," I said, folding my glasses and sitting motionless so Oliver wouldn't have to wag his tail, "I'm not alone—ever."

It was impossible to continue as Oliver's keeper forever, never able to leave him, never able to travel. The decision was made to give Oliver to Diane a history teacher at the Academy who had fallen for him. When I asked if she would like to take Oliver on she couldn't believe her luck. To make the transition I lived in her apartment for a week with Oliver while she was on summer holiday. In that way I thought Oliver would not feel so insecure in a strange place. When Diane returned we both stayed for two nights, with Oliver very much at ease.

The transition was made, Oliver stayed with a devoted Diane until he died at an advanced age for a dog, especially one with such a bad beginning.

Now we could travel. The horses were put out to pasture with friends near Hiram, the rooster died of a heart failure when he was attacking someone, the hens went to another friend, the cats found homes, the rabbits were long gone, and the old poodle obliged by dying at fourteen years.

Kimon and I were alone for several trips to Greece and I was with Coola when she furnished her house in Portoria.

Coola's terrace.

Kalderimi.

Fountain in Portoria.

Portoria

F OR YEARS COOLA had talked about a summer property on Pelion, a house she saw us returning to forever.

Now Coola's letters changed. The concern was not so much for Kimon, "to find job where he would be respected as professor in Greece is respected," but the trials of finding property to buy in Portoria, the village she had determined "for the good of all" was the best for our summer home. It is a lovely village with huge plane tree protected square, picturesque kalderimia and remarkable fortified houses all on a high slope of the mountain with long views across the Bay of Volos. It was after all, the first village I had visited when I came to Greece with two infants, where Coola and I had spent many peaceful days exploring or enjoying the *platea*. It is however removed from the sea. On one side a descent to Volos and the beaches there, or on the other, a tortuous drive to the Aegean side of the mountain. This was not a problem for Coola. "Easy to take taxi or drive car to beach," she said with ease. But driving round the mountain over questionable roads as they were in those days was a test of nerves.

On a trip to the Peloponnese I had fallen in love with Monemvasia, the name means single entrance, a semi deserted Byzantine town on a rock outcrop surrounded by clear blue sea. When we visited, the town was in ruins and everything for sale. It was the most romantic spot I had visited in Greece, as a place to live. Cobbled streets, ruined houses hanging over the sea, exploring to do; walking the ramparts, searching out the Byzantine churches, finding the best swimming. There were derelict houses to repair, and best of all no crowds of tourists. I could imagine the fun of restoring one of the old stone houses, the fascination of the sea, as close as the deck of an ocean liner, but stable. I imagined sipping wine while watching the moon silver the water, right at my feet; sunrise, with walks through the twisting streets, and the feeling of security from the mainland, which was the reason for building and living on the rock since the first Spartans built fortifications and made it home, after fleeing Slav invaders. It took only imagination to populate the decaying town with the merchants, seamen, languages and energy of a flourishing Byzantine port.

That was then. Coola was right. Monemvasia has since become a tourist hang out with Flying Dolphins running from Piraeus all summer. The decaying houses are modernized, fancy boutiques line the streets and excess has taken over the mainland side of the causeway. Portoria, however, remains a Pelion village despite widening of the roads and the ski resort of Agriolefkes at the top.

Coola wrote, sometimes in Greek for Kimon to translate, of the latest negotiations for property. She was going to Pelion from Athens at every opportunity and helped by lifelong connections, finding possibilities on every visit. It was the usual problem, one we had found whenever we had half heartedly inquired about property, they were owned by several members of the family, most of whom lived abroad. There was no one person with the authority to sell. She described a property owned by seven brothers two of whom lived in Canada, the only ones who wanted to sell, another in South Africa, two in the States, and two in Australia. It had taken months of haggling long distance between them all before Coola had given up.

Then there was the house she most fancied.

"Yesterday I find very nice house not too much destroy, on main *kalderimi* near *platea*." The trouble here was that the old man wanted to sell but he also wanted to stay in the house until he died. The deal was that he would take over the ground floor, Coola would make all but the last payments, she would make all necessary repairs and upon the old man's death the house would be hers. "House is like house we saw together, old style but much stone fallen down. Now I find engineer to tell me how expensive to make new." Theodore did not like this plan. He had many objections. How long would it take for him to die? Then what? If he had no relatives what was to be done with him? If he gets sick who cares for him? Theodore wanted things certain. "This house will be for my darlings to come to Greece. Be Happy—Your Mother"

Next she wrote of a house at the top of the village. The house involving a geriatric waiting to die had been vetoed both by Theodore and the engineer who had said it would cost too much to repair. She liked the house of this new prospect but it could be reached only by *kalderimi* and mule. "Good for now but not good when old." The other snag was that the water came from a communal spring, which meant that it could be redirected by anyone.

These water conduits running beside the *kalderimi* offered the unique balm of rushing water, in Pelion villages. There were ancestral arrangements for the diversion of water done by placing a rock in the channel, to cut off the water from its main course into a garden or plot of ground. Generations had worked out the days, hours, and need for the irrigation. Unfortunately, with depopulation, these arrangements have been forgotten or neglected, resulting in bad blood between new tenants and surviving land owners.

At last she wrote: "Have bought good house in Portoria. Very good on road but must have much repair." She went on to say that the house had been burned out during the occupation and had stood in this state of decay ever since. "Very beautiful view from house. Come in from road into big room will make balcony from there across front to enjoy view and make *tsaiki* (the raised fireplace of the typical Greek house) then down stairs to three small bedroom. Nothing there now but have decided this best. Then down again to kitchen, bathroom and door to terrace. All will be perfect. Just take time. Theodore thinks this good house. Good he think to be on road, no mule up and down, water in house, also close to *platea*."

So that was it. Coola finally had her house on Pelion.

She was ready to start the renovation immediately. (Her dress shop Style was a huge success in Athens and gave her the funds). The engineer explained, since the earthquakes, strict building codes mandated that all the walls must be repaired with reinforced concrete. "But this not difficult." Now that the work was started, Greek style, there were constant arguments with the engineer. We heard about most. Coola wanted a balcony the length of the south upstairs wall and the engineer refused. He insisted on retaining the Pelion style even though the house was being recreated from scratch. He did not want to make a villa. The traditional balcony held no more than a few chairs and a table and that is what was built. For more people, he explained, there was the terrace and grape arbor below. There were discussions over stairs, kitchen, plumbing, the building of the fireplace, almost everything. I wondered that anything was ever accomplished—but it was. After months of letters detailing every event, Coola wrote that the house could withstand any earthquake and was clean and new with modern plumbing and kitchen. "Now my darlings must come to enjoy."

With the three girls now young women we were taking our trips to Greece separately, that is Kimon and I or Helen and friend. The house had to be furnished and it was on one of the childless summers that Coola and I went to Portoria to find furnishings, leaving Theodore with his routine and Kimon with his books. This time I drove.

Coola had decided to find the simple furnishings in the artisan lanes of Volos: chairs, tables, linens, cushions. She was as excited as a bride to find just what she was looking for among the dozens of tiny shops all making exactly the same thing on the same street. Everything was bargained for and haggled over which was exhausting to me, exhilarating to her and took time.

The twisting drive down the mountain to Volos was like a trip from Ohio to Florida. In that half hour the apple orchards miraculously become orange groves. I was unaccustomed to this dramatic vertical climate change. These drives took on more danger than the mere narrow bends in the road as I looked for the wildflower or crop changes around me. Coola was immune to erratic driving and remained at ease when I veered too close to the edge. She even took up my plant spotting and filled me in with stories of the specialties of the area.

"There," she would point. "So many hortensia. You know why? Because Kyria Metatopoulos lived in France where husband was merchant, and when she return she brought some with her and now everyone have them."

She was right hydrangeas hung from every wall and cottage of the village we drove through.

The first things we needed were chairs and what better than THE Greek chair, the rush seated chairs seen at every cafe and restaurant all over Greece? Frayed seats often indicate the popularity of the establishment.

We parked the car on one of the side streets of *palio* Volos. Here, Coola told me, we would find the craftsmen, every street saved for a specialty; woodworking, copper, stone, weaving, basket making. We found the chair making street, where Coola headed directly to the three man garage-sized workshop of Alex Papandreou, she had dealt with previously. The owner took us over, calling a small boy to bring chairs to sit on, then sending him off to the cafe for coffee which was brought back on the swinging tray of Greece. The thimbles of coffee consumed he took us on a tour; one man cuts and assembles the wooden frames, in a tiny loft another weaves the rush seats and the third stains or paints the chairs to order. Simple variations can be made on the same theme. The cafe chair can become an arm chair, with a change in the slatted back it becomes more elegant. Remove the back and you have a high or low stool or even a table. Even though Coola had said from the first moment that she wanted only the classic chairs, we had to see the full inventory and listen to construction details. The final order was for four cafe chairs, unstained, and three low stools to serve as seats or tables. Once back in the village, it was our job to arrange for delivery, so after hours of negotiating, we were still perhaps days from having a chair to sit on.

Coola had told me of the lamp maker who could turn any vase or crock into a lamp. Between us we had a variety of objects to try; a brass candlestick, a dried gourd, a ceramic vase and an old wooden bracket. The shades could be made to order from our material and were cleverly designed to slip off for easy washing. We were shown a number of completed shades ready for delivery, created from fine needlework the customers had done themselves.

Bowls, pitchers and vases for the kitchen we bought in a shop which specializes in terra cotta on a street devoted to ceramics and I even found an earthenware casserole which reminded me of my old Ohio oven proof antique.

In another ceramic shop I looked for egg cups, to replace the paper napkin stuffed into a Greek coffee cup. At the show room end of the shed-like work shop I recognized the lively folk art tiles. It was like meeting old friends. Our daughter Io had bought several when she had meandered these artisan streets in Volos. Later she fitted them in with the early American antiques of her Ohio farmhouse. In their naivete they resembled the folk art of Quimper pottery of France, but these designs of saints and village life were taken from carved stone decorating the exterior of the churches of Mount Pelion.

By now we were exhausted and shutters were being drawn for the midday siesta. So it was up the mountain again taking what we could with us and postponing the other jobs until next day. Coola was impatient with the intimate method of the Greek merchants. She had been buying in Switzerland for years and was an admirer of Swiss efficiency where the choices were presented, prices fixed and sales made in an impersonal deal. What should have taken half a day she predicted would take several and it did. The drive up and down the mountain could be frustrating as well. There were always the episodes of landing behind a bus or truck with the relevant drama. The bus for instance stopping to let off a passenger on a tight curve, not only the passenger but bags and boxes from the roof which had to be untied and tossed down. A Greek driver would have welcomed this pause to get ahead of the bus with a blind dash around it, but I stayed safely tucked in watching the arguments, augmented by a force of locals, who appeared mysteriously to take part in this drama of the day. Coola, suddenly very much in tune with this Greek inefficiency, laughing and translating for me some of the more humorous language. "People who know him ask what he is bringing home. Why so much? Presents for family? When he tell them he bring new clothes and covers they tell him he don't need these things. Po,po, po."

We were early next day driving to Volos, hoping to finish the errands and still have a bit of time to explore the mountain. It was not to be.

We passed the street of weavers to negotiate for sheets.

"Here, look," Coola stopped in front of a sign that said in Greek, WEAVER OF GOAT HAIR. Fotis Kolokithopoulos. "You must see. Very special." Coola wanted me to explore the Greek crafts even if it meant taking another day. Instinctively she knew that this way of life would end, that machines would take over and yes—it would be easy to go to one place and buy everything under one roof. It was the same ambivalence she had about Kimon doing any kind of house work. In theory she wanted desperately to be "modern," she admired the American way of life until she saw her son doing house work, and much as she admired the efficiency of the Swiss and ease of doing business there, she was hesitant to see a wholesale overturn of Greek ways.

We were on a street of low plastered buildings where a bewildering commerce is conducted in dark interiors. A few woven rugs hanging in the doorway advertised this remarkable craftsman. Fotis, a big man with a smile that split his face, compensated for the gloominess of his shop by his eager welcome.

Coola introduced me as her American daughter-in-law who was interested in all things Greek especially Greek crafts. Fotis was delighted to tell me that most of his weavings he sold to America. I wondered to whom but before I could ask, he called into the obscure depths and in a minute his fifteen year old son Gregory came carrying two chairs for us to sit on. Gregory, shy and sensitive, I knew at a glance, would not be following his father and grandfather at the loom. No, he told me in school English, he liked mathematics. The father said with pride that his son was a good student.

As I questioned Fotis about his weaving he jumped around as quick as a goat himself, dragging out one after the other of gunny sacks of hair for me to feel. To make sure that I understood the difference between sheep and goat—the two Greek words I do know—he would baa like a sheep his face contorted with repugnance, then changing to the bleat of a goat needing only horns to transform him into a Pan. He had Gregory drag out huge balls of natural brown, grey, white and black spun hair, which was most of what he sent to America. To explain this craving of Americans for goat hair he asked me if there were no goats in America. Proudly he told me that it was rough, inflexible and never wears out. His supply is all local, clipped from the goats in May and sacked just as it is taken from the animals.

Further explanations took a vehemence not to be contained. Fotis nudged us past the looms and gunny sacks back into the dark, calling over his shoulder to Gregory to bring the chairs. Opening the door by feel he delivered us into a shed extension, lit only by a small window near the ceiling. Gregory seated us onto the chairs and closed the door behind us. For a moment I wondered if we had been too trusting. The door had been closed behind us, so there was no escape. I would have panicked if it had not been for Coola sitting as calmly as she did when Theodore drove the car, or when I drove down the mountain identifying wildflowers, or when she was passenger in a bus while the driver talked, both hands off the wheel.

In the corner I was facing a trap, a cubicle with a curtain across the front. As my eyes adjusted to the gloom the hunched forms against the wall (murder victims? insane?) changed into sacks, but the stick with ropes attached lying in front of the cubicle turned my thoughts to the "Avengers" of TV and I tried to summon the courage and calm of Emma Peel.

Fotis emptied a sack onto the floor in front of the cubicle and picked up his three foot long stick with four ropes attached at one end. It was not an instrument of torture after all, but a flail to beat the goat hair. Each rope, about eight feet long pegged to the floor at four inch intervals, fanned from the stick. The hair was piled under, Fotis backed to the limits of the ropes and as he raised his stick up and down the hair was beaten sending it back to be caught in the cubicle, forming a separate pile of light fluffy hair, unrecognizable from the untreated hair on the floor. The process was repeated. That sack was mostly white, the odd strands of black he picked out by hand. Any dirt seemed to fall to the floor. The hair is not washed. After the second beating the hair is rolled into a sack. Now Fotis climbed an unsteady ladder into a narrow loft running the length of the shop. He fastened on a belt to which he snapped a rope which was attached to various wheels and pulleys, then tied the sack to his waist. Using both hands he twisted a bit of hair from the sack onto a starter strand tied to one of the wheels. As he moved backward the 24 foot length of the loft the whole system of wheels was set into motion, causing the threads to twist as he rubbed the hair between thumb and forefinger. How effortlessly Fotis twisted the hair into a manageable strand the required thickness. It seemed so easy I wanted to try—and I did. It can only compare to my futile efforts at throwing a pot on a wheel when the clay seemed to take on a life of its own. As I twisted, the hair sprang from the sack like a mischievous genie, unwilling to take directions from me, in the end only to be tamed by the master. What a thrill, even if Fotis did have to retwist my uneven strand. It had been an exciting insight into, even then, a vanishing trade.

The beds, foam mattresses on wooden frames, Coola had ordered and installed months before this visit, but even with the chairs and terra cotta dishes and buys from the day before, we still needed so many small things, like a tray to take our meals out to the terrace. On the coppersmith's street we stopped at a shop where a prophet-like figure with full black beard sat on a bench surrounded by the glowing products of his own hand, working a delicate design into a bowl. Christos worked alone at a craft which has been passed down through his own family from his grandfather. Coola and I finally selected a tray of the right size to hold what we thought would be essentials without being too big to be practical.

Baskets were not on the list but I have such a weakness for them we had to stop at the basket weaver's shop. The wife of the owner showed us the wares while her husband sat on the floor transforming a pile of sticks and brush into baskets. There was nothing more I would have enjoyed than to sit beside him to try my hand. We ended by buying a small assortment to use for wastebaskets and containers for wood.

We didn't want any of the hand carved furniture from the little factory of Yannis Hatzopoulou, but we stopped to see the work that went on there. Yannis himself, bubbling with pride, showed us round starting in the yard of the little factory where some ten people were employed. The chestnut timbers are cured for two to three years, all the wood coming locally from Mount Pelion. The chests, chairs, cabinets, tables and bedsteads are hand assembled and beautifully carved with motifs Yannis has collected from all over Greece. The richest source of design comes from the Pelion churches where some of the finest of the original wood carving may still be seen.

Coola was too impatient to wait for a hand made flokati rug. "It just the same," she told me. "Hand woven too heavy and hard to wash." She was probably right but when I took one back to Ohio with me I made sure that it was hand woven as there is a difference in quality. That day we bought a yellow ochre flokati to place in front of the fireplace. "Nice place to sit with fire," she explained and when we returned that evening to put it down we both sat on it just imagining the fire. The warmth the color gave to the room was the only warmth we had on a cold night.

Peaches

WE WERE TO spend Christmas in Greece and it was decided to celebrate in Portoria in the newly built and furnished house.

Again Coola, and I went to Pelion together to make sure all was in order, but most especially to install some sort of heat as the fireplace would not be adequate for winter cold. It took a full week of constant haggling and frustration to buy, deliver, install and finally make Peaches (the word that sounded like peaches to me) do her work.

On Saturday, the morning after our arrival, we set off to Volos, and the zig-zag drive to the foot of the mountain, to enquire about heating a house. Accustomed to the segregation of shops, Coola headed to the stove vendors street to find a merchant who had been recommended to her. She explained the situation; the family of her only son from America coming to Portoria for Christmas, they were accustomed to central heat and must be warm. At great length he told to her that an oil space heater was what we wanted and assured us that it was what everyone in Portoria used. We believed him and instead of comparative shopping in stores nearby, Coola promised to find someone from the village to pick up the stove on Monday. Carefree, thinking the heating problem settled, we splurged on groceries before returning up the mountain to await the stove delivery on Monday. We went to Coola's favorite cheese shop where seven different fetas were sold, to the green grocer for fresh horta and another grocer for staples of pasta, rice, cofee and tea, a huge jar of Pelion olives and bread with thick brown crust, fresh from the wood fired oven. Sunday the clouds came down, the view was of thick cloud and the house was damp and cold. With all our clothes on we huddled by the fireplace burning wood which I had found stacked in the garden and had cut with a saw I found under the stairs.

"We must have more wood," I announced, rationing the twigs. I was used to fires in Canada where huge logs are burned in the summer cabins.

"That's easy," Coola answered. "There is much wood here."

The mountain is heavily wooded with chestnut and beech trees which grow where the olives cannot survive and it was as simple as she said. Next day she asked a man passing with a string of mules where we could get wood.

"I'll bring it."

He was as good as his word. That evening we returned from a walk to find two large gunny sacks of neatly cut wood at our door. Coola was horrified at the extravagant quantity. I did not tell her that at home we would go through that much in an evening.

Monday morning Coola found Philipos at the square who agreed to fetch the stove the next day from the stove shop in Volos and recommended Dimitri, the local smith, to do the installation. With sun restored and view in place we sat on our terrace at lunch looking out over the sea and mountains, feeling smug that everything was going so smoothly. That was before we met the local builder on our evening walk who introduced us to Peaches or so it sounded to me—the best stove made, he told us.

At breakfast Tuesday morning, Coola announced that our decision had been too hasty. We didn't know what we were buying, perhaps it wasn't Peaches, which the builder had convinced Coola was the only stove to have. So it was back to Volos, for the comparative shopping we should have done Saturday. In other shops, we were introduced to "Esquimo" a much too plausible name, as well as to thermal units. I was side tracked by a display of old wood burning tile stoves ranged along the wall of one tiny store and was willing to sacrifice all practicality to have one—until I was told the exorbitant price. Even if we couldn't afford one, I was pleased that these wonderful stoves from the past were valued. Satisfied with her investigations after visiting at least five shops, we returned to the original merchant. His stove was Peaches after all and it had all the thermal units we needed. The deal was confirmed and the necessary pipe ordered. Up the mountain again to be on time for Dimitri who was coming to size up the installation. We needn't have hurried; we eventually had to track him down in his shop. Agreeably he followed us home, looked at the pipe hole in the three foot thick concrete wall and stated calmly that the hole was in the wrong place, too close to the electric wires. To install a pipe would be dangerous.

Wednesday morning at eight, back to Volos to find the electrician who had originally wired the house. He contradicted Dimitri and said that the wires were far enough away and there was no danger. He seemed to remember the house and location of the wires, although I did suggest to Coola that perhaps he should look at the space again. An idea that was refused by a tst and upward nod of the head, eliminating all discussion. So back up the mountain to be home on time for the delivery of the stove which should have come the day before. There it all was now—pipes and stove at the door. Three hours later a black hairy bear of a man came to say that Philipos, had sent him to move something. Coola pointed to the stove and fittings which were still where they had been dropped outside the door. "Endaxi." With much grunting and me carrying most of the weight we, the bear and I, moved the stove the three flights down to the ground floor. The light pipes he simply let slip. Accidentally? The fifteen sections tumbled down taking bits of plaster from the walls and danced about on the flagged floor, almost taking down Coola, before coming to rest. Coola took this carelessness calmly; this was not Athens, and there was no one else to call.

No sooner had Philipos left and we had picked up the bits of plaster than Angelos, Dimitri's helper, arrived. He unpacked and positioned the stove then settled in to wait for Dimitri who turned up an hour later. During this wait of course coffee had to be served with English biscuits, the only ones we had. Finally the installation was made, and with Dimitri there, I decided to have heat that very night and light the stove under the eye of the experts.

Of course we had no fuel. Just getting and installing the stove had taken all our thoughts and energy, kerosene to feed it had never been considered. Insisting that they wait until I returned with fuel, I left with a two litre container to a shop in the *platea* where fuel oil was sold.

"I want oil," I said in my best Greek.

"What's it for?"

"For a stove," I answered, delighted to be understood.

"For a stove?" he questioned as if I had said I wanted to bathe in it.

"Yes, for a stove."

"Do you want clean or unclean oil?"

"Clean oil," I said, thinking unclean had come from someone's crankcase.

"For a stove?"

"Yes, for a stove."

"You don't want clean oil then."

"I don't know what I want," I said in desperation, "just oil for a stove."

"She wants oil for a stove," an old man spoke up who had been sitting in the shadows next to the glowing space heater of the shop.

"It's unclean you want," persisted the shopkeeper.

I felt that I was conversing with the Queen of Hearts.

I finally returned to Dimitri and Angelos with the container filled with some kind of oil. They filled the stove and lit the taper. Nothing happened. Half an hour later they started reading the instructions. Half an hour after that they left in defeat.

In ten minutes Angelos returned with his sister. She had two space heaters and was therefore an expert. With assurance she turned the valve, adjusted the gauge, threw in a bit of flaming cotton and turned to us smiling. We all smiled in return. The stove burned.

It burned beautifully all night and was out by morning. It was taking more oil than we had counted on. Obviously we needed large containers.

Next morning Thursday, we bought from our village grocer what looked to me like 5 gallon tins. We were told that they could be filled in Volos. If everyone on Pelion used space heaters, I wondered why no one seemed to know how they worked or why we had to go to Volos for oil. But there was nothing for it—back down the mountain we went to the man who sold oil. There it was the same question.

"Do you want clean or unclean?" the man at the pump asked as he filled the first tin.

"It's for a stove."

"Then you want unclean," he told us filling the second tin. "I only sell clean. It's too dangerous for a stove."

We paid. He kindly loaded the two tins of dangerous clean oil, not before dropping one container to give it a rocking bottom and slow leak, as I found when I lifted it from the trunk of the car upon our return.

Seeking advice, back at the stove shop, our merchant confirmed that it was unclean oil we must burn and where to buy it. Where oil is sold, of course the tins to put it in are not. After a foray down the street we found and bought two more tins, filled them with unclean oil and loaded them next to the others.

At home in the kitchen I faced Peaches with a funnel and a five gallon tin of oil and tried to pour it down her throat. There was oil everywhere; all over myself, the floor and the stove. Why we didn't blow up when we finally did light the stove I don't know. I, who had lived intimately with space heaters back in those grim student days at the Cabin Camp should have known better.

On Friday we left Peaches simmering our beans and took advantage of the beautiful weather to drive to the picturesque village of Zagora on the other side of the mountain where the car ran out of—oil!

On Saturday I waved good-bye to Coola, as she left on the bus for Athens, a new plastic pump in my hand. Now I could give Peaches the nourishment she required in easy doses.

Alone now in Portoria with Peaches drinking oil like a baby its bottle and exuding a gentle warmth, I felt that I had all the conveniences of Hudson, even if achieved in a different way.

Silence

NOW THAT I had heat I decided to stay on in Portoria to explore the mountain. It seemed a cozy idea. I had the car for trips to Volos, maps of the mountain, watercolors and pencils, books and provisions. What I didn't expect was to be snowed in. It was the first time I had experienced snow in Greece and even though Theodore had told me stories of huge snow storms in the mountains where villages were isolated for weeks, I had not thought of Portoria as being that sort of place.

The snow came on for two days. The road in front of the house filled. Snow piled in front of the front door and the back door; snow blanketed the terrace, snow made me a prisoner. I have coped with snow all my life but always in places where everyone had a snow shovel, where snow plows cleared roads and houses were never shut off from the rest of humanity.

For those two days of the snow fall I didn't even try to go out and if I could have gone out there was no where to go. On the third day I woke in the morning to complete silence. The wind had dropped and snow covered the world with an insulating blanket. There were no birds cheeping, there were none of the usual village sounds; the crowing of a rooster, braying of a donkey, shouts and calls, cars, trucks or any engine noise. It was as if every moving thing had been suffocated by the snow.

Silence. The most perfect silence. The ticking clock which I had never been aware of now took on a personality and during these days became a friend, a perfect friend: steady, never asking, ever faithful, always there willing to listen without argument, never demanding or moody, always on time.

After being shut in for two days, I couldn't wait to go out to explore this new world. I did have a broom and the shovel from the fireplace to clear the thresholds of the doors. With hiking boots, socks pulled over my trousers, scarf around my head I stepped out into a world that seemed to have just been created. The worn, old, trashy and ugly one had disappeared. The road had disappeared to become a clearing between beautiful white trees, branches scraping the ground from the weight they carried. Houses looked as if, like a chick from the egg, they were struggling to emerge as dwellings. I felt that my footsteps scared this perfection. Perhaps more snow would come to cover them. Scar or not I couldn't wait to explore and enjoy the clear air but lifting every foot high through the drifts was exhausting. While I stood to catch my breath, a robin fluttered along the branch of a tree scattering the snow, care free it seemed, then light as one of its own feathers it hopped onto the snow in a vain search for its usual meal. There was nothing that I could imagine that the bird could survive on until the snow melted. I turned and hurried back to the house to bring something to the one living creature I had seen for days. With a pocket of oatmeal and piece of bread I returned to find the robin in the same search for food. When I tossed the oats onto the snow the bird came immediately to peck at them. My joy was complete. Every day I repeated the ritual with the bird now waiting for me and coming to perch on my arm the quicker to find the food.

At the house I had a guest. A small window had been built in the thick side wall of the kitchen, which could be opened from the inside, for what purpose I never knew, but a mother cat with two kittens took shelter on the stone ledge outside the window. The three crouched uncertainly the mother looking through the window at me in desperation, ready to run if I threatened. I poured tin milk into a saucer with a bit of bread, the only cat food I had. When I opened the window the kittens backed off hissing, but the mother crouched ears flattened, in fear. She cleaned the saucer and as quickly as they had come, the cats disappeared. I would have thought I had dreamt the whole thing if it were not for the empty saucer. Where had they come from and where did they return?

The cats became regulars and the mother became quite tame but never the kittens. They hissed and growled every time I offered food. Perhaps with more time they could have been tamed but it was as well for them to be wary as they were wild cats and not apt to find kindness again.

With these jobs and eventual forays to the *platea* for provisions I passed the time in silence. (No radio then).

I had the clock, the cats from time to time but always at a discreet distance, and the robin who waited for me. Finally the roads opened. I had made phone calls to Athens from the kiosk on the street the first day I went out. In Athens the family had lived by the news. After hearing that all the villages of Pelion were snowed in they imagined me in some sort of Swiss avalanche buried forever, so it was a huge relief for them to hear my voice.

"You come back to Athens now," Coola ordered.

"We are warm and we can go anywhere in Athens. Now is not the time to be on the mountain." Theodore was practical.

"I don't know why you wanted to be there to begin with," Kimon.

This unforeseen snow plunged me into a void of silence I had never experienced. I awakened to the creaks of the house, and was surprised at how much noise I made in this new world just walking about. Why did I not miss the give and take of daily conversation? I wondered about things I had never thought about, at least not consciously. Having married at an early age and produced children right away, I had never been alone, ever. There had never been time it seemed for introspection. Until now I had never thought about it. But now I could reflect, and I was reflecting on everything I had taken for granted, my children and their abilities, the life I led, most especially my marriage. Why was Kimon so keen to take on a full time appointment in Greece? He had always said that he had the best of both worlds, summers in Greece, real work in the States in a pleasant atmosphere with respected colleagues.

With typical optimism and dismissal of anything that might be unpleasant, I cleared my mind of subversive thoughts, left the cats a bowl of meat scraps, wound the clock, tidied the house and left to return to civilization.

Death in the Family

IO DID IT first—fell in love. Ted came around frequently to visit or pick her up for dates. He was good looking, voluble, enterprising, of Greek descent and very much in love as was she. They were married in the Episcopal church on the corner, with reception in our own garden, had a cruise honeymoon and went to live in Medina where Ted had his business. It wasn't long before they bought a farm where Io could start her lifelong pursuit of training horses and rescuing animals.

Next was Alice who fell for Panos, a Greek who was studying and visiting with his sister at Oberlin College. After their marriage at the same church, with reception in the same garden, they moved to Washington D.C. where Panos completed one of his many degrees, this one in international affairs.

Then Helen graduated from Western Reserve Academy and was accepted at Earlham college in Indiana.

The summer after Helen's graduation from Western Reserve Academy in Hudson, she went to Greece for the summer with a friend to join Kimon who was already there winding up an academic year abroad. Due to my mother's failing health I had returned early to Hudson. No sooner had Helen left than my father called to say that my mother was to have open heart surgery. Alice and Panos decided to drive to Florida with me even though Panos had booked a flight to Greece where a job was imminent. He was to stay as long as he could, leaving Alice to help with the convalescence. Io and her husband Ted in Ohio, were in touch by telephone.

As it turned out my mother did not survive the operation. Panos had left, Alice, my brother Leonard and his son Roger were with my father and me and during the painful aftermath. Kimon was not there. In a telephone call to Greece to tell him of mother's death he asked if I wanted him to come. If he had to ask, I realized the comfort would be nil. It is like asking when the trash is overflowing on the floor if it needs to be taken out.

During that wrenching summer my solace was the St. Augustine beach. I wrote of two episodes, the first a swim.

The Florida beaches are inviting for their vastness and for the purity of hard sand washed twice each day by the tides. To me, more beautiful than the famous Miami or Daytona beaches, is the St. Augustine beach where the hotels and condominiums have not completely encroached on the dunes. My favorite is the Anastasia State Park, about 3-1/2 miles of wide white sand. To the end and back gives a walk or drive (during low tide) of six miles, which if not enough for the whole day, is a good stretch.

I've walked this beach, as well as the St. Augustine Beach proper, about a mile farther south, in almost every weather and at every time of day; in winter, huddled into a biting north wind, watching the gulls sweeping over a white-capped ocean, on hot, humid summer evenings when the water's edge is the only place to find air and enjoy the magic of the summer phosphorescence, when each step leaves a saintly glow in the sand. I have collected shells, watched the bird life and ever-changing tides. Even if the water is too rough or too cold for swimming, the long miles of sand are varied. Even someone who has never watched birds will have to stop in awe as a group of pelicans play their languid follow-the-leader over the crest of the waves. The wind-up-soldier performance of sandpipers advancing on a retreating wave in military formation, only to scatter before an advancing wave like a battalion dispersed by an invisible enemy, never fails to amuse no matter how often it is repeated. There is the thrill of finding the perfect sand dollar or other shells. Most importantly is the expanse of horizon where the imagination may roam. Each visit is an expectation. How will the surf be today? What will have been washed ashore? Will there be fanciful cloud formations? How many pelicans will I see? Will there be porpoise fishing close in?

Florida summers are oppressive, with high temperatures and high humidity. As the thermometer rises, my vitality dwindles so that after a few weeks, I find that I must will myself into activity. The only pleasant time for walking is before sunrise or after sunset. We had a run of suffocating days so bad that even my father, who likes heat and hates air conditioning, had grudgingly agreed to "turn the darn thing on." This meant that the rest of us could survive, but we were as confined to house as one is in the winter in the north.

None of us were sleeping well but when I awoke before dawn to find the house quiet, I dressed in my bathing suit and left for the beach. The predawn hours are always magical, those moments before the world awakes and when it seems to be at its deepest rest, but that morning when I started out in the grey light there was something eerie in the calm. Then I realized that it was not the hour but the sea and the air. Never had I seen the ocean so at peace as I did that morning. Even in a calm waves are breaking on the shore; that morning the waves had been reduced to a gentle lap. It was no longer an ocean but a lake. The silence was intense, the constant breaking of the waves, which one takes for granted was missing. The birds were not yet on the wing and I felt that I was the only living thing on the beach. In that unnatural calm, I was Eve waiting for the wrath of God. The sky was cloudless, there were no signs of hurricane or tornado, but that oiled surface of water stretching to the horizon brought to mind the Ancient Mariner's painted ocean, and held something of the same ominous calm.

I started to walk, pushing through the grey silence as through a fog, but it wasn't long before the sky on my right slowly, took on color making me wonder if the conch shells took their colors from the dawn as they lay on the beach staring at the sky and catching all those delicate varieties of pinks and reds. By the time the sun and sky had changed from pink to yellow I had been walking for half an hour or more and my skin was sticky and hot. I sat down on the sand to steep myself in this clam, less eerie now that the sun was up. The vast expanse of ocean was so without tremor, it would have seemed quite reasonable for a swimmer to strike out for the horizon and Africa. These must have been the waters that Christ walked upon. I could no longer sit and look. Just as a field after a fresh snow fall invites footsteps, so that oiled water invited a disturbance. In I plunged and swam and dived and floated as if I were the first human to dare the mysteries of water. How clear the water was that morning, unusual on the Florida shore where the breakers churn the sand into a tawny cloud. There swimming with me were schools of little silver fingerlings. I felt like a usurper. I was the one who didn't belong, so I stopped splashing and diving and floated calmly hoping to blend with the fish. Around me the water speckled like rain drops and so much did it seem like rain that I looked up to see if perhaps one of those shower clouds hadn't suddenly appeared. It was the little fish breaking the surface. I floated, thrilled to be in the midst of such teeming life which ignored me. The birds too seemed to ignore me. Diving repeatedly almost within arm's reach, the little terns simply picked the fish from the water while I watched them flash like a strip of foil before being swallowed. Most thrilling and startling was a pelican who glided past, made his spearing dive with a splash almost next to me, then calmly floated like a huge cork while he tossed his head back to swallow the fish. The thought did cross my mind that the terns and pelicans would not be after the same meal. No doubt the pelican was gobbling up something larger than those delicate fingerlings and my mind did go on to the next and obvious step—that there must be large fish too that would be feeding on this sudden abundance. Then I would be distracted watching another bird and excited to be part of this nature drama, this churning life in such calm. I looked out to see where the pelican had gone and saw the surface of that unusually calm sea cut by a fin. I looked at the shore. I was close in. This was the summer of "Jaws." "Don't panic," I told myself. "And don't make a disturbance. Just quietly get out as fast as you can." My heart was pounding. I hate to admit it, as I have always said that wild creatures are more frightened by man than he by them. I told myself that again and quietly and purposefully struck out for shore. Above my own heartbeat I heard a sigh. A human sigh that I recognized from a previous fish watch from the sea wall in front of my father's house. My God, I turned around and to my relief I saw the blunt head of a porpoise and not the shark I had expected. If I had seen a herd of elephants rise out of the dunes I could not have been more thrilled. The porpoise were not coming toward me at all but swimming languidly parallel to shore going on about their own business. I delayed my rush for shore to watch the graceful arcs of the mammals until they were gone and I realized that the sun was high and strong and I still had to walk back.

I was so excited by my adventures and eager to tell the family what they had missed, that I jogged half the way down the beach and had to take two dips before finally going home. The family was just beginning to come to life and was appalled by my story.

"Supposing it had been a shark?" Roger asked

"Anyway," I countered, "it was one of the loveliest walks that I have ever had on the beach."

That was during those days of uncertainty, waiting at the hospital, visiting in intensive care, all of us fearful of the outcome.

The evening of the day that my mother died, we were showing the strain. Io and her husband Ted had been reached by phone in Ohio. Somehow my brother and I and the two cousins had survived the dreadful day, each of us trying to ease the grief of the Pater, my father. We had made the rounds with him, (he insisted on seeing to everything himself) of hospital, funeral home, cemetery. We tried to shield him from some of the worst funeral commercialism and help him through the grim procedures. After tea the Pater had retired to his room and the rest of us too strung out to think, jumped when Alice suggested a swim. We plunged into the waves without our usual gaiety, but rather to wash the day from our bodies. We came out feeling at least physically better and without a word we struck out along the beach. For some time we walked in silence, each with our own thoughts. I was feeling especially sorry for myself because my husband wasn't with me to give me the support I so longed for. Alice had been an angel through everything; willing, thoughtful, compassionate and practical but as her mother I somehow retained the habit that I should be supporting her, not she me. There was only one person who should be supporting me, and my anguish was most acute because of his absence. My brother and I had lost a mother, and there was in this the loss of part of ourselves. For us, each near fifty, it was the end of our childhood. We sensed that never again would there be anyone in the world who would hold us in that very special maternal regard. We both felt, even with grown children of our own, alone in the world for the first time. In our silent walk we were with our own thoughts, each turning inward, each thinking of his own grief. For my own part I realized for the first time how very dependent I had been all these years, while so sure of my independence. The attitudes and values which I would try to pass on to my own children were from this mother who was now gone.

As if reflecting my thoughts Alice spoke first. "I told Io to bring something gay to wear for the funeral. You know what Grumps always said. She wanted everyone to have fun at her funeral. She said that things were backwards, black should be worn at weddings because problems were just beginning and white at funerals, where we know the troubles are all over."

"It's the Pater, he seems to have given up, is there nothing we can do for him? You know," I went on, "It is for him much worse than for any of us. So much older, he had never expected to survive mother and now he's at a complete loss. Here we are with our children, and a good bit of our life ahead. For him it has all been accomplished. He has had his career, raised his family, planned his old age and at 85 he has lived it. The person he loved most in the world is gone, what is left? We have our children still to watch mature and they, much as they loved their grandmother and were influenced by her, cannot feel her loss in quite the same way. For them, an old person has died, at twenty almost everyone seems old; and for them there is the whole world ahead."

"You're right, Len said. "It's tough for him. I hope he gets through it. He was in a daze today."

"The Pater will be all right." Roger said, with conviction. "He has his faith, and even if he was tottering today he'11 come through."

"I'll tell you one thing," Len said. "It would have been a darn sight harder for Grumps to go it alone, than for Patie. When I told him that today he listened, it seemed a comfort."

We talked and bared our hearts and our grief and walked who knows how far. By the time we found the car again it was dark. We had walked that beach, for the first time, oblivious of birds, shells or tides. We had plodded on until exhaustion had driven us home. It was the needed physical exhaustion that had mitigated the emotional strain. We returned home ready to cope again, ready to sustain the person whom we all loved so dearly and around whom we all rallied so willingly. In sitting at home or lying in bed, or indulging in alcohol, food or anything else that I can think of, could we have soothed our misery as well as that long walk on the beach?

Grumps sketching.

Travels With Grumps

DURING THOSE DAYS after the funeral in St. Augustine, after Alice, Len and Roger left, I stayed to make sure that my father recovered from the shock of mother's death. Again I turned to the beach for comfort.

Walking, swimming in the sloughs, watching birds, waves, or fishermen I thought back to the previous summer when my mother and I had taken a trip to Scotland and Ireland. The two summers before that she and Alice had travelled together and returned with so many stories of people and places, each with a different take. Alice telling how quickly Grumps had everyone on her side, how she put up with less than desirable B&B's, (no reservations) of huge breakfasts and long hikes. My mother had her own stories of busses not on time, of the cold, (she was coming from Florida) of the graciousness of everyone, of pub encounters, of Irish humor.

Now I had my own memories of my mother and I flying into Prestwick Scotland, then with me at the wheel of the rented car, continuing first to Ayr where we were welcomed like old friends at the hotel where my mother and Alice had stayed the previous year. The plan was to visit the Yorkshire Dales, which I had never explored and where Grumps was keen to meet James Herriot, author of the recently published book *All Creatures Great and Small.*

There are twenty main dales all very individual, some wide with pastures, others rugged and narrow. After browsing through these valleys the weeks we were there, I fell in love with the area very reminiscent of Vermont, and the people. On our way south to Yorkshire, and the Dales, we were to see the Ruthwell high cross which Alice had researched when she was studying abroad.

The Ruthwell Anglo-Saxon cross in Dumfrieshire was well worth the effort of driving hours along single track roads over cattle grids, through sheep pastures, sweeping barren landscapes with accompanying winds, never sure if we were even on the right road. Called a preaching cross it now stands in its own apse in the small church at Ruthwell and is remarkable for the Runic alphabet and figurative reliefs. After this visit Grumps was not to be held back on her quest to meet Herriot. We took back roads, to explore one dale after another. After a pub dinner, we were strolling through a village enjoying the long northern evening. Grumps saw a shingle with the name of the resident veterinary hung out over a stone wall. There behind the wall was a man we took to be the vet himself trimming a lavender hedge. (To be able to trim a lavender hedge I thought the utmost luxury as my lavender only grudgingly makes it though the winter). Grumps introduced herself and stated that she wanted to meet James Herriot as she had read his book back in the States.

He laughed. "Oh you mean Alf Wight, Herriot is his pen name. Quite a splash he's made with that book. So you want to meet him?"

"I saw him at home interviewed on television and found him delightful. He had a wonderful sense of humor"

"Well, he lives in a small town called Thirsk, Darrowby in the book is a fictitious name, it's not far and I do think that you would like him, we all do."

I took directions and after the usual breakfast of oatmeal porridge, bacon, eggs, toast, marmalade and pots of tea we meandered through North Yorkshire dales to Thirsk. When we saw a man and dogs spilling from a small car it was only too natural to assume that we had found Alf Wight. My mother undaunted as usual at making new introductions, presented herself.

"You must be James Herriot," she said holding out her hand. "I saw you back in the States and as my daughter and I were coming to England I knew that I must meet this charming author."

He corrected the name to Alf Wight, shook hands with genuine pleasure, delighted to meet an elegant elderly lady, who had been so impressed with a TV interview in the States, that she wanted to meet here in Thirsk. We were taken into the surgery with explanations of what and how things had changed since the book descriptions. We met the partner, in real life Donald Sinclair, Siegfied in the book, who took some teasing from my mother, were introduced to various dogs and heard a few more stories. We left as if lifelong friends.

My mother was thrilled and over tea and sandwiches in town she told me that from watching Herriot interviewed on TV she knew that he was someone worth meeting. "Anyone with such a knack for picking up on human drama, sense of humor and a care for animals has to be. There is a joyousness to his life." It sounded like a reflection of her own life.

Our next stop was Harrogate to meet with Dermot MacManus first cousin to my grandfather. He had become a family legend as a survivor of gassing in the first war and for his acquaintance with figures of the Irish literary Revival, Lady Gregory, W.B. Yates and others. His youth had been spent at the family home of Killeaden in County Mayo. For years he had been living in Harrogate with his wife Enid. When we arrived for a visit Enid told us that we could not stay long as the previous few days had been tiring. The BBC had come in full force with cameras and very hot lights to interview Dermot as the last living link to W. B. Yates. He had just had a nap and would love to see us but we were not to stay long.

We entered a high ceilinged Victorian room. The wheel chair was near long windows hung with heavy red velvet curtains. We approached tentatively and waited while Enid bent over a frail figure wrapped to the chin in a steamer rug.

"You have visitors my dear, all the way from America." If ever there were an example of mind over body, Dermot was it. The body for all we could see was nonexistant, but the head which turned to us was ruggedly beautiful, even at this time so near death. Most startling were the bright, penetrating blue eyes with such a twinkle, they seemed to take over the room, mesmerizing, holding us as if we were waiting for the greatest poet to recite. Not even my mother could break the spell. It took Dermot himself. He disentangled his thin hand from the rug and held my mother's in a surprisingly firm grasp; his voice however was barely audible.

"You are so welcome my dear Helen. I hope you have come to buy Killeaden." Although spoken with a hint of laugh, for one of the few times in her life my mother was completely taken aback.

"It depends on the ghost. Is he friendly?" she said recovering instantly. The ghost of Killeaden had been a story my father had delighted in telling.

Dermot's face glowed, his own most delightful form of laughter. "Sit down, Enid will bring us tea. I'll tell you about Killeaden." Which is what happened.

We were afraid of wearing him out but Enid told us that she had not seen him so animated, even when reminiscing with the BBC. We learned of the fairy ring, and how we must walk around the thorn tree at the end of the house or trouble would follow. The blind poet had been a frequent visitor when he was a lad, and if we visited the pub nearby we would see a tribute to him. We were told that the ghost was a very friendly ghost and only appeared on rare occasions. Then we came to the property and how it had been neglected and what a joy it would be to see it back in the family again and restored. Mother was intrigued and promised Dermot that we would visit.

It was with genuine regret that we left Dermot and his dear wife. It had been a remarkable visit with a man so much alive so close to death.

Before changing our itinerary to take in Ireland, we took in the Harrogate farm show. This was county fair at its best. The animals sleek and groomed shown by handlers in white coats; huge draft horses, pigs, cows and sheep neither of us had ever seen before, with spots, streaks, horns or shapes that were like animals from the ark. Most wonderful were the carriage displays, four in hand, six in hand stage coaches with passengers in period dress. The coaches were thrilling with fast turns and smart stepping horses but the smaller carriages were equally wonderful right down to the pony traps with children holding the reins.

We had so much to discuss with Dermot and Killeaden and the excitement of a trip to Ireland, it was hard for either of us to sleep that night.

Next day we set off for Stranraer our ferry port to Larne in Northern Ireland. Someone with the usual Scottish concern for visitors had told us over tea, that we would enjoy Port Logan, just a few miles from Stranraer. We were told that it might be a pleasant resting point either coming or going from the ferry. Port Logan turned out to be nothing more than a hamlet with a dozen houses strung along a quiet waterfront. We found a pleasant bed and breakfast and while Grumps had her nap, I took my usual walk.

A lonely farmhouse perched on a barren cliff just at the end of the shingle intrigued me. I took the farm path, dodged the mud of the cow yard and saw that a track continued past the farm and seemed to be a sort of cliff path with a drop to the sea on one side and the close cropped pastures on the other. I was glad that for the safety of the animals a fence held them short of the cliff, especially when they all cantered toward the hedge and bunched close to inspect me in the way of curious young cattle. In the middle of July, a chilly breeze was blowing from the sea which looked forbidding and cold stretching toward a sky made dramatic by cloud masses pierced by fans of sunlight, those floodlight sky effects which are so common in Britain. I wondered who ever followed the little track I was on and why. It seemed to lead nowhere, just followed the cliffs which rose vertically from the sea. Usually heights don't bother me but I had a turn of the stomach standing carefully from the edge, knowing what my fate would be if I missed my step. I lay flat on the green turf to peek over at the green sea relentlessly pounding against rocks, no soft beach or inlet to mitigate the force. The sea birds nesting in the cliffs rose screaming around me. Their cry was so insistent and raucous and so entangled with the breaking of the waves below that I became mesmerized there on the cliff edge and for a few moments I could understand how in ancient times a frequent suicide was the leap from a cliff top. The birds, the wind with spirit-like whistle and the insistent sea below all seemed to coax. How easy to feel called, just as Odysseus had heard and felt a physical tug from the Sirens.

Breaking the spell, I rolled onto my back and watched the gulls circling against the sky overhead. I had heard that men and boys lowered themselves by ropes and stole the eggs from these cliffside nests. Never I thought would I be that hard up for an egg. "Don't worry about me," I cried to the gulls and continued on the path which became rough in places where there were cuts and run-offs. A variety of miniature plants that I could not identify were flowering in these sheltered depressions. From tine to time I sat on the cushion-like turf to inspect more closely the flowers growing here and there in this inhospitable place. The blue, yellow, and white flowers reminded, me of Alpine meadows, or spring in Greece. I picked a sample bouquet for my mother. The path was springy with a turf which must never have been grazed and which hid unevenness. I trod with care after I had almost lost my balance by sinking into a hole and thought thankfully that my warning had come where the path had turned in some six feet from the edge.

As I walked the gull-watch continued, new groups passing on the duty as I passed. I must have walked several miles and there seemed to be no end to the path. Reluctantly I retraced by steps, panicking again each colony of gulls. As I passed by the farm house which had led me to this beautiful walk the farmer's wife came out and I told her what a memorable walk I had had along the cliff. She was delighted to hear that I had enjoyed her bit of the world. She told me at length that she could never live in the city and how she would miss the wind and smell of the sea if she lived inland.

As much as I had enjoyed this experience I could never imagine living in such a forlorn, rugged place. With all the modern encroachments on this traditional life it was sobering to hear that there are still people who not only enjoy but thrive in a windswept outpost. The wildflower bouquet was a hit with my mother and our hostess who knew exactly where I had gathered them. It seems that I had found a well known cliffside footpath.

Driving through Ireland was the way it must have been when the automobile had first taken to the roads; donkeys and horses had the right of way. Northern Ireland when we visited was still wracked by violence, town centers were closed to cars for fear of car bombs, and we didn't dare to go into any pub. At one B&B our hostess asked if we were not afraid to come to Ireland.

"We are from America," I told her, "where we have every kind of violence from serial killers, to political assassins, child killers and children killing. We have it all."

The countryside was so beautiful it was difficult to imagine violence of any kind. We made our way to county Mayo and found Dermot's Killeaden. In pouring rain we slogged down an overgrown lane to the house, a once lovely beautifully proportioned Georgian, now derelict. Peering through broken windows was enough to know that to make it even habitable would cost a fortune. Taking care to walk around the thorn tree, we found the stable yard which we decided would be more manageable for restoration; the box stalls and groom's quarters above, carriage house, tack and feed rooms would easily convert into a charming small hotel. After a miserable meal at the local pub where the only recommendation was a mural of the blind poet Anthony Raftery, the last of the wandering bards, we landed in an equally miserable B&B.

Poor Dermot, nothing could have persuaded us to linger in what seemed a God forsaken patch of Ireland. We took off for the north to visit the Giant's causeway, a geological wonder; huge basalt hexagonal stepping stones reaching out to sea. It was a scene of complete calm, not another person in sight, the usual wind and call of gulls, making the place more lonely. We spent some time scrambling around and could quite understand the legend that the giant Finn MacCool had made these stepping stones himself to reach Scotland to fight another giant. The large hotel on a hill overlooking the desolate coast gave us a delicious tea to fortify us for the coastal drive to Larne and ferry back to Scotland.

That drive was one of the most beautiful in the world. The equal of any on the Riviera of France, the California coast, or Greece. The difference here was that there was no traffic. I could enjoy the magnificent coast without worrying about meeting a crazy driver head on and it was a fitting culmination to our pilgrimage.

Back in Scotland we both regretted having to leave and perhaps to placate this wish the plane was delayed. The airline treated us to rooms at the the Turnberry golf course hotel for the night, where we were offered dinner and huge breakfast next morning. Although my mother was tired after our driving she was delighted with this unexpected bit of hospitality from Air Canada, only dismayed that without our luggage, she could not change for dinner. When a fellow diner complained of the delay she took him gently to task, when after a delicious fresh salmon dinner, the band struck up and she invited him to dance. The two of them were the stars of the floor and the traveler acknowledged that this delay had made it the best flight ever.

All through Scotland my mother had won friends. Tall and erect she would poke her head into the male precinct of the bar and ask, "Are ladies allowed here?" There was an immediate shuffling, scraping of chairs and seat offered. It was after we were seated that the fun began.

"I'm from Canada," she would say in answer to "Where are you from?"

"Just two months of poor sledding." That brought out comments on Canada good and bad but when she recited Robert Burns Wee, slecket, cowran, tim'rous beastie I remembered so well from childhood, the drams of whisky appeared on the table, soon followed by my mother leading in the Highland Fling, with the entire bar exploding in laughter and clapping.

To travel with my mother was an education. She took the bad with the good, always looking for the good, talking to everyone from any walk in life. On one occasion she made friends over tea with a couple she corresponded with for years and whom I had to notify of her death. Despite her intolerance of old age; the limitations of activity, the changing body, fading looks, she kept up a vital front and continued to enjoy life to the fullest. People were her stimulation. In five minutes she knew more about the person she was talking to than they had probably revealed to anyone. It was not idle curiosity but true interest. The broken marriage, bad job or education, plans for travel, relatives alive or dead, I had listened to these dramas since childhood and now I had lost not just my mother but all the humor, teasing and verve which I knew I would never hear again.

Walking the beach that summer of her death I had to acknowledge that I was on my own for the first time in my life.

Alone

I DIDN'T KNOW WALKING that beach, how alone I was to be. Kimon had been talking about taking a full time appointment in Greece with an American college year abroad. He seemed restless, distraught and homesick for the first time in our twenty-five year marriage.

That year my mother died I had resigned my teaching job at Western Reserve Academy, Helen was off to college, Alice and Panos were in Greece, Io and Ted on their farm in Ohio. Kimon's teaching appointment at the Athens institution was supposed to be temporary but he informed me by letter that he would be staying on for another year. There was no consultation. No asking me to come when I could. What was I to do? There were still the responsibilities of the house in Hudson and the concern for my father whom I did not want to leave for too long. It was impossible for me to join Kimon in Athens at this critical time in my life, which he knew all too well.

After many sentimental letters from Kimon, about the beauty of our marriage and his deep love for me he acknowledged that he was happy with his new position in Greece. In all this there was no concern about my state; still reeling from my mother's death, worried over my father, alone with all the bills and care of the house, in disbelief of the sudden rupture in our marriage, in deep guilt struggling to understand what I had done or not done to cause it all. I was also without a job.

The most wretched for me, was the tone that this was something he had to go through alone without my help or consultation. I was the old shoe so easily tossed off after all the years of wear; the cabin camp years, the child rearing years, the first Hiram years, the difficult travels with infants to please Coola and Theodore.

I returned to Hudson to ramble the rooms, live with the objects we had selected or found together on various trips, dust the books lining Kimon's study and try to pay the bills. I sank into increasing deep depression, avoiding even old friends, refusing invitations, unable to say a word without bursting into tears, sinking into a morass of self pity and guilt. When a colleague of Kimon's told me that Kimon had sent a letter of resignation to the Dean at Hiram College, the self pity that I had not been consulted or informed before anyone else, took the form of anger. And what anger. I sent vituperative letters and lettergrams (an overnight inexpensive communication before email) to Kimon, wrote vituperative letters to myself, and in a fury of activity gathered his possessions to throw away, give to Goodwill, or shred. I cleared his office at the college in minutes, tossing everything into the trunk of the car; long hand notes for lectures, more notes for a monograph he was writing, books, student papers treated with the same disregard, all jumbled together, speaking to none of the faculty who stood back not daring to interfere with this once compliant wife acting so viciously.

These violent emotions made me realize how superficial our gentler emotions are and how easy it is to tip over the edge. My outlet in fury was to clear possessions but it might well in someone else have taken a more violent form. I now understand how fragile the human condition is, and how an emotional dependency can lead to emotional unravelling. And it was emotional dependency I had. As with many housewives of my era I had not paid or worried about bills, the car and its expenses, insurance, any of it. Now with no warning the bills came to me and the bank account was empty. Dribbles came in after desperate night letters and longer regular letters—none of them kind.

We had been a small family but tight. Grandparents on both sides were very much part of our daughters' life. They had endless stories to tell of adventures, quirks, attitudes of their grandparents. For me Coola and Theodore were my devoted second parents. Now all that changed. I was cut off from them and from Greece, my adopted country, as easily as I had been received. My loneliness was profound. I put myself into mourning for all that I had lost through the utter selfishness of the man who had been my husband, my confidant, for whom I would have done anything; this trust was misplaced I now knew. What had all these years meant only to be destroyed on a whim? I am sure that their love for me was not diminished but a Greek mother could never side with wife over son. It was not in me either at that point to be magnanimous. I was hurt and bewildered and gave no ground to compromise. Put simply—it was a bad time.

I made frequent trips to St. Augustine to hover over my father who insisted that he was just fine. "The Lord helps those who help themselves." Nevertheless I found that indeed he did need help as most would at ninety. He continued to drive but I noticed one side of the garage smashed and dents in the car. Finally I was able to hire someone part time—Jeanie who would come in the morning and make the main mid day meal leaving enough for supper. He had her phone number and promised to call her if anything went wrong.

While I was there I had to do something other than walk the beach. I was told that deliveries for meals on wheels were always needed so I took that up while with my father.

It had been a long hot summer. Children were back at school and night temperatures down to seventy but my hand sticks to the paper as I write to my girls. It's been a long hot summer for everyone. At the church where I pick up the meals to be delivered to the shut-ins, the kitchen volunteers are sitting in front of whirring fans, resting for a few minutes between packing the meals-on-wheels and setting up the eighty-five places for the dinners served in the church hall. "Your route is the same dear," Florence tells me. "Salad and desert today."

My first stop is at the Colonial gas station where Mr. Corkhill is waiting. Square faced, work shirted Mr. Corkhill has every ailment and is surprised to greet a new day.

We discuss books and politics together and exchange reading material, although reading is difficult for him.

"They tell me I won't be able to see much longer so I better make the best of it," he told me once. "Here's that New Yorker story I was telling you about. You'll like it."

"And here's an article from the Wall Street Journal." I pass it to him in the back seat.

"That's great, I haven't seen that for years."

We stop at a cabin where wren-like Lorenia Smith lives with her niece who calls out when she sees me, "dinner here." I walk in through the screen door carrying the dinner. Lorenia tells me that next week she brings home her two new legs.

"Only trouble is fixing them on, it not easy." Lorenia is seventy-six. "Ah just prays, all ah kin do,"

The next stop out past the county jail is for a couple— Jack Sprat and his wife—I called them. Mrs. Sprat has spread out over the kitchen chair. Her round friendly face with hair pulled into a tight bun is flushed.

"Jest finished-ma warsh." I see the faded shirts and cotton dresses hanging from a line on the back porch. "It's the way ah were brought up—al'ys warsh Munnay 'an ifn not Munnay then nexday."

Her emaciated husband calls, "Thanks Mam fer dinner."

Back in the car Mr. Corkhill drawls, "Hear they had no water there all week end." Mr. Corkhill collects gossip and I wonder where he gets it.

In front of Mrs. Lyon's trailer he says, "Hear her grandson wants to kick her out."

"Who? Mrs. Lyons?"

"You know it was in her daughter's will that the son had to take care of his grandmother but I guess he didn't expect it to go on so long."

"I don't believe it! No one would want to kick out Mrs. Lyons." We watch a smartly dressed, perky little woman lock her door and make her way across the yard to the gate where she quiets the barking dogs before joining me in the front seat. I shout, "That's a pretty blouse you're wearing."

"Glad you like it. I make all my own clothes," she smiles.

"She always looks so nice," Mr. Corkhill remarks from the back.

Mrs. Lyons comments as we drive that most of those we take meals to would feel better if they would get out more. Mrs. Lyons herself is ninety-four. Several miles down the highway we turn off down a sand, ditch lined road which dead ends in a grove of slash pines hiding an abandoned shack. I pull into the shade of a lone live oak to protect the two passengers from the fury of the noon sun. The ditch beside Lucy's gate is filled with beer cans. Several mongrel dogs crawl from under the shack and tentatively wag tails then give up to scratching.

"Co'n in," Lucy calls. She has heard my steps. This little corn shuck of a woman lost her sight when she tried to put life into the cook stove by pouring kerosene on it. I sidle round the same stove to place the dinner on the tidy kitchen table and notice that the drunkard son is in his usual place on the back porch staring over the lifetime of debris to the outhouse. "Ah do thank 'ee fer a dinner," is Lucy's inevitable parting remark.

"Do we stop today for that fella who runs around naked?" Mr. Corkhill asks. I look at my chart.

"No, he isn't on."

"Well they must have done something with him then."

Ruth Sherman is lying on a cot in her stuffy living room with the gown pulled away from the sores which ring her body. She wipes her neck with a wash cloth. "Are you any better today?" I ask.

"It's just the same. Sometimes I think I can't bear it, but what is a body to do?"

I wonder what the life drawing class would do with the Goya grotesqueness of the sagging breasts melting into the swollen, diseased stomach and the legs flung wide to avoid the damp touch of flesh on flesh. Ruth talks on—the chatter of someone who is too much alone and suffering and with no one to attend her.

At our next stop the tiny wife is always in the same chair and the husband with no nose and most of his face eaten by cancer, is always in bed. A friendly little dog scampers at my feet, a good subject for conversation but my constitution fails and my cheer dries up. The putrid odor is so strong it is all I can do to get out of the house. On one occasion I had to nip behind the car. It is so bad that all day I dread the few minutes it will take to run in and put the dinners down.

"Do we pick up Minnie today?" Mr. Corkhill asks.

"No not today."

"Good. She never stops jabbering and no one can understand her. She phoned in and complained about us—said we never talked to her—said she wouldn't ride with us any more."

"I wonder who's loss that will be?"

Mr. Corkhill laughs, he doesn't like Minnie.

We arrive back at the church where I leave off my passengers and return the empty containers. Some of the dinner guests are arriving as I leave, so before going to the car I help the most wobbly cases into the church hall. My cotton shift is wet and I feel the trickles of perspiration inside. Gratefully I return home to the air conditioning and lunch with the Pater.

"How did you get along with those poor old women today?"

"Fine, they all got their dinners."

"That's wonderful, you certainly are the good Samaritan. You must be dead, I think we should both flop down."

When the Pater flops down I take the car and go down the street to pick up Chris for a visit to her sister in the "geriatric" center. Chris and Flora, widowed sisters, lived together until Flora became bedridden. Chris lives with a companion but neither drives and the center is on the other side of town.

We make our turn onto Sunrise Avenue and pull up before what looks like a new suburban kindergarten building grounded on a sand lot effectively bulldozed clear of the surrounding pine scrub. The children are eighty, not five year olds. We make our way through a group of the more fit who are sitting in wheel chairs in the shade of the portico looking out at the shimmering white glare of the concrete parking lot. One calls to me, "Are you the Avon lady?" Pasted on the wall inside the door is a verse, hand written on construction paper and decorated with flowers cut from a magazine which reads: "As a white candle in a holy place, so is the beauty of an aged face."

We pass into a room with the construction paper label, "Our entertainment center." Chairs are ranged round the walls of a room bare except for the TV staring from a far corner, a few chairs pulled in front of it, the occupants dozing. The halls are cheered by more hand copied notices, inspirational or cute sayings. "Activities" with a reinforcing arrow is repeated at intervals and even turns a corner. We dodge some of the bundles tied into their chairs with sheets to keep from falling face forward. The chairs are stalled in the halls or bumping into the walls or each other. The less active we don't see behind doors labeled, "Encourage liquids," or " Diet # 2 only." The noises are as disturbing as the sights—a constant rumble, like a school corridor, but the sounds here are not the sharp vital voices of youth but croonings, moanings and wailings, seemingly from another world. At times individual words come clearly through the static of keening—help, repeated without notice.

As I wait outside Flora's room for the sisters to discuss their dwindling resources, I talk to Gertrude May. She looks fresh and bright and no more than seventy. I wonder why she is here.

"Will you be out soon?" I ask.

"I'll be here to the end I guess, I'm ninety-one."

"You're not sick are you?"

"I'm fine, nothing wrong with me—nothing for me to do here but my daughter comes to visit often."

"She lives in town?"

"Just down the road. A widow, lives alone but she don't want me. You see she's just at the age where she can come and go as she wants."

I've brought one of the Herriot books to read to the sisters, both of whom are deaf. Chris settles into a chair, Flora is propped against pillows too weak to sit up. She is dying of cancer. I start reading wishing I had the knack to project my voice. I shout instead. The fiber glass curtains are drawn against the west sun beating on the wall of window. The whine of the air conditioner set too high gives the background music.

When I glance up Chris smiles and nods, Flora can't see well enough to know that I have looked at her. My throat is dry and I feel the trickle of perspiration again. I reach for a tissue to dry my wet face. I wonder if it is menopausal hot flashes—my audience seems comfortable.

I read of spring in the Dales; the miracle of life, two or three lambs issuing from hardy ewes; the sharp winds sweeping over the stone walls and the intimacy of the farm kitchens. The chapter is finished. My voice is hoarse but the looks of expectancy are too much.

"You'll love this chapter," I call and start again.

"I just know we will," Chris says and settles into her chair.

The Pater is waiting for me to return for tea. We sit on the porch looking out over the water, "This is a beautiful, peaceful spot. Don't worry about the lawn when I leave for parts unknown."

Soon after 8:30 the Pater retires for the night with, "Leave me comrades, here I drop," and a kiss.

On the porch the wet-blanket air envelopes me. I blot the trickles with my blouse and stretch on the hammock. A cricket sings companionably. There is the heavy plop of a fish jumping in the water. The cricket will be dead by morning, killed by the invisible fence of poisons and the fish I know is not jumping for joy, but for his life, pursued by a voracious enemy. He is probably dead already.

This was not the place or the recipe to fight the depression I lived with.

Ireland

I HAD TO DO something about myself. Even in my depression I knew that. Alice wrote inviting me to Ireland, insisting that I come to Ireland and enjoy the life she and Panos were having there.

One of the best things about having daughters is that they grow up to marry your sons-in-law. After a brief afternoon ceremony you have an instant son at a companionable and work force age. What an easy way to have a boy! If you're lucky you'll delight in this new, and you hope permanent addition to your family, but not to your household.

Alice and her husband Panos spent a year in Athens where Panos studied for the civil service exams and came through with top scores, while Alice put herself into total immersion in her study of Greek. When not studying they haunted antique shops for Greek folk art and assembled a collection of everything from icons to embroideries.

When Alice phoned excitedly from Athens that Panos had been posted to Ireland we all rejoiced. It was a country she had travelled with her grandmother, for me it was the closest and cheapest air fare abroad. What luck, she wrote.

They arrived in Dublin July 1977 where Greece was to open its first embassy to Ireland. This meant the purchase and renovation of the chancellery and residence. The first was a lovely Georgian house just off Fitzwilliam Square. The residence was south at the exquisite seaside town of Killiney. Panos, as second to the ambassador, was involved with the confusion such renovations bring in Ireland, while Alice was house hunting which presented its own problems.

The letters came. Mostly about finding a house to live in.

She took it all as a great adventure.

Shelbourne Hotel Dublin July 1977

Dear Mummy,

We arrived yesterday. Today is Sunday and we have been walking around the city. I doubt that we will get a house in town, but tomorrow I'll start to see what is available. We move to Charles's place, the Golden Vale tomorrow. We came here for the first few nights because the Ambassador is here. You can write to us at the Greek Embassy, Shelbourne Hotel, Dublin. I'll keep you posted on all our news.

Love, Alice and Panos

Shelbourne Hotel, Dublin, July 7

Dear Mummy,

This is a quick note to keep you informed of our progress with house hunting. There are lots of houses on the market but few you would want to buy. The ones you would are expensive. There is almost nothing to rent so we don't have that as an option. I have several appointments today, so we'll see.

Last night we saw a fabulous one, an old Tudor house set in 60 acres. It is all to be turned into flats and we would buy one flat. Joan Kennedy Ireland's alternate for the Olympic equestrian team lives in the gate house and has taken the stables as her riding school. It is fantastic. There are some definite negatives though. It has been gutted by fire, it's an hour from town and there is a mad neighbor. Also it would be tiny. I don't know where we would put everyone. Still it has atmosphere. Panos says almost too much. We're still looking.

Love, Alice

July 15

Dear Mummy,

We have a marvelous man, Paddy Rooney, an architect to help us. He said the Tudor had rising damp, needed a new roof and that something "was going on" with the mad neighbor. Now we have decided to rent and I think I've found a semi-detatched town house. It sounds awful but it's in a good location, near where the boats come in from Wales. There are lovely vistas of lawns including tennis lawn, thick velvet curtains in the drawing room, dripping chandeliers, high ceilings with elaborate moldings. It needs some painting which the landlord says he will not do but I will. It is spacious—room for everyone.

Love, A.

P.S. Disregard everything I've said about this. Paddy Rooney says that we will all have rheumatism if we spend a winter there.

July 17

Dear Mummy,

We're trying to buy a car. We can't get one for two weeks and that is fast, done especially for us. Nothing is done quickly here. Of course everyone is sweet and kind but that doesn't change the fact that you might want some things done quickly. As for houses everything so far has problems. Now there is a Georgian house in town, a Queen Anne in the country on 600 acres with pastures, horse boxes, absolutely fabulous. It belongs to a terrific young man who is farming. It has no central heating, just peat fires. Needless to say it's marvelous.

Love, A.

July 22

Dear Mummy,

Finally our house problems are over. We have found a little stone mews in Monkstown to rent. No more Queen Anne houses without heat. Unfortunately one has to be more practical and as we are not here only for our own enjoyment we must have a house that is accessible. When you come I'll take you to see all these other places. They are lovely. Our mews is an old stable, all stone and wood, secluded behind huge gates and high stone walls. Downstairs is one large room with fireplace, the fireplace wall being stone, the other walls are white plaster with beamed ceiling. The kitchen is at one end separated by a brick wall with swinging saloon type doors. Upstairs there are two bedrooms and two baths. It is partly furnished with primitive pine antiques that one would like to own. Our Greek primitives will fit in beautifully. The tiny garden has a lovely old apple tree and roses along the walls and the walk from the gates is bordered with wild flowers and fuchsias. The train for Panos is across the street and the sea is a block away. We will sign the lease Monday. There is plenty of room for everyone.

Love, Alice and Panos

While this was going on Panos needed his ready sense of humor to cope with the misadventures at the embassy. On my first visit, three months after the embassy had opened, he was amusing us every evening with stories, like the flag pole which when installed turned out to be more like a battering ram, or the endless conflicts with telephones which never worked as they should, if they worked at all, of workmen who never turned up, of electricians who spent the day crawling around then left behind a trail of dangling wires to be sorted out at their convenience. "The trouble is," Panos said, "they are all so pleasant and talk all the time."

In Ireland they bought their first car.

Dear Mummy,

Our new car is fantastic, a Renault 5TL, tiny, marvelous. We have it in a fire engine red. We ordered yellow but in Ireland things don't come exactly the way you want them. Anyway it is very smart. We just love it.

Love Alice

Their first dog.

Dear Mummy,

Helen arrived. I made a mistake and mentioned that we expected to get a dog. That was all she needed. I should have known better. She forgot all about Trinity, the Book of Kells and museums I had sent her to see. She returned with a female black lab, so she was told, but it had pointed ears and legs like a German Shepherd. She took it back. We now have a yellow female lab. She is very good and sweet and also extremely intelligent. She couldn't be better.

Love Alice and Panos

My depression faded after a few visits, after all I had to take advantage of easy flights to Ireland and on one visit in October 1977, I had thought that I would take off for a week or so on a bike trip while I was there so as not to wear out my welcome. This was the response.

Dear Mummy,

    I don't think it's safe to bike on Irish roads. Ireland is not England. The Irish are crazy drivers. Last week-end (not even a bank holiday) 27 were killed in car accidents. I'll organize a horse for you but I don't approve of a bike. I'm postponing everything until you arrive so that we can do them together. I'm going to get the names of horse people and dog people and we'll visit breeders. When will you have time to disappear on a bike? Read up on monasteries and castles and we'll visit them.

Love Alice

One of the distinctive features of Ireland is that no one, in any occupation is far removed from the land and that means horses and dogs. You won't hear cronies, as you do in England, discussing roses or dahlia varieties. More likely they'll be comparing greyhound bitches or discussing winners at the latest race meet.

Riding had always been part of Alice's life, now Panos developed the passion. It was inevitable in Ireland.

Dear Mummy,

    Panos has started riding at Bel Air, Rathnew, Co. Wicklow. He rides a huge, raw boned, hairy footed black gelding named Mercury. About eight of them GO for two hours or more up and down, galloping through fields, forest paths, jumping logs or anything else. It is just what Panos needed to give him confidence. All this happens Sunday afternoon. The front of the stable is a hotel (Irish style) a beautiful Georgian house, but decorated in what Panos calls "early itinerant." After the ride everyone comes in for a drink at the bar or has tea (usually just Panos the tea) with scones and apple tarts. The house is in a beautiful setting and has the remains of lovely gardens. Today they grow lettuce in amongst the rose beds—so that's how we pass Sunday afternoons.

Love Alice

They made close friends.

Dear Mummy,

I have been meaning to write but have been very busy. Vivienne has done something to her back and must stay in bed 15 days without moving. So I go there daily and naturally besides taking care of the various horses and ponies, sit by her bed and chat.

Love Alice

In December 1978 she wrote:

Dear Mummy,

Please don't worry about us for Christmas. We are spending Christmas Eve with the Rooneys and all Christmas Day with the Butlers. Vivienne is doing it this year so her sister and her children will be there too. It should be lots of fun. I've made two huge puddings (your recipe) for the occasion.

Love Alice and Panos

Alice took up riding again.

I've gone half half with Vivienne on a big Irish horse. A bay three quarter bred gelding with a huge "leap" in him. It's fun to try these horses, saddled up and ridden down country lanes until there is an opening into a field, it doesn't matter whose, then over banks or ditches, water, brambles, anything.

And hunting:

I've joined the Tara Harriers, they hunt Co. Meath, but hares, not foxes. There we all were about thirty of us at one of those Irish cross road towns, the men on huge hairy horses some steeple chasers "out for the sport," Vivian on her new chestnut gelding and me on a marvelous Connemara pony I have for the winter. I've been preparing her every day for two weeks, getting her fit, clipping and walking. It was one of those beautiful clear grey days, clouds but light. At the first field the hounds got a run so we were "tally ho" across a ploughed field, huge ditch and the woods. Bushy, my pony, never hesitated over the first ditch and the next two hours were the same, jumping everything, even wire. If the ditches were too big for her, she slid into them and reached for the other side. Probably the funniest part of the day was when we all jumped into someone's back yard, scattering ducks, chickens, and calves. We picked our way around heaps of coal, garbage and a discarded bathtub, over sticks and under the clothes line with nappies blowing in the breeze all to the delight of a handful of half dressed toddlers, the mother holding the youngest.

Alice did volunteer work, teaching riding to the handicapped.

It is wonderful how they respond. My little boy patted his donkey today and everyone was amazed. He's never responded to anything before. It's really wonderful. It's all done Irish style, very disorganized, anyone who has a pony or donkey brings it.

After my first trip with so many experiences to draw from, none on a bicycle, I was at a loss to sum them up.

In Ireland if you want to meet the locals, take the dog for a walk. Exercising Tara, the yellow lab, to the end of Dun Loaghaire pier and back every day we met unforgettable personalities, human and canine.

Tex, the big boned red setter was usually waiting for us at the gate in the morning. He would turn in circles barking then run on ahead announcing our progress like a medieval cryer, spilling over into the frantic traffic of Seapoint Avenue. I could only hold my breath as he avoided cars by a hair. There was no controlling Tex; no one ever had, not even his owner. Tex favored various families in the neighborhood with visits, once staying a month with a man who had lost an old dog, taking over the empty bed and dish and filling an empty heart. Often he would appear in the garden, we never knew how, as it was surrounded with a nine foot wall. He would make himself at home on the oriental rug for half an hour or so, then as if remembering an appointment, he would ask to leave.

Along the pier Tex settled down to smells and running off dogs that came too close to us. He tolerated Tara's frenzy for retrieving like a modern husband whose wife engages in activities outside the home. He watched over the wall, tail wagging when she plunged off the steps into the harbor to retrieve sticks, then greeted her with licks of pride when she came up and shook all over him. These daily walks with the dog out to the end of the pier in sun, or more frequently drizzle and high wind, took a good bit of time, not for the length of the walk but for the length of conversations with other dog walkers who all knew Tara.

There was the unforgettable Dublin Show week, like no horse show in the world, horses all day, and marvelous people and diplomatic dinners and receptions every evening, as the horse show is the highlight of the Dublin social season. There was the luxury of starting each day with the Irish Times where journalese is sacrificed to a good story. There were the outings to Moone and Glendalough, unspoiled and romantic, the cliff walk from Bray to Greystones, Monasterboice with its magnificent high cross and lonely setting. There was tea at the Kilkenny shop, tea with Alice in her kitchen reading Sommerville and Ross, the Purty Kitchen for Guiness, shopping at Paul Costello's, polo matches in Phoenix park, riding with Vivienne's children on Pella and jogging with them in the mornings down misty lanes. Vivienne's kitchen with children, dogs, Andy or Anne. Dinners en famille with the Rooneys or with Alice and Panos at home. The daily rounds where people have time to chat or watch puppies play, where there is always time for a cup of tea. A country where nothing matters, and where life continues very well. Very well indeed.

Their first baby

> Dear Mummy,
>
> Another present from you. You are overdoing it. We have just returned from a film on birth. Panos will be present and help beforehand. He has attended Father's class and is all prepared. I wonder how much help he will be but I feel he should participate and see it all. You'll be glad to hear that I've prepared for the baby. It has a lovely wicker basket to sleep in and be carried in and hand woven wool blankets from Avoca. I also have nappies.

The news reached me in Boston where I was waiting with Helen, all the closer to an Aer Lingus terminal. Helen was as excited as I. Her words as she saw me onto the plane were, "take pictures every day. She'll never be the same again. Remember I'm her aunt."

What happened was the birth, January 11, 1980 at Mt. Carmel hospital Dublin, of a healthy granddaughter, my first grandchild. It was as ever, like coming home, to fly into Ireland. Although I had especially pleasant memories from previous visits, I don't think that anyone could feel strange dropping into Shannon over putting-green perfect fields dotted with sheep. It is more like stepping into a romantic nineteenth century painting than an international airport.

At Dublin airport Panos was waiting for me in the inner enclosure, exercising his diplomatic privilege, and was on a loquacious high as we drove to the hospital through mists, which had just cleared enough to allow my plane to land four hours late.

Panos is never at a loss for words, in almost any language, now he rattled on, "It was really something I can tell you—look at that bloody idiot—I was there for everything—you remember the Custom's House over there, arm stretched across me to point,—my God it was something—there is the Mansion House and now St. Stephen's Green—why doesn't that fool stay in his own lane—then they just handed the baby to Alice like that—covered with everything—now we cross the canal, and Dr. Mullen talking all the time—my God it was really something I can tell you."

Set in spacious gardens, the hospital has more the air of a luxury hotel. There are no set visiting hours and even the no children prohibition Panos explained, was enforced like most rules in Ireland, if necessary, but not automatically. Alice looked drawn but radiant. Her bright private room, with large window view of the Wicklow Mountains, would be hard to rival in a resort. Asleep in a wheeled cot next to her mother's bed, lay the black haired mite who had taken so long to come into the world.

It is hard to say who the baby resembled, but in that moment I saw her mother as a newborn and relived the exhilaration of giving birth and the languid sense of fulfillment, with none of the pain or fatigue. Perhaps that is what is so special about being a grandparent; through a perspective which deletes difficulties, child rearing is distilled into pure joy. Holding my granddaughter I remembered the sweet of raising her mother and none of the bitter; the sleepless nights, diapers, incessant demands, the endless energy and all the trying fazes of adolescence. If Alice flags, as she must, she has only to think back to herself, as I now can, and say it is all worth it—it all comes right in the end. The grandchild indulges us in a review of the past and in the effortless continuity with the future, proclaims to us a surging optimism.

On my daily visits during the next week, (Alice remained in hospital the usual seven days) I was impressed with the gentle and personal attention given to mother and infant. It was so unlike my own maternity experiences where fathers were excluded, and nurses had no time for help or explanations, and infants were kept like rare plants behind glass, handled by masked professionals.

At Mt. Carmel the babies stayed with their mothers, the nurses assisted with feedings and helped mothers to bathe and dress the infants and swaddle them in the no-cry bundles, "Ready for the post."

The meals and manner of serving them was elegant; no paper cups or disposables here. Dinner at noon was brought in three courses on trays with heavy silver plated rims and handles, reminiscent of ocean liner days. The food was hot under silver covers. Every dessert was enriched with huge dollops of Irish cream. Intervals between meals were broken with frequent cups of tea and biscuits served by a rosy cheeked country woman announcing, "Here's a cuppa."

On one morning the head sister visited, like the Duchess of a country house welcoming her guests. She shook hands with me, the grandmother, and listened with delight to my account of the thrill the news of the birth had caused with Aunt Helen in Boston who, "Can't stand kids."

"It's a wonder the joy a child brings," she smiled, then looked into the cot. "God be praised, it's perfection." She turned to Alice. "The mother is the perfect artist," she said in her soft Irish voice, "only a woman can create a baby—with the help of God," she added. The father was not mentioned.

When Alice and her baby were finally allowed to leave, Dr. Mullen, himself a father of eight, instructed Alice to take a cue from the animals. "It takes time, a baby, try to be as available and relaxed as a bitch or a mare."

The homecoming of my granddaughter warmed me spiritually, but most especially physically. Panos turned the heat way up to 55. If it had not been for the baby, we could never have basked in this extravagant waste. Anticipating a shortage, fuel had been limited to a winter's supply of 200 gallons per household. In a stone house, with temperatures outside hovering at between 35 and 50 degrees, I felt that I had been entombed prematurely. After huddling before a gas jet, trying to capture the faint warmth before it dissipated into the room, I was at last thawed enough to look appreciatively around me.

The antique Greek weavings covering the white plaster walls of the beamed room were complimented by the vivid Caucasian rugs. These had the effect, as Synge had said of the red dresses of the Aran women, "Of bringing untold joy to the eye of those who live in gloom and damp."

Only Alice could have produced a festival dinner the first night home, so effortlessly. She had written that we would celebrate Christmas upon my arrival. However, I never expected the complete menu: roast chicken with her special dressing, roast potatoes, sprouts and flamed plum pudding with hard sauce. Before dinner we sat before the peat fire listening to music and sipping egg nog, heavy with Irish cream. The babe slept and Tara, the lovely yellow lab, lay stretched before the fire, her tawny head on a Turkoman pillow. This scene was repeated every evening. The baby Daphne slept and grew, causing no one anxiety.

The humor and tenderness experienced by Alice are best revealed in comments. There was the young mother in the hospital delivery room who was having her fourth child—unplanned. "I think I know what my problem is," she said to Alice between contractions, "I don't wear nighties."

There was seven year old Sarah who sat back and sighed when she first saw baby Daphne, then whispered, "She's just gorgeous." Her brother, twelve year old Hugh, tried hard not to be interested but when he did take the baby in his arms he was reluctant to hand her back. "I'm not finished with her yet," he said giving her a grubby finger to hold.

The grocer, who had seen Tara as a pup and watched Alice's lump grow admonished, "Mind you make a fuss over Tara when the baby comes home so she won't feel left out."

The roofer who, Irish style, had been repairing a leak for as long as the pregnancy, replied when I told him the good news, "I expect your daughter will be looking better by the day now won't she."

Eifa, the neighbor child and Tara's friend, said on holding Daphne for the first time, "She makes noises like a pup, but I'd rather have a pup."

Walking Tara by the sea in the evening and looking out at the yellow lights across the bay stretching to Howth, I think of the uniquely Irish way of viewing life that has affected all of us. I am pleased that Alice had her first child where it is not the fashion for young women to feel that they must excuse themselves for reproducing, where birth and death, good and evil are as evident as wind and rain. Surrounded by such unfailing kindness and good will, surely it is a good omen to have had an Irish Happening.

With Jan in Iran.

Trip to Iran

BACK IN OHIO I continued to commute to Florida where my father was doing as well as could be expected. I had arranged for Jeanie to come in and as far as I could see, she was doing a great job. My father was delighted with her and looked forward to her daily visits and outings in the car to the bank, Woolworths, grocery stores. In other words he was on to his usual routine while Jeanie did laundry, cleaned and supervised.

When my friend Jan Herbert asked if I would accompany her on a rug buying trip to Iran I felt that I could leave my father for a month, asking Helen and Len, my brother in Miami, to check on the situation in St. Augustine.

The condition I made was that to pay for the trip, Jan would select rugs which she thought I could sell. It was with great excitement that we set off, with a full itinerary; stopping first with Alice and Panos in Ireland then on to a rug symposium in Munich. The original plan was to travel first to Iran where Jan had connections in the rug business, then to Afghanistan crossing the Khyber Pass to Pakistan for more rugs. The Khyber had a romantic connotation for me; Kipling's Ballad, the exotic trade route, Alexander the Great's passage in 997 B.C., and all subsequent struggles between east and west. I was thrilled that this trip had come up—one I had never thought of taking.

Off we went.

Despite telephone and post office strikes, Alice was at the Dublin airport to meet us looking smart in an Irish wool cardigan she had knit herself, tweed skirt and Tara as accessory.

Alice gave Jan a quick tour of the mews house which seemed to have been designed especially to display their Greek folk art collection. The brilliant weavings looked stunning against white plaster walls, the copper disks glowed from the stone mantle and the carved peasant implements repeated the wood of the ceiling beams. Fresh spring flowers were bursting from vases, reflecting the daffodils blooming in the stone walled garden. Jan's assessment of the oriental rugs scattered over the floor was interrupted for a quick lunch of Irish cheese, soda bread and a glass of creamy milk. Alice had a program for us and we had to keep up—a quick tour of Dublin starting at Phoenix Park where Tara watched deer and ending at the Greek Embassy and Fitzwilliam Square, where we picked up Panos.

I couldn't turn in without taking Tara on my favorite walk to the end of Dun Loaghaire pier. It was with the mewing of gulls ringing in my ears and lungs filled with brisk sea air that I fell asleep.

Alice had kippers for breakfast as well as eggs, Irish bread and homemade marmalade. Panos took his train to Dublin and we bundled into Alice's sweaters and drove into the Wicklow hills to visit her friend Vivienne and of course the half bred hunter Alice had been riding and hunting.

As we drove through the primrose bright lanes, Alice explained how a hunter is brought along in Ireland. The first season cubbing, next season following the field, and finally the two week visits to other counties to master another terrain, stone walls in Limerick, banks in Wexford and rides with the local farmer to master ditches or in the farmer's words "the problems to make 'er like 'em."

Vivienne greeted us, gentle and pretty as ever. We admired the children's ponies and the dogs and I rode the big mare. She jumped like a dream with power and certainty. I could imagine how she would be in the hunt field. Leaving Vivienne and the fields we were, in a matter of minutes walking the beach at Killiney. Dublin is the only capital city I know where unspoiled hills and coast are so easily available.

Alice drove us along the coast road through Dalkey and past Yeats's tower to have a quick lunch at home before turning Jan loose in Dublin.

We visited two antique shops and a rug shop which Alice considered to be the best. Jan found the Waterford lamp she was looking for and we ended the afternoon with teas at the Kilkenny shop, my favorite. That evening we had a gay reunion with Hudson's Charles McKinley and Trudy and John Strassburger who are in Dublin for a term with Hiram college students. Included in the party were Mary and Paddy Rooney from whom the Strassburgers are renting. It was a cheery and late evening, the dinner a masterpiece from mushroom soup to Irish coffee. It was good to see old friends and to hear John's account of conducting a college course abroad with all notes and clothes lost somewhere between Cleveland and Dublin.

Our last day in Ireland was saved for the country and a visit to a round tower and high cross, both monuments peculiar to Ireland. The round tower at Glendalough, which preserves even its conical roof, is in a setting of mystical beauty associated with Christianity from earliest times. There are monastic and church ruins as well as an early stone church, all linked by footpaths through tree studded lawns where new spring lambs challenged Tara.

At Moone the path to the magnificent high cross led across a stile and bordered a cow pasture. The cross serene among the Abbey ruins and venerable yews is one of the most pleasingly proportioned crosses. We read the bible stories depicted in primitive carvings on the four sides of the base and admired the intricate Celtic intertwined designs. Friends of Alice and Panos who own the early Georgian house and lands adjoining the cross had asked us to stop. The wrought iron entrance gate had to be carefully closed to keep in the hunter and cob grazing the lawn which swept around a twelfth century tower to the river.

The chickens scattered from the imposing steps leading to the door. Our host and hostess greeted us in blue jeans and very worn sweaters, but with courtly charm and manners. Alice had told us that they are Polish-German refugees who having lost all their money and lands in the war have made their livelihood since by farming the 300 acres. We sat in a small room huddled round a peat fire for warmth and looked into an untidy but extravagant garden.

That evening we stopped to admire Strassburger's flat and greet little Trudy and Sarah, now in Irish school, on our way to the Gate theater. In the shabby, musty not too clean theater we enjoyed a brilliant performance of Equus.

It was with a pang that I saw Dublin recede below me on our way to London and Munich. I was leaving more than a city—I was leaving people like the Rooneys, and Vivienne witty, talkative, warm, the Dublin Bay, the Wicklow hills, the untouched meadows and serene monuments, tea in Dublin, gentle confusion, contrasts and downright fun.

From Tehran I wrote home to Helen.

> Tehran May 4, 1978 Dear Helen,
>
> Please pass this on to Io and Ted. I am so full of all we are doing I haven't time to write to everyone.
>
> Tehran. Immediately at the airport it is the Middle East. The greetings are noisy and extravagant. Babies passed round pinched and kissed; the returning are greeted not just by the family but by the whole clan. Everyone embraces and weeps and laughs, old men, women in chadurs. Bouquets of flowers, as big as trees, wrapped in shiny plastic are held by everyone meeting the plane. It all seems so warm and friendly and natural after Germany where the greetings were no more than discreet smiles and gentle hugs.
>
> Teheran is not attractive, nor even chic like Athens. It is general confusion, everything mixed together. There is no elegant shopping area for instance like Kolonaiki in Athens

and very surprising to me, no cafe sitting or endless restaurants. The traffic is like nothing you could conceive. Congestion like Athens but no regulations, a free for all, U turns, lights which mean nothing.

Today was the highlight. Jan's broker, Mr. Etessami, picked us up and took us to the bazaar where we looked at rugs until two. It is amazing and fascinating. The bazaar is incredible, Athen's monasteraiki 100 times over. Everything is there and goes on there—a whole world, a warren of lanes and streets, shops and artisans. Rugs are traded, washed, woven and repaired. We saw three men weaving a pure silk rug, sitting cross legged on a trestle—it will take them 3 years. Unbelievable.

I'm exhausted now, suffering from sensory overload so will close. I've so much to tell you. By the way I'll be home late probably June 1.

Teheran and Iran have eclipsed the three days in Munich at the International Oriental Rug Conference. The conference was interesting; the delegates a combination of the scholarly and arty, as if a group of historians met at a New York gallery opening. The two rug exhibitions were worth the trip. Munich is orderly, clean, prosperous, open, easy to navigate and pleasant to walk.

Nothing could offer more contrast to all this than Teheran. The traffic is a mechanized version in all its grizzly variety of the busy and varied hell which challenged the ingenuity of medieval sculptors.

Jan and I have so far been fortunate enough to survive (we've seen those who haven't) and with Helen's specific words of caution ringing in my ears, we have also survived a day at the bazaar.

Helen's advice.

1. Remember that in "those" countries the dark-haired men lust after blonds of any age (I thought the modifier rather unkind) so never go anywhere alone.

Dear Helen I did try to keep eyes forward and stride on but it is all so new and fascinating and to tell the truth I forgot your words until Jan, who is very dark, would grab my arm and hurry me on. All I ever saw on turning round were dark eyes and bearded faces, curious but not lusting.

2. Never eat or drink anything in "those" countries. Why do you think all those shots are required?

Dear Helen, My appetite for meat is gone. After seeing lambs slaughtered by the roadside while the shepherd stands with the remaining live animals. It doesn't take long for the remaining flock to reappear in the bazaar, pushed by vendors in wheelbarrows. One with legs, another feet—need I continue? Everything else is delicious and I've tasted from street stalls, almonds, nuts and seeds of every size and shape and succulent dried fruit. It is impossible to resist the fruit drinks mixed in a blender while you wait and do you think that I can pass up melons, oranges, cucumbers, tomatoes, mint and green onions just because they are grown in night soil?

3. Above all Mum never, ever, go to the bathroom.

Dear Helen, I've really tried very hard to follow this bit of advice—God knows I don't want to. More specific details on this subject when I see you. Also Helen, we are not going to Afghanistan and the Khyber Pass. They are in the process of murdering everyone so it seems to be dangerous for westerners.

It was a great disappointment to miss the Khyber Pass but despite our visas and preparations the revolution in Afghanistan made travel there too uncertain. It was the beginning of the suffering which lingers until this day.

Despite not being able to cross the Khyber we were lucky to have been able to travel as much as we did and for me, years after this, to travel to many countries now prohibited by conflict or politics. The world has become more restricted since Freya Stark, one of my favorite travel writers, made her excursions into uncharted Iran and Arabia in the 1930's.

Our rug buying in Iran continued although even there unrest was evident. With our gracious merchant and host Mr. Etessami we spent almost every moment of the day. He had arranged accommodations at the best hotel, patronized by foreigners, oil men we gathered from casual conversation; many Americans but French, British and German as well.

Our days started early with a car picking us up before eight to meet at the shop in the bazaar. The traffic was frightening and completely without control whereas the bazaar seemed, in all its intricate alleys, very organized; different alleys or areas for each product. Jan told Mr. Etessami what she thought she could sell and what she wanted to buy and we would follow him to the merchants he thought had the best quality Shiraz, Sarouk, Herez, Ispahan. We were in the company of a Swiss merchant from Basel also on a buying trip. All of us would stand behind a pile of rugs while an attendant flipped them over, rather like flipping the pages of a wall paper book. Our Swiss merchant who had apprenticed in England with an Iranian dealer, was so astute and quick in his assessment of a rug it was a marvel to watch him. He told us that during his apprenticeship he had to be able to identify carpets in a dark room simply from the feel.

The process was quick. If a rug was of interest it took only a nod and that rug was folded back to be examined more closely. If it passed that inspection it was taken out of the pile to be carried by a porter on his back with others for final testing in the evening. To see these porters, old men, carrying on bent-double backs loads that would crush a donkey, passing down the gloomy alleys of the bazaar took me into another world of human suffering.

Lunch was quick and delicious in Mr. Etessami's office with hard boiled egg, cucumber, tomatoes, flat bread and yogurt soda drink. After a siesta which we took at our hotel we continued the rug viewing. At the end of the day we assembled in a warehouse where the porters had carried all the rugs selected that day. Now each in turn was laid out for inspection. Our Swiss crawled on hands and knees running his hands over every inch, sometimes looking up to comment on a flaw, sometimes to comment on the superb quality of the wool. Jan too crawled over the carpets she had selected. If a fringe was shredded or missing the rug would be put aside for repair. It was immediately folded and removed to a corner of the room. These days were so intense, concentrating every second on the carpet displayed, my faculties could not take it in; my relief was to look about at the bearded Persian faces like those on the ancient friezes, the alleys lit by domes, casting pools of light, the hierarchy of the shops with, as in Greece, small boys running errands, fetching and carrying, tea, soda, messages.

We were treated to a lavish dinner en famille with Mr. Etessami. The house behind high walls was surrounded by a fragrant Persian garden. The food was delicious and never ending. A beautiful daughter newly engaged to a man she had not met joined us along with a son who was on brief leave from his military service. Jan, a rabid feminist took on the daughter asking how she could allow her father to choose a husband. "Why would I not trust my father who only wants what is best for me?" she answered. We were told that two other sons had been set up in the rug business, one in New York, one in Italy. "It is their college education," the father said. "If anything happens we have sons established." It was yet another lesson in survival. The entire family preparing for another route, another disaster.

Jan and I flew to Ispahan where Jan was given introductions to another merchant. The roses lining the streets from the airport into the city seemed a miracle after the forbidding flight over desert. Ispahan is a beautiful city and between rug buying contacts we visited the mosques, squares, bridges. The beauty of the city itself, the restful atmosphere of our hotel caravanserai gave me the exotic, romantic Persia that Terhan lacked.

It was with real regret that we left this beautiful city, impossible to appreciate in the short time given to us. Back in Tehran trouble was brewing. The bazaar was closed but we were told that we could still visit certain merchants, which we did. It was all very spooky, with Mr. Etessami leading the way down now deserted alleys of the bazaar to knock on a door, to have a shutter opened a crack, to be admitted quickly. At the main entrance to the bazaar and here and there throughout the city trucks were parked filled with soldiers.

"It is nothing." Mr. Etessami assured us.

In fact it was the beginning of the revolution. After we left, the country was in turmoil with strikes and demonstrations against the Shah. In January 1979, the Shah left for exile, in April 1979, the Islamic Republic was created.

We had only a glimpse of the country and despite the hospitality we were given there was a feeling of repression, of unease. In Ispahan we were told that a woman had been hanged from a lamp post for so-called indecent behavior. We were lucky to have been able to go at all.

The atmosphere in Istambul, our return stop, was like coming from a cave into the light. To walk the crowded streets with women unveiled, street cafes, restaurants, strangely was like plunging into Western life with a vengeance. In travel everything is relative. Istambul, with its minarets, calls to prayer, roosters crowing, donkeys braying, even in the center of a thriving city, would have seemed very Eastern if we had arrived from the West. As it was, the confusion only made the city more friendly and indeed hospitality was evident even on the bus or street where strangers were ready to offer help.

From this first visit I fell in love with Turkey.

The Pater

A S SOON AS I could I flew to St. Augustine to check on my father, the Pater. I found him well and very much in the hands of Jeanie. When I was away Len had stayed with his father and found that indeed Jeanie had been most solicitous especially on trips to the bank. Len, examining his father's check book became suspicious of large withdrawals and installed a recording machine on the telephone.

He heard on one recording. "Pater I need an air conditioner."

"Do you Jeanie dear? Don't you have air conditioning?"

"No Pater and I can't sleep at night it's so hot."

"That's dreadful Jeanie. We can get one tomorrow. We'll stop at the bank when we do our commissions and withdraw the money. How much do you think they cost?"

"About five hunnert."

"Well, we can certainly do that."

That was enough for Len. The next time he heard his father complaining to Jeanie, "I want to give you the five hundred you wanted, but they are on to me and watching all the time so I'll put the money under the chair cushion on the porch."

"You do that Pater. I'll come around the side no one will know I'm there. If anyone comes around I'll just tuck it into my buzeer."

"Now Jeanie be careful, Len is watching all the time. If he tries to take the money just give him an uppercut."

With this information Len set up a trip wire on the side of the house so he would hear Jeanie when she came for the money. And come she did. About four in the morning, Len was awakened by a cry as Jeanie stumbled into the wire. He waited until she had found the money then confronted her but fortunately did not try to search her but called the police instead. The search was conducted by the police and the money found. Jeanie spent the night in jail but was back again at the house in the morning to take the Pater for a drive.

Len told her that she was not welcome and in fact fired.

"Only Mr. Strong can fire me," she said.

After more police threats she backed off, but the episode made us realize how vulnerable the aged are. Jeanie had promised to stay with him to the end, most especially never let him go to a nursing home. For this he was willing to pay anything.

I tried to persuade my father to live with me but it was not easy. What he wanted was for me to move in with him. A survival instinct took over. I knew that I could not spend my days patting the trickles under my shift, delivering meals on wheels or even walking the beach. I had to live in my own home. As much as I adored my father I realized that he had done what he wanted all his life and I had to have mine now.

It was Roger who travelled with him to Ohio where I had arranged his room in the house I had moved into and renovated with him in mind. It was a wonderful arrangement. Helen was part of the household from time to time, Dee who had been house sitting for me during the commutes, moved in permanently, and I had at various stages of the stay, wonderful help from Mrs. Limbaugh first, then Lucy and finally Doreen. The household revolved around him. All of us planned for his welfare.

I knew before he came to live with us that I would feel trapped if I had to do it alone, so from the first day he arrived I had arranged for

Mrs. Limbaugh to arrive in the morning to prepare him for the day with shower, dressing and breakfast. It worked. I could enjoy taking care of my father without feeling oppressed.

The real reason why it worked was because of my father's personality. He was uncomplaining, cheerful and grateful for everything.

Once showered, shaved and dressed he would sit at the kitchen counter waiting for breakfast with his current helper. It was his custom never to start a meal without a prayer of thanks. It was also his custom to have a hearty breakfast; boiled egg, toast "slathered in" butter, marmalade, coffee with lots of cream.

"Now we'll just say the blessing. What a delicious breakfast you have made. It is so good of you to do so much for a poor old man. For these and all his mercies, God's holy name be praised."

"Oh Mr. Strong I love having breakfast with you every morning."

It happened that his three caregivers were all very religious, had fallen away from the daily prayer ritual, and were delighted to be able to start the day with my father over breakfast and prayer.

Lucy took over when Mrs. Limbaugh became ill and added to the morning with stories of misfortune. My father loved them.

"Mr. Strong the reason I was late is because little Lavon fell all the way down stairs and I had to take him to the hospital."

"That's dreadful Lucy. What did the doctor say?"

"He gonna be alright but he have a big lump on hiz head."

"That's dreadful. Did I ever tell you the story of the little boys about twelve years old who were on the railway bridge?"

"No, you never did."

My father delighted to add to Lucy's repertoire, settled in with coffee laced with cream to tell the details.

Lucy had a habit of burning the first breakfast. As I was making my escape through the kitchen I would pass through a cloud of smoke. Lucy reassuring my father, "Don't worry Mr. Strong the next time it won't burn." And she was right it took two efforts to produce an edible breakfast. My father sat at the counter oblivious of the smoke only waiting for Lucy's next tragedy to cheer his day.

Lunch with the hermit.

Cappadocia

I F RUGS HAD proven a possible income once, I thought that it could be repeated. With the Pater happily settled in Ohio with Helen, Dee and the daily help, I felt that I could leave for a few weeks. With encouragement and instructions from Jan who could not go herself, a rug buying trip took me to central Anatolia in February of 1982. The purchase of tribal kilims was expected, unexpected was the spell cast on me by the mystical lava landscape of Cappadocia, a plateau 185 miles southeast of Ankara.

"You're crazy."

"A woman alone?"

"Don't you know what men think of women in THOSE countries?"

These were the warnings I heard from friends and even veteran middle-east travelers when I said I was off on my own.

"Especially blond, blue-eyed women," my daughter Helen warned, herself a veteran traveler, repeating her former warnings.

Undaunted, I packed my knapsack, tucked in a map and with a few phrases memorized from a tape, left Hudson Ohio, for Turkey via Switzerland.

The few days spent with friends in Basel made an easy transition from home and during the five hour Swissair flight to Ankara the Swiss efficiency was prolonged. There was no time to prepare for the contrast between Europe and Asia.

Travelling by air one is thrust into black and white, with none of the mediating grays. There is no natural progression from west to east, no relationship with all those who have preceded through the ages, overcoming the vicissitudes of terrain, customs, language and villainy.

Dropping out of the air between those desolate mountains, one arrives with all Western mental trappings in tact. There is no time for a shake up; no time to toss out familiar attitudes to make way for fresh experiences. No time to think "otherwise."

Unlike the Swiss playground of mountains which rise from cultivated valleys and tamed slopes, these Turkish mountains under their dusting of snow, were inhospitable mountains of survival, an impression which was reinforced by the barrack-like airport.

It all looked so dismal in the late afternoon light. The cold from the bare concrete floors penetrated the soles of my shoes and my nose started to drip. Looking forlornly for my knapsack I had a moment of panic, asking myself what in the devil I was doing there and where was my handkerchief? My spirits rose though when an airline assistant sought me out to say that someone was waiting for me outside.

Sure enough there was Muammer. A handsome, smiling young man who was to be my escort and guide.

"Welcome," he said in English.

"It's you who are welcome," I countered.

"If you like to rest we can go to hotel. If you are not tired we can catch bus to Urgup."

Of course I wasn't tired. I was far too excited by my surroundings and anyway, who could postpone arrival in a town with such a name?

"Then we go," he said swinging my knapsack into the nearest taxi, an old Chevy Impala. We took off full speed across the plain.

After ten minutes Muammer looked at his watch. He smiled when he said, "Bus has left." Then he relaxed against the seat.

"Then where are we going?" I asked, the warnings of home surfacing.

"We catch bus," he said and offered me a cigarette.

I shook my head and hung onto the front seat trying not to worry about what we were, or were not, doing. After twenty minutes we pulled up on the deserted road beside a telephone pole.

Muammer grabbed my sack and jumped out and before any more of those reminders of what happens to women alone could disturb me, a bus pulled up.

It came out of nowhere, like a genie from Aladdin's lamp. I had seen no cars on the road, not even signs for Ankara, the capital city. I learned later that Ankara is 26 kilometers from the airport on the other side of a mountain. But the bus, shiny and capable, had somehow found us, or we it, and the driver was in a hurry to be off. Once settled in our seats Muammer chatted for a while then leaned back to doze and I was able to look around and absorb my surroundings.

I was the only woman. This was the rule almost everywhere I went in Turkey and although I was certainly the object of curiosity, I invariably met with only the most formal kindness.

Endless Turkish pop tunes whined, Mideast fashion, at full volume from the radio. The air was suffocating from cigarette smoke. After a stop the conductor, no more than a boy, would make his way down the aisle sprinkling outstretched hands with scented water—a simple and very pleasant custom, followed by little sweets to suck.

Through the black pit of night we followed the ancient silk route into central Anatolia. The road we were travelling had been followed since time immemorial by migrating tribes, invaders and traders. This land had seen the fulfillment of every human virtue and vice—of building and destruction.

In another age we would have swayed along on camel back or pony and stopped the night, according to the rhythms of nature, at a caravanserai. I seemed alone in an infinity of time which I was unable to comprehend, isolated as an astronaut in the void of space.

Somewhere we changed buses. It was colder now and snowing. We hunched into the station for a glass of hot tea. Then more travel through the unknown until we reached Urgup about eleven.

Stepping out of the bus into the sepia light of the square I lost my link with the twentieth century. It could have been an old photo from early expeditions into Mongolia that I was looking at. I felt a quickening at entering alone into an unknown world where nothing is familiar; not the language, dress or food. Not even the dwellings. The one story flat-roofed houses and shuttered shops trailed away down one end of the dark street, at the other, houses were plastered onto a hill like the daubs of a social insect. Even the air was different. Perhaps it was those first burning cold draughts, heady as strong brandy, that gave me my initial intoxication with Cappadocia.

The town lay sleeping under its light dusting of snow in a snapping clear night. The silence was complete. Nothing hung in the air, not even the voices of the other few passengers who had been absorbed into dark lanes.

"We go to best restaurant," Muammer said as he picked up my sack and led the way across the deserted square.

We entered a variation of the bus; a smoke filled room of men playing cards or taula. Every wisp of heat from the coal stove was cherished in the tin pipe, bent into intricate abstract shapes across the room, before it was allowed to exit through the wall. Prominently displayed was a stern portrait of Ataturk, father of modern Turkey, incongruously flanked by a series of girlie pictures.

It was daunting to be the focus of so many dark eyes, assessing me from the gloomy recesses or from the table I had to sidle past. Every man in town must have been there. They so much resembled nineteenth century paintings of Turkish warriors: lean they were and strong, mustached, unsmiling; I would not have been surprised to see scimitars in their belts.

But there, close to the stove, was an old fellow who so much reminded me of the aged father I had left at home, his face gentle, eyes mellow. He looked at me, first solemnly, then he smiled that vulnerable, toothless smile I knew so well. I sifted through the phrases memorized back in my Hudson kitchen.

"Good evening," I said in Turkish and shook his hand.

All those other faces which had seemed so intimidating a moment ago, flashed smiles—literally flashed—white teeth showing under black mustaches. The tension broke.

The salad I ordered was perfect; grated carrot, red cabbage, green onions, olives and cheese arranged on the plate like flowers in a garden with a sophistication which would have rivaled a House and Garden display. The plate of thick yogurt was not our insipid stuff diluted with flavors to disguise the fact that it is yogurt, but the real thing; a creamy crust and rich as clotted cream, with a nutty flavor reminiscent of mountains and flocks.

Kadir, the merchant I had come to do business with, joined us for dinner. He explained that at this time of year the hotels were closed but he had arranged for me to stay with friends who ran a motel on the edge of town. The rug business could wait, he said, tomorrow Muammer would show me some of the wonders of Cappadocia.

By now, well past midnight, I was exhausted and only the thought of stretching in a warm bed sustained me through the introductions with the family who ran the motel. At last I was shown to my room. It was like stepping into a tomb. In summer it would have been adequate; a new building of concrete block construction, but now—in February! Any heat left from the summer sun had seeped away months ago.

It was useless to complain, there was nothing else. Besides there were two family members lighting a kerosene heater, all smiles and concern. The concrete floor and walls wicked away the faint heat. Unzipping my knapsack I pulled out my sporting gear: wool tights, wool socks, sweater, jeans, sheep skin gloves, wool hat and finally I untied the down jacket Helen had strapped on at the last minute. Then I dressed for bed.

The cold concentrated in the mattress under my back. Sleep was impossible and only dawn brought the relief of stepping out of bed already dressed and ready to explore.

A few hundred yards from my door a fantastic valley fell away, spreading out to a plain and a rim of distant mountains. There were no trees, no habitation, no roads or animals. Nature, with eons at her disposal, had sculptured the valley and peopled it with her own fantasies: tawny needles, bulbs and cones which rose from a dusty white floor in a clear light and stood silhouetted against a bleached blue sky.

The miseries of the night evaporated with the exhilaration of the scene. It was like stepping into the beginnings of time; as if I could see down the tunnel of infinity. There was so much of nothing.

In the office, huddled next to the coal stove, I relished a breakfast of bread, cheese, olives and honey served by the same small boy who had stoked the fire to life. Warming my hands with a cup of cafe au lait, I was finally comfortable enough to read the brochures on Cappadocia.

It is a 1500 square mile area in central Turkey. Millions of years ago five great volcanoes erupted covering the earth with lava, ash and cinders from which erosion has fashioned the surrealistic landscape.

Man is known to have cut dwellings into the soft tufa both above and below ground, since prehistoric times. The cave villages are mentioned by Xenephon in 401 B.C. Peter spoke to the Cappadocians in the first century when the converts practiced their ritual in underground cities. During the Byzantine era Cappadocia was a monastic center and produced scholars, mystics and saints, even today there are over 1,000 churches. Christians found sanctuary here from Arab harassment from the sixth to tenth centuries. The last Christians, Greeks and Armenians, were uprooted in 1924. Today the caves are virtually uninhabited.

By the time I had done my homework Muammer arrived with a taxi. No one could have been a better guide. Not only did he know the valleys but he loved them. At various points we left the car and hiked for miles in a colorless sun under a remote and cloudless sky. As it must have been on the first walk after the expulsion from Eden we saw no form of life, not even a bird.

I had to remind myself that only a few days ago I had been in Ohio, that there was such a place as Ohio, and as I saw fantasy after fantasy, that it mattered.

Like a soul dispossessed I almost floated, weightless, through those endless valleys, with no sense of fatigue. Each had its own personality. One had been eroded into what looked like a giant Henry Moore throw away, all rounded and smooth, others were like a child's sand castle dribbles, and still others like a succession of Irish round towers.

Into the cliff sides of these valleys the dwellings had been cut; elaborate tiers of caves which we climbed into—whole cities of caves—with passages leading up, down, along and opening into rooms where benches, tables and beds had been cut into the rock.

At intervals, openings framed views and depending on the location, were either of an intimate cul-de-sac where grass showed green under the snow, or a panorama of distant blue mountains and rosy erosions. Every group of caves had elaborate dove cotes cut into the rock which, I was told, were a substitute for the more vulnerable chicken house.

The day advanced imperceptibly in the thin light that defied shadows.

We returned to reality at villages where we visited artisans or rug shops and drank endless glasses of tea. At a potter's we entered through a door which let into the cliff side. The utilitarian terra cotta ware was stacked into the walls. In a loop back the passage opened into a small, dark room. At the far end, the potter was working in a shaft of light which fell from a small window high in the solid wall creating a chiaro scuro scene reminiscent of Rembrandt. Three small boys were busy round the inevitable tin stove, two were sanding plates, the third no more than a tot, was stuffing twigs into the fire. How could I keep my promise to buy nothing, to travel light?

Returning along the deserted road to Urgup, the car stopped.

"Up there is a church." Muammer pointed to a cliff. "You want to see?"

"Yes, of course."

We scrunched across a hard frosty bit of land to look up at a Byzantine cross carved over an opening into the cliff face, the only suggestion of a church. After climbing a flimsy wooden ladder, we stepped into a perfect Byzantine church, cut from the rock: columns and domes, apse and aisles. Most striking, startling in this bleak landscape, were the frescoes covering the walls in a testament of faith, painted in primitive colors, as brilliant as if they had been created yesterday.

There was the Pantocrator floating in the dome, supported by the most heavenly angels. On the walls the twelve apostles bent six by six leading the eye to a central Christ. The lines had the simplicity of folk art. It was all so unexpected, pure and spontaneous and as moving as many more sophisticated Byzantine frescoes.

I looked out the rectangle of door at the world which lay like a mystery below. Now I understood why the world's three great religions had come out of the desert. Here there was a similar desert atmosphere of space and light, of a vast world canopied by a sky which was as easy as a breath. There was nothing to intervene between man and his God. There was no clutter—not even of cloud.

Standing in the presence of the saints and apostles and of Christ himself did I detect a lingering fragrance of incense, that essential of Orthodox ritual?

The rug business was done over endless glasses of tea and dizzying designs and colors. Kadir and Muammer were the perfect hosts although there was nothing to be done about the miserable cold of my room.

On successive days Muammer and I visited the churches of Goreme, the monastery of Zelve and explored more valleys. In this otherworldly landscape, without the shackles of pattern, vegetation or even movement, the senses were freed. The inner self was released to float through a pale light from horizon to horizon over a sterile world.

Sitting one evening in the shop on a pile of kilims we had examined, a doll-like young Japanese woman entered. She was introduced to me by her Turkish nickname of Sultan. She was so amiable and soft-spoken I took to her immediately.

"What on earth are you doing here?" I asked first off.

"Come to make carpet," she answered simply. "Live in house where 'ooman' willing to teach."

Next day I was invited for a visit.

Much better with head scarf.

"No shoes in house," Sultan smiled as she slipped off her own. I untied my shoes and walked stocking footed into a small room filled with women. Divans ranged two walls where five or six trousered women sat comfortably doing needle work. Three small girls stood in a corner, not daring to speak or even approach.

"Neighbors come to see you," Sultan explained.

The landlady greeted me, patted a place on the already crowded divan and glanced at the older of the girls, no more than ten, who shyly set a bowl of fruit and nuts beside me. The women giggled and asked questions. Where was my husband? How many sons? No sons, only daughters? What misfortune—long faces and shaking of heads. This was like Greece.

The child helped me tie knots at the loom against the wall, her fingers deft with experience. The women laughed at my ineptness no doubt wondering what I did with my hands for I was just as clumsy when I tried spinning the raw wool from the hostess's spindle.

By the time we had sipped tea, served by the same child, the women had loosened up enough to tell me that I could improve my appearance if I wore a veil. I felt like the new girl, not yet in uniform, surrounded by well meaning class mates. Sultan's teacher fetched a veil from a shelf and tied it round my head to the applause of everyone. We parted like old friends, with kisses and good wishes all round.

It was Sultan who took me to the hermit. "My friend. You must meet."

Next day as we followed the road out of town, Sultan told me of her life in Urgup and the life of other Turkish "ooman."

She had been brought up in modern Japan, had studied abroad and found the restricted life of the women here stifling. "No friend with girls. They not allowed to walk with me to fields or to shops. Very lonely for me, very boring for them. All conversation just gossip. They not know where is Japan or any country."

Several kilometers out of town she turned off onto a track which followed to the edge of another of those world vistas. Here we descended crude steps to come out below a terrace.

Sultan called in Turkish, "Old man, where are you?"

Then appeared the reincarnation of Noah, the Prophets and Saints of all ages. I looked up at a face tanned black, where any skin at all showed through the beard and eyebrows. He was a big man, but lean, with horizon-seeking eyes. He stretched his arms to us as if in embrace and we scrambled to his terrace.

I was welcomed with the same easy acceptance he would give a bird, not caring where I was from or where I was going, but caring for me nonetheless.

"Come see how nice house is." Sultan led the way into a cave room, soothingly dark after the glare outside. A tin stove in the center provided heat. Cut out of the walls were couches strewn with bright covers, The usual portrait of Ataturk was surrounded by post cards and snap shots of young people who had visited the old man from all over Europe.

"So he is not a hermit," I said.

"Oh yes," Sultan nodded. "He live all alone except when student come in summer, then he take all in to sleep and eat. He like young people and they water garden and bring him food."

"Come see kitchen," Sultan danced ahead like a child. We returned to the terrace to enter another smaller cave room where tin plates, mugs and a few staples were neatly arranged on the rock shelves. Sultan set water to boil on a gas ring as if she were mistress of the house.

"Everyone work when they come here, then always welcome," she explained. "Look there." She pointed to a water trough outside the door. "Everyone decide Musa need water, so pump is brought and now water come from pipe below and Musa very happy he can share water with his pigeons." As she spoke one perched on the rim and drank. "He love all animals and very angry if farmer kill pigeons."

She made tea and we sat on little stools sipping it from tiny glasses, looking out at the lavender and white valley and mountains. Sultan chatted on, her voice blending with the cooing of the pigeons.

"That boy cat Musa love very much and all village know." The boy cat she spoke of, a scarred old tom, was purring on the old man's lap while a dainty, very female cat circled his feet. "Boy cat go away. Old man very sad. He think boy cat dead. But boy cat go to village to find girl cat. Small boy see boy cat and bring back to old man with girl cat. Now boy cat stay home and old man very happy."

Our peace was disturbed by four farmers who came up the path, one carrying a pail and another two circular loaves. They greeted me easily and set about making a meal. The pail was full of fresh smelts which were cleaned, the innards thrown to the mewing cats.

Soon the fish was on the gas ring boiling with onions, lemon and tomato paste. When it had boiled enough, the kettle was placed in the center of a large round tray surrounded by the loaves cut into wedges. One of the men took the low table where they had been playing cards, into the sun; we each carried our stool to set around it.

The cook carried out the tray, set it on the table and handed me the first fork and a hunk of bread. Then we all dipped into the common pot using the bread to blot the juices. It was delicious. When I said so with much smacking of lips they laughed as if they had been able to give me a rare treat—which indeed they had.

After the meal the few plates were washed (I wasn't allowed to help) and the men resumed their card game. We sat in silence broken only by the whirring wings of the pigeons as they fanned in and out.

The farmers left. Sultan, Musa and I sat on that terrace above the world and watched the lavender and rose deepening over the valley to deep purple and blue. The pigeons ceased their intimate gossip until at last we were left with nothing but the vault of heaven luminous over a fallow land.

When the rugs arrived in Ohio, I sat on the floor to open the bales. When I saw the first geometric design I returned immediately to Musa's cave, and sat, within my own kitchen, caught in the violet evening light of Cappadoccia and the gentle murmur of pigeons.

The End

THIS YEAR 1984 my father was ninety-six. His father, for whom he was named, Rev.J.L. Strong was missionary to the Indians of the Six Nations on the reserve near Brantford, Ontario. His son James Leonard Strong was born there at the rectory, Kanyengeh, in 1887, on the feast of Saint Simon and Saint Jude. This was fourteen years before the death of Queen Victoria.

That my father lives with me has elicited many comments. Friends wonder how I can submit to the confined routine so recently outgrown after raising three children, as well as trying aspects of personal care and meals. By most I am considered either foolishly stubborn in not committing him to a nursing home, or a special sort of heroine. In fact I am neither.

I do not deny that the household revolves around this ninety-six year old man. It takes the unanimous effort of three of us as well as devoted outside help to mediate the care. The situation does pose problems; it is tedious, at times irritating, exhausting and always depressing. To see a once vital and independent parent progressively enfeebled is heart rending.

For him each new day is a miracle to be approached with help. Help to sit up in the morning, help to shower and dress—and waiting. Waiting for someone to come, waiting for the circulation to start before standing, waiting before taking the first step. It means the putting in of teeth, the putting on of glasses which do little good, shaving by feel, walking with pain, sleepless nights and lonely days enforced by the failing senses.

Unable to read the daily paper, excluded from conversations, he leads an inward life and physically is limited to a short hobble with a walker or an outing in the car. This prison of old age would be enough to make the rest of us depressed, self pitying and irritable.

My father at ninety-six has balanced the restraints placed on his life, and thus those he has placed on ours, with inspiration and example. He is positive and cheerful, appreciative and undemanding. He carries with him the grace and manners of another age when such virtues mattered.

He is attired every morning in tweed jacket and tie ready for anything, even though anything may be nothing. "Excuse me for not standing," must be explained to grandchildren's friends. "You won't think me rude if I thank you now and don't write," after receiving a birthday present, is incomprehensible to the youth who seldom write much less send thank you notes. Even though almost sightless, he still answers letters when he can and sends cards on the appropriate occasions.

Within his capabilities he clings to the conventions and forms of life, and his self imposed obligations to family, friends and God.

Much of his strength of character is derived from his faith which offers serenity in the anticipation of, "meeting my Maker." He is still able to hold an erratic household, forks poised, until he has said the blessing, and still assembles us for a prayer of safe deliverance before any of us start on a trip.

From another age he draws, "Let not the sun go down upon your wrath," one of his many quotes and recitations. The young people for whom learning by heart has been taboo, are in awe of his memory and recitations of, The Wreck of the Hesperus, Lord Ullen's Daughter, Lucy Gray and many others.

In our household we do not wash our hands but "perform our ablutions." We do not write a letter but rather an "epistle." We do not go to bed, but "retire." We do not go out but "on our way rejoicing." Women of any age are "dear darling girls," men more simply, "darlings." Anyone who helps him is either "sweet and thoughtful" or a "good Samaritan."

If we have made a commitment to Patie, he has made a greater one to us. He has drawn a code, now considered outworn, of restraint, formality and kindness to spare us the whines and snappishness he might try us with as he reminds us daily that a kind word is more effective than a curse, good manners make life easier, thoughtfulness and appreciation are always welcome.

In an age when it is difficult to find anyone to emulate we have Patie.

Through his example we have all become more patient and considerate and we have learned the meaning of dignity. He has shown us too that when our time comes, even though we know we can never do it as well, of how it can be done.

We are honored to have Patie with us.

The following year at age 97 he died at home peacefully in his bed, as he had wished.

The void was huge.

For me it was another beginning.

Tea with friends my grandmother has given me.

Epilogue

IT WAS MANY years later that my grandmother's neglected portfolio was found and her talent displayed on the walls of my house. Before I could find the time for a leisurely tea with these friends, I had created a new career as landscape designer, and published a book of those adventures, travelled in Egypt, Cyprus, Jordan, Italy, France, the Netherlands, and of course England.

Through luck it has been an honor and gift to have shared a bit of the life of my mother and Coola, both unusual women who each in her own way, were ahead of their time.